GETTING OUT

CLARENDON STUDIES IN CRIMINOLOGY

Published under the auspices of the Institute of Criminology, University of Cambridge; the Mannheim Centre, London School of Economics; and the Centre for Criminology, University of Oxford.

RECENT TITLES IN THIS SERIES:

Sentencing Policy and Social Justice
Henham

Cold Case Reviews: DNA, Detective Work and Unsolved Major Crimes
Allsop

Justice, Mercy, and Caprice: Clemency and the Death Penalty in Ireland
O'Donnell

Young Criminal Lives: Life Courses and Life Chances from 1850
Godfrey, Cox, Shore, and Alker

The Chinese Mafia: Organized Crime, Corruption, and Extra-Legal Protection
Wang

Dirty Money: On Financial Delinquency
Ruggiero

Getting Out

Early Release in England and Wales, 1960–1995

THOMAS C. GUINEY

OXFORD
UNIVERSITY PRESS

OXFORD
UNIVERSITY PRESS

Great Clarendon Street, Oxford, OX2 6DP,
United Kingdom

Oxford University Press is a department of the University of Oxford. It furthers the University's objective of excellence in research, scholarship, and education by publishing worldwide. Oxford is a registered trade mark of Oxford University Press in the UK and in certain other countries

First Edition published in 2018

Published in the United States of America by Oxford University Press
198 Madison Avenue, New York, NY 10016, United States of America

British Library Cataloguing in Publication Data
Data available

Library of Congress Control Number: 2018941408

ISBN 978–0–19–880368–3

General Editors' Introduction

The *Clarendon Studies in Criminology* series aims to provide a forum for outstanding theoretical and empirical work in all aspects of criminology and criminal justice, broadly understood. The Editors welcome submissions from established scholars, as well as excellent PhD work. The Series was inaugurated in 1994, with Roger Hood as its first General Editor, following discussions between Oxford University Press and Oxford's Centre for Criminological Research. It is edited under the auspices of three centres: the Institute of Criminology at the University of Cambridge, the Mannheim Centre for Criminology at the London School of Economics, and the Centre for Criminological Research at the University of Oxford. Each supplies members of the Editorial Board and, in turn, the Series Editor or Editors.

This book makes timely contribution to the Clarendon series in light of events surrounding the case of John Worboys (known as John Radford) and the proposals of the Government to reform the Parole system in England and Wales. John Worboys, known as the 'black cab rapist', was jailed indefinitely in 2009 with a minimum term of eight years after being found guilty of nineteen offences, including rape, sexual assault, and drugging late-night passengers, committed against twelve victims. Worboys served ten years in prison before the Parole Board recommended that he be released. But two of his victims of the serial sex attacks succeeded in forcing the Parole Board to reconsider its decision to release him from prison. Three judges at the High Court in London ordered the Parole Board to carry out a 'fresh determination'—with Worboys remaining in prison pending the outcome. Sir Brian Leveson, Mr Justice Jay and Mr Justice Garnham, subsequently ruled in favour of the two women who brought the challenge, and indicated that the Parole Board should have undertaken 'further inquiry into the circumstances of his offending'. Nick Hardwick, the Chair of the Parole Board, was then forced to resign after David Gauke, the Secretary of Justice, told him that his position was untenable. This landmark case prompts us to delve into the history of the Parole Board and its decision-making processes.

Thomas Guiney provides us with a hugely interesting and scholarly historical exploration.

As the author notes, there is always much attention given to 'front end' decision making in the criminal justice system, who gets stopped and searched, who gets an out-of-court disposal, who gets charged, prosecuted, and sentenced in the courts, but the process of 'getting out' of prison has attracted much less interest. This book offers a rich and detailed history of early release policy and practice in England and Wales between 1960 and 1995, years which saw major mood changes in the criminal justice system, from the rehabilitative ideal of the 1960s through to the Law and Order years of the 1980s and early 1990s, culminating in Michael Howard, then Home Secretary, claiming that 'prison works' which perhaps made Parole Board members question even more rigorously whether and when to release someone from prison early.

The author looks at three critical junctures: the introduction of the modern parole system in the Criminal Justice Act 1967, the complex policy debates surrounding the extension of release on licence to short sentence offenders in the 1980s, and the steps taken to rationalize the operation of early release in the Carlisle Committee and the Criminal Justice Act 1991.

This work will undoubtedly appeal to academic researchers with an interest in early release, parole, and the administration of justice. We also think that it will appeal to those interested in institutionalized analysis and to modern historians and political scientists alike. As Editors, we commend Thomas Guiney's book for making significant contribution to the field of criminology and to our understanding of the complexities of early release from prison. We warmly welcome *Getting out: Early Release in England and Wales, 1960–1995* to the *Clarendon Studies in Criminology* series.

Loraine Gelsthorpe and Kyle Treiber
Institute of Criminology,
University of Cambridge
May, 2018

Preface

Introducing the very first 'Report of the Parole Board' in 1968, the chairman Lord Hunt noted, no doubt with one eye to posterity, that

> social reform is a continuing process, but certain measures are seen in retrospect, to stand out as milestones on the main road to progress. As first members of the Parole Board, we appreciate the opportunity to play our part in introducing this new measure for offenders, because we believe it will prove to be one such milestone. (HMSO 1969)

More than half a century has elapsed since these words were written. As the parole system reaches another significant milestone it is timely to reflect upon these events and consider what lessons history may reveal about the challenges that await us in the future. Like so many areas of criminal justice, the policy and practice of early release has become an altogether more complex pursuit since the 1960s, and the 'main road to progress' has proved far bumpier than even the most cautious members of the Board could have anticipated. Nonetheless, the questions that motivated an earlier generation of social reformers remain just as relevant today as they were when the parole system was established by the Criminal Justice Act 1967. In what circumstances might it be desirable to expedite the early release of a prisoner from his or her sentence? Who should make these decisions, and what conditions should be placed upon individuals when they return to the community? There are no easy answers to these complex public policy questions. As anyone who has debated the high-profile cases of Myra Hindley, the release of John Worboys, or the international furore that surrounded the prosecution of Oscar Pistorius will know, the arguments for and against the termination of a prison sentence go hand in hand with deeply held assumptions about justice, fairness, and the morality of punishment within our liberal democratic system (Padfield 2007). At a time when so much public discourse on crime has focused, to a significant degree, upon the powers of the police or the sentence of the court, discussion of early release forces us to contemplate the day after tomorrow and the reality that the overwhelming majority of men and women sentenced to imprisonment can expect to be released before the end of their term of imprisonment.

It is this juxtaposition between the everyday and the contested that has inspired this book. The profound socio-economic transformation of post-war Britain continues to shape the contemporary world and early release offers a largely unexplored vantage point from which to view the stepping stones that led from the confident penal-welfarism of the 1960s to the altogether more contested politics of law and order that emerged in the mid-1990s (Garland 2001). As such this book should not be approached as a legal text. It is first and foremost a historical study of policy change that uses a case-study approach (Yin 2003) to illuminate the complex ideas, trade-offs, and moments of political controversy that defined the evolution of early release in England and Wales between 1960 and 1995. The case studies featured in this book offer a unique insight into the inner workings of government during this turbulent period in British history and draw heavily upon documentation held at the National Archives as well as files released to this study by the Home Office, Ministry of Justice, and Parole Board under the Freedom of Information Act 2000. Making use of recent advances in smartphone technology it has been possible to develop a substantial library of digitized archival records and this book represents, in focus and presentation, an attempt to showcase this hugely important public resource in a more creative way than would have been possible even a decade ago. This journey has been as important as the destination. Detailed archival research remains uncommon within the field of criminology and there is little methodological guidance for those seeking to negotiate the competing demands of social science and historiography. Nothing can fully prepare the uninitiated with the practical skills, instinct, and craft that are needed to make real-time decisions within the archive. As Michelle King has noted, even the best laid plans do not survive first contact with the archives,

> ... the researchers own fear, boredom, inexperience, frustration and loneliness can shape decisions made in the archives, and the resulting contours of research. Nicholas Dirks recalls the moment of panic he has in going in the archives for the first time, having no idea 'how to control the chaos' of documents, 'both endless and banal'. (King 2012 p.20)

This work offers one possible reading of the chaos of documents that accrued during the evolution of early release in England and Wales, a little understood area of public policy that continues to shape the everyday lived experience of prisoners and their families. Insofar as it achieves these aims it can be considered a study of what goes on behind the scenes of our criminal justice system. It is a study of what happens in the shadow of our prison gates.

The book is structured into five substantive parts and proceeds as follows:

Part I outlines the central concerns of this book. Chapter 1 builds the case for the study of early release in comparative historical perspective and highlights the important, but often overlooked, role early release has played within the criminal justice apparatus of the liberal democratic state. It situates early release within a broader policy context and concludes with an overview of the three case studies that provide the substantive focus of this book. Chapter 2 expands upon this theme and sets out a theoretical framework for the systematic and historically grounded analysis of early release in England and Wales between 1960 and 1995. It considers the mediating role of political institutions in shaping complex policy outcomes and goes on to offer a critical appraisal of the challenges facing a criminologist doing historical study. It concludes with a brief overview of the primary and secondary data sources that have informed this book.

Part II examines the period 1960 to 1968. This case study is split across two chapters and reflects upon the events that culminated in the introduction of a modern system of parole in England and Wales, a period of policy development that is fundamental to our understanding of how early release developed in the decades that followed. Chapter 3 explores the long-term historical evolution of early release administration and how these enduring policy problems gave rise to a reform agenda that was infused with the prevailing optimism and confidence of the 1960s. It goes on to examine growing criminological support for indeterminate sentencing and the influence of the landmark Longford Committee Report *Crime: A Challenge to Us All* (Labour Party 1964a). Chapter 4 considers the impact of Roy Jenkins' appointment as Home Secretary and the detailed legislative planning that resulted in the complex system of parole given legal effect by the Criminal Justice Act 1967.

In Part III, the focus shifts to the second case study period, from 1975 to 1983. This case study is split across two chapters. Chapter 5 explores the delicate negotiations that led to the 'Jenkins initiative', a reform package that extended the scale, scope, and reach of the parole system in England and Wales. It goes on to consider the rise and fall of the 'partly suspended sentence', a policy innovation intended to extend the benefits of early release to short-sentence prisoners. Chapter 6 explores the ever more complex policy debates that enveloped the efforts to extend a system of early release to short sentence prisoners. The chapter reflects upon the Home Office (1981b) *Review of Parole in England and Wales* and an extended period of policy inertia which culminated in the Criminal Justice Act 1982 and wide-ranging changes to the operation of parole in England and Wales.

Part IV deals with the period from 1987 to 1995 and the decision to undertake a root and branch review of parole following the 1987 General Election. This case study is again split across two chapters. Chapter 7 opens with a discussion of the piecemeal modification of remission arrangements in April 1987, a measure to relieve pressure on the prison system that ultimately came at a high cost for the Home Office. It goes on to critically appraise the proceedings of the Carlisle Committee and the compromises that came to define their landmark report *The Parole System in England and Wales* (Home Office 1989). Chapter 8 examines the legislative planning process that resulted in root and branch reform of early release in England and Wales. The chapter traces the post-election planning process that culminated in a Home Office strategic 'away day' held at Leeds Castle in September 1987 and goes on to trace the evolution of the collective vision for management of the criminal justice system set out in the White Paper, *Crime, Justice and Protecting the Public* (Home Office 1990a). It concludes with an account of the turbulent passage of the Criminal Justice Act 1991 which gave legal effect to a radically altered system of early release in England and Wales.

Part V returns to the questions posed at the outset of this book and reflects upon the deep-rooted institutional structures of power that shaped the historical trajectory of early release in England and Wales between 1960 and 1995. Chapter 9 investigates the 'spatial' dimensions of this mediating role and builds the case for a sharper focus upon how policy-makers operate within, and interact across, institutional settings. The chapter re-visits the 'stewardship function' of the Home Office and examines how functional tasks were assigned, interpreted, and resolved within the Department. It then looks outwards to better understand the complex and fluid balance of power between the various actors with a stake in the administration of early release. Chapter 10 turns to the 'temporal' dimensions of this mediating role and discusses how historical factors have influenced the development of early release in England and Wales. The chapter considers the central role of path dependency in shaping the trajectory of early release policy and practice in England and Wales between 1960 and 1995, before turning to the less well understood catalysing role of 'timing and sequence' at key moments of policy reform (Pierson 2004 pp.54–78).

Finally, an extended postscript will trace the evolution of early release since the events described in this book. The postscript examines the growing influence of a 'strategy of bifurcation' (Bottoms 1977) within penal policy and considers how the differential treatment of low-level and serious offenders has transformed the policy and practice of early release in England and Wales.

Acknowledgements

This book was completed during a Visiting Fellowship in the Mannheim Centre for Criminology at the London School of Economics and Political Science. I would like to place on record my deep-felt gratitude to Tim Newburn and Robert Reiner, neither this book nor the PhD research it is based upon would have been possible without their continued support, guidance, and encouragement. Over the last eight years the LSE has become a home from home for me, and I would like to thank all the staff and students in the School of Social Policy and the Mannheim Centre for helping to create such a friendly and intellectually vibrant environment for academic study.

I am indebted to the many librarians and specialist archivists at the National Archives, Churchill College Cambridge, British Library, London School of Economics Special Collection, and the Bodleian Library, Oxford for their help and assistance with this study. I am also grateful to all the civil servants at the Ministry of Justice, Home Office, and Parole Board who dealt with my numerous freedom of information requests with such skill and professionalism. I would like to express my particular thanks to David Faulkner whose personal papers have offered an invaluable insight into the more recent events described in this book. This study is richer for his assistance and personal reflections.

Finally, I would like to extend my appreciation to those interviewed in the course of this study and those who provided comments including David Downes, Nicola Padfield, Michael Moriarty, Jennifer Brown, and Peter Dawson for being so generous with their time and thoughtful in their responses. I hope I have done justice to the incredible wealth of information they have shared with me. I am grateful to the general editors of the Clarendon Studies in Criminology Series and the anonymous reviewers for all their constructive feedback, as well as my Oxford University Press editors Lucy Alexander and Amy Baker for their endless patience and guidance during the preparation of this book.

As always, my biggest thanks are reserved for my family: Pauline, Dennis, Max, Grace, Evie, Matt, and Alexandra.

Table of Contents

List of Figures xix
List of Tables xxi

Part I Introduction

1. Early Release in Comparative Historical Perspective 3
   - Introduction 3
   - When to Release: Justice, Fairness, and the Limits of the Liberal Democratic State 6
   - Situating Early Release: Criminal Justice as a Public Policy Concern 10
   - Case Studies: Three Defining Moments of Reform 25
   - Conclusion 28
2. Conceptualizing Policy Change 29
   - Beyond Structure and Agency: The Mediating Role of Political Institutions 29
   - Historical Institutionalism: Organizational Factors in Political Life 36
   - The Criminologist as Historian 44
   - Conclusion 51

Part II Penal Optimism, 1960–1968

3. An Idea Whose Time Had Come: Parole, Indeterminacy, and the Personalization of Punishment 55
   - A Brief History of Early Release in England and Wales 55
   - Criminal Justice in an Age of Optimism 61
   - A Recognizable Peak: The Coupling of Parole and Indeterminacy 67
   - A System of Parole Takes Shape: *The Adult Offender* White Paper 73

4. A Very British Compromise: The Criminal Justice Act 1967 79
A Change at the Top 79
Managing the Crisis: A Home Office on the Back Foot 83
The Criminal Justice Act 1967 87
Cautious First Steps for the Parole System in England and Wales 91
Conclusion: A Victory for Principle or Pragmatism? 96

Part III An Age of Uncertainty, 1975–1983

5. Squaring the Circle: Early Release and Short Sentence Prisoners 103
The Long Shadow of Disinvestment 103
The 'Jenkins Initiative' 110
Policy Innovation: The Partly Suspended Sentence 115
New Government, New Direction 119

6. The Politics of Inertia: The Criminal Justice Act 1982 124
On the Horns of a Dilemma: The Question of Short-Term Prisoners 124
The Home Office Review of Parole in England and Wales 132
'Whitelaw Mark 1 and Whitelaw Mark 2' 137
The Criminal Justice Act 1982 140
Conclusion: Administrative Realpolitik 145

Part IV Breakdown and Renewal, 1987–1995

7. Truth in Sentencing: The Carlisle Committee Review of Parole in England and Wales 149
A Restricted Operating Space 149
The Introduction of 50 Per Cent Remission 155
The Carlisle Committee Review of Parole in England and Wales 159
Managing the Fallout 166

8. A New System Takes Shape: The Criminal Justice Act 1991 171
The 1987 General Election: From Penal Pragmatism to a Strategic Approach 171
A Fragile Consensus: The Green Paper and Ditchley Park 175
The Criminal Justice Act 1991 181
The Backlash Begins 187
Conclusion: Penal Policy at a Crossroads 190

Part V Discussion

9. Organizational Factors in Early Release Policy and Practice 195
Inside the Home Office: From Plurality to Action 196
The Mediations of Political Power 201
Law's Empire 205
Conclusion: Criminal Justice as Statecraft 210

10. Temporal Factors in Early Release Policy and Practice 212
Policy-Making in Real-World Settings 212
Path Dependence 216
Continuity and Change 219
Conclusion: The Merits of Comparative Historical Study 226

Postscript 230
Context 230
1997–2003 232
2004–2009 236
2010–2017 240

Appendix 1: Early Release Key Event Timeline, 1960–1995 247
Appendix 2: Biography of Key Actors 250
Appendix 3: Carlisle Review Committee Membership and Terms of Reference 254

Bibliography 257
Copyright Acknowledgements 283
Index 285

List of Figures

1.1 The operation of parole in England and Wales for determinate sentences, 1968–1995 9
1.2 Total recorded crime, England and Wales, 1900–1995 12
1.3 Crime survey for England and Wales estimate of overall crime, 1981–1995 13
1.4 Persons sentenced to immediate custody in England and Wales, 1950–2001 18
1.5 The average prison population and 'Certified Normal Accommodation' of the prison estate in England and Wales, 1960–1995 19
1.6 Home Office 'organizational chart', August 1963 22
1.7 Functional breakdown of Home Office expenditure, 1968–1990 (2017 prices) 23
3.1 Government spending as a percentage of gross domestic product, 1960–1995 64
3.2 Number of persons held either two or three to a cell, 1965–1995 66
3.3 Lord Gardiner's note 'A Parole System' to the study group on crime prevention and penal reform, March 1964 72
3.4 Home Office computation of parole release eligibility 77
4.1 A 'Young Home Secretary' under pressure, 1966 85
5.1 Home Office annual prison population projections 1970–1973 104
6.1 Home Office options appraisal of early release for short-term prisoners 134
6.2 Letter from the Lord Chief Justice to Home Secretary, 9 October 1981 138
6.3 The use of partly suspended sentences, 1982–1990 142

7.1 Media response to Hurd's introduction of 50 per cent remission 158
7.2 Summary of Carlisle Committee recommendations 164
7.3 Home Office impact assessment of the Carlisle Committee recommendations upon the prison population 169
9.1 Caricature of Home Secretary William Whitelaw in *New Society*, June 1980 203

List of Tables

2.1 National Archives, key file series 48

4.1 The first ten years of operation, parole decisions made in determinate prisoner cases, 1968–1978 94

Source: TNA: HO 303/98 © The National Archives, 1975

PART I

Introduction

1

Early Release in Comparative Historical Perspective

This introductory chapter outlines the central concerns of this book. It builds the case for the study of early release in comparative historical perspective and highlights the important, but often overlooked, role early release has played within the criminal justice apparatus of the liberal democratic state. It goes on to locate the evolution of early release within a wider context of policy change and, using a case study approach, identifies three critical periods of reform that exemplify the evolving ideas, trade-offs, and political controversies that exemplify the evolution of early release in England and Wales between 1960 and 1995.

Introduction

> It has been said with truth that it is easy to imprison a man; the difficult thing is to release him. (Home Office 1959 p.19)

In the second half of the twentieth century, England and Wales, like many liberal democratic jurisdictions, experienced a profound readjustment in both the aims and techniques of criminal justice. The broad contours of this historical shift have been well mapped within the criminological literature (see Bottoms and Stevenson 1992; Garland 2001; Newburn 2007b). As classical and utilitarian justifications for punishment fell into decline in the late nineteenth century a modernizing project began to gather pace and this saw punishment re-cast primarily as a means of rehabilitating offenders (Allen 1981; Garland 1985). Over time, this perspective grew in sophistication and exerted increasing influence over the administration of criminal justice. So much so that by the 1960s it had crystallized into a policy framework Garland has described as 'penal welfarism', a complex web of

Getting Out: Early Release in England and Wales, 1960–1995. First Edition. Thomas C. Guiney. © Thomas C. Guiney 2018. Published 2018 by Oxford University Press.

values and attitudes united by a common belief that, 'penal measures ought, where possible, to be rehabilitative interventions rather than negative, retributive punishments' (2001 p.34). Just as this framework reached its highpoint in the early 1970s, it began to break down (Garland 2001). Disrupted by significant socio-economic and political change, a rise in recorded crime and negative research findings that challenged the rehabilitative value of prison, many of the underlying assumptions of penal welfarism began to unravel (see Downes 1992; Morris 1989). In time, the temperature of penological debate began to rise and the expert driven discourse of a metropolitan liberal elite gave way to a more populist law and order agenda and new forms of criminal justice governance (Loader 2006 p.561). The politicization of criminal justice has fundamentally re-shaped the terms of crime debate. Where the operation of the criminal justice system had once been seen as a bipartisan matter with a strong humanitarian impulse, the emergence of a highly charged 'penal populism' has often seen 'penal effectiveness sacrificed at the altar of electoral advantage' (Roberts et al. 2003 p.5; see also, Bottoms 1995; Lacey 2008).

Comparative historical analysis allows us to look with fresh eyes upon these continuities and dislocations with the past. In the introduction to his critically acclaimed novel *The Go-Between*, L.P Hartley (1953) observed that 'the past is a foreign country: they do things differently there' and this neatly encapsulates the appeal of historical study. It reminds us of the contingency of seemingly stable social structures and forces us to confront our ideas and assumptions about the political world. Making sense of contemporary historical events, or to use Peter Hennessy's (2012) colourful turn of phrase, 'distilling the frenzy' of the world we inhabit focuses our attention on the changing knowledges, understandings, and techniques of government as well as the various actors, ideas, and struggles that came to define the administration of criminal justice in the latter half of the twentieth century. For this reason, Loader and Sparks have argued that, 'an account of change in the criminal justice arena is best approached as a special case of an historical enquiry into politics' (2004 p.6). It draws attention to the 'struggles over the meanings and import of such ideas as order, authority, legitimacy, freedom, rights and justice' that go to the heart of public policy (Loader 2006 p.562). More importantly perhaps, it speaks directly to competing conceptions of the 'right' or 'good' society (Rawls 1999; Sandel 1998).

How do we account for these changes? How can we gain traction within this debate given the proliferation and density of existing criminological research? In his seminal work *The Culture of Control* Garland draws attention to the unavoidable tension between 'broad generalization' and the 'specification of empirical particulars' when studying complex social and political structures (Garland 2001 p.vii). The broad terrain of criminal justice may have been well mapped in the literature but the 'capillaries' of power which connect individual action to macro-level social structures remain relatively uncharted (Foucault 1980 p.39; see also Hunt and Wickham 1994). This book explores these lesser-known capillaries in order to build an empirically rich and theoretically informed account of one discreet area of penal policy-making in England and Wales. In so doing our point of entry will be the evolution of 'early release' policy and practice between 1960 and 1995, a period of thirty-five years punctuated by episodes of intense legislative and administrative reform. Contemporary discussion of crime control and penal policy has focused to a significant degree on the entry points into the criminal justice system; the police as criminal justice gatekeepers (Newburn 2003b; Reiner 2000) and the increasing punitiveness of sentencing practice (Bottoms 1995; Roberts et al. 2003). But this is only one feature of a much wider panorama. Criminology has had relatively little to say about the termination of prison sentences and the inherent ambiguity of 'getting out' as the state begins to loosen its grip on those held in custody (Padfield 2007; Padfield et al. 2012a). The extract above from the White Paper *Penal Policy in a Changing Society* (Home Office 1959) is so interesting (and seemingly counter-intuitive), because it shifts the locus of penal enquiry from the sentence of the court and the quantum of punishment to the day-to-day operation of the penal system and the most appropriate moment to release an individual back into the community. There has been little exploration of the historical development of early release, the key periods of reform, crisis, or political controversy (Maguire 1992; Shute 2003). We know very little about how policy-makers themselves approached this task or the challenges they faced in seeking to shape this area of criminal justice administration. This book sets out to answer two simple questions that, it is hoped, will help to illuminate this complex area of public policy: First, in what ways did the policy and practice of early release develop in England and Wales between 1960 and 1995? Second, how might these changes be accounted for? In turn, we will find that these questions offer a promising point of departure to look afresh at the changing aims and techniques of criminal justice administration in post-War England and Wales.

When to Release: Justice, Fairness, and the Limits of the Liberal Democratic State

For the purposes of this book, early release is defined broadly as the various legal and administrative mechanisms by which the custodial element of a sentence may be reduced by executive action, with the remainder served either in the community under licence or terminated unconditionally (Shute 2003; West 1972). This definition captures a number of practices including the exceptional use of emergency powers, adjustments to the tariff for offenders serving life sentences and the Home Secretary's residual power to exercise the Royal Prerogative of Mercy. While important, these mechanisms have accounted for a relatively small proportion of the prisoners who have benefited from early release arrangements in England and Wales and will not be the focus here. Instead this book concentrates on the routine, 'steady state' operation of early release for adult offenders serving determinate prison sentences. Between 1960 and 1995, this largely consisted of 'remission' and 'parole', supplemented over time by various forms of 'release on licence' that will be discussed later in this book. While each of these mechanisms resulted in the reduction of the custodial portion of a determinate sentence their historical antecedents, legal basis, and practical operation of these mechanisms differed markedly. In part, this reflects the challenge of justifying early release in principle and delivering a viable system of executive release in practice. Early release has always been bound up with societal justifications for punishment and the limitations placed upon the use of imprisonment within the liberal democratic system (Padfield 2007; Padfield et al. 2012a). It draws attention to the uneasy constitutional balance of power between the judiciary and the executive, and forces us to reflect upon the administrative challenge of governing large captive populations where the hopes and expectations of inmates do not always align with the interests of prison authorities or the community at large. The termination of a prison sentence will always be a significant penal decision where disparate concerns collide, but the early release of prisoners can feel even more disorientating. In an age of 'penal populism' (Pratt 2007), where crime has become increasingly politicized, early release inverts our usual way of thinking about punishment and challenges us to consider the circumstances in which it may be desirable to reduce the custodial element of a sentence rather than extend it. We will see that even where there has been a working consensus on the overarching objectives of early release, translating these principles into practice has proved to be extremely difficult. Like many spheres of governmentality that involve the exercise of discretion (Foucault 1991), the early release of prisoners in England and Wales has developed a complex legal-administrative apparatus with its own bureaucracy and internal logics that have exerted considerable influence over the development of policy in England and Wales.

The concept of remission time has a long history in English penal practice and the term is still in use despite its abolition in the Criminal Justice Act 1991. Remission developed as a tool of control to assist by prison authorities with the maintenance of order (Padfield et al 2012a p.968). A prisoner could earn remission of a prison sentence if they engaged positively with a prison regime, an incentive that was amplified over time since indiscretions would typically result in the forfeiture of all accumulated benefits. Originally conceived as a discretionary privilege in the gift of a Prison Governor, remission slowly evolved into a presumptive entitlement only to be withheld from inmates in cases of serious misconduct (Home Office 1989; McConville 1981). This entitlement was eventually codified after the Second World War when the Prison Rules were amended to the effect that all prisoners in England and Wales serving determinate prison sentences were eligible, subject to good behaviour, for unconditional release after serving two-thirds of their sentence (Fox 1952). The universal operation of remission can make quantitative analysis difficult. Since remission time applied to all determinate sentences, subject to good behaviour, the Home Office did not routinely collect information on remission, or report annually on its operation, making it almost impossible to trace the development of remission with any degree of confidence. In this sense, remission represents one of the many 'black holes' of British penal policy, for while it exerted a strong gravitational pull over the wider system it cannot be observed or measured directly.

In contrast, the modern usage of parole has tended to evoke a future-orientated quality concerned with the discretionary release of a prisoner back into the community (Hood and Shute 2002; Shute 2003). Derived from the French chivalric tradition, parole was originally used as a term of art in times of war when an officer gave his 'parole d'honneur' or word of honour, not to escape from captivity, or to refrain from certain other actions to which his captors might object (Hansard *HL Deb 12 June 1967 vol 283 c721*). In more recent times parole has acquired a more specific legal meaning and this led Professor Donald West to propose the following widely accepted definition '[p]arole, as it is understood in the United Kingdom, is a procedure whereby a sentence imposed by a court of justice may be varied by administrative action' (West 1972 p.1). While remission provided a reward for past deeds and resulted in the absolute termination of a prison sentence, the parole system looked forward with parolees released on licence with the possibility of recall for breach of their parole conditions. Given the instrumental benefits of parole, it is perhaps unsurprising the system has demonstrated remarkable plasticity as a tool of public policy. It has expedited the safe release of prisoners who pose no further risk to the public, or whose rehabilitation would be better served in the community. It has been offered as a reward for those who have cooperated with prison authorities and relied upon as a safety valve of last resort when demand for prison places has outstripped the capacity of the prison estate. Perhaps most controversially, the parole system has, in some high-profile cases, insulated government from politically motivated decisions to keep in custody, 'for comparatively longer periods, not only those who apparently continue to pose a high risk to the public but also those whose crimes were notorious, even though they have apparently been rehabilitated or no longer pose any significant risk to the public' (Hood and Shute 2002 p.836). Over time, the relative importance of these considerations has shifted in response to the changing pressures placed upon the criminal justice system and these moments of policy reform can have significant implications for the lived experiences of prison inmates and their families. As Figure 1.1 reveals, the number of cases processed through the parole system, by either the Parole Board or prison-based Local Review Committees under delegated powers, fluctuated at around

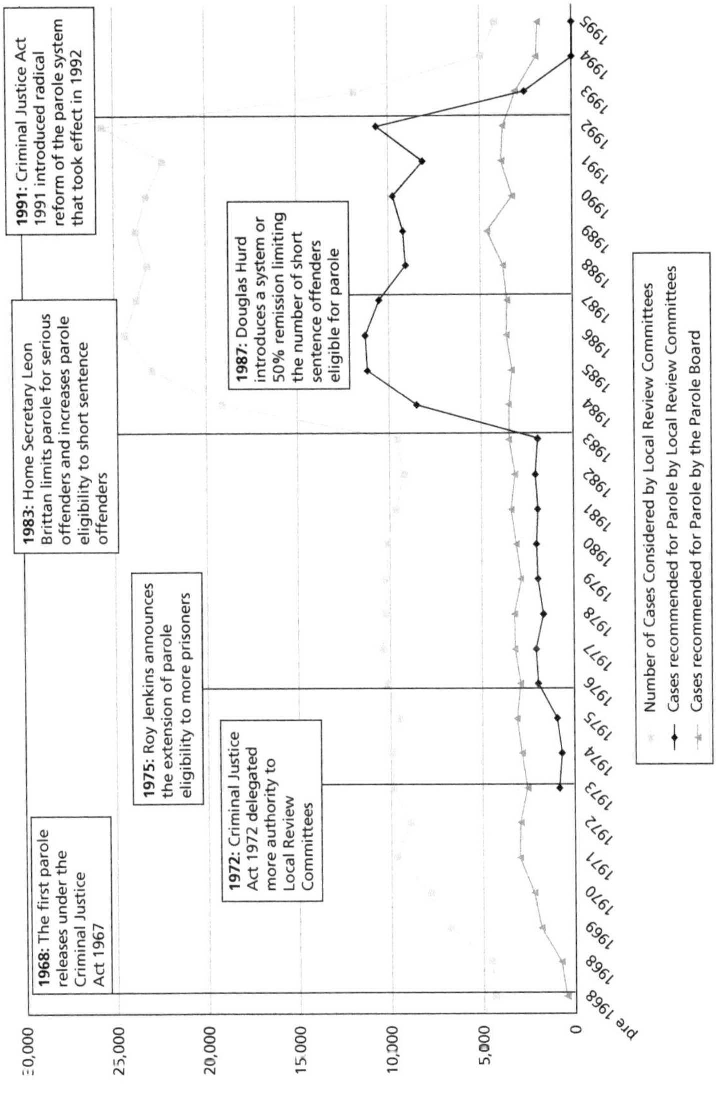

Figure 1.1 The operation of parole in England and Wales for determinate sentences, 1968–1995

10,000 applications per year in the 1970s. During this time, the number of cases approved for parole increased steadily from 2,210 in 1970 with a 28.3 per cent success rate, to approximately 5,000 in 1980, representing a success rate of over 50 per cent (HMSO Report of the Parole Board, 1968–1995). After 1983, the volume of cases considered for parole increased dramatically following the decision of Home Secretary Leon Brittan to reduce the minimum threshold for parole eligibility to six months. As a direct consequence of this decision the caseload of the parole system peaked in 1986 when 24,380 cases were considered and approximately 15,000 prisoners were granted parole, a success rate of over 60 per cent that bore little resemblance to the risk-averse instincts of the early Parole Board. Following this high-water mark, more cases were dealt with automatically and the number of cases subject to discretionary release by the Parole Board began to decline. Reform of remission arrangements in 1987 removed many short sentence prisoners from the scope of the parole system and this downtrend accelerated after 1992 when the Criminal Justice Act 1991 came into full effect.

Situating Early Release: Criminal Justice as a Public Policy Concern

These short historical vignettes are helpful because they remind us that 'early release' decisions were not made in a policy vacuum. On the contrary, the evolution of early release policy and practice in England and Wales was, to an important extent, an expression of wider policy forces and a response to the challenges, both immediate and long term, of administering an effective criminal justice system. As Hood and Shute have noted:

> The weight accorded to these different considerations, and the resolution of conflicts between them, has been affected by changes in the structures and objectives of the sentencing and prison systems. It has also been affected by changing conceptions of the problem of criminality, by changing social and legal values, and by changing public sentiments. (Hood and Shute 2002 p.836)

To really understand the complex historical trajectory of 'early release' in England and Wales it is necessary to locate these events within a wider picture of criminal justice change. As we have already seen, criminal justice, like many areas of public policy has become an altogether more complex pursuit since the 1960s and the breakdown of the post-war consensus (Dutton 1997; Kavanagh and Morris 1994; Marsh et al. 1999). But this has always been a contradictory picture of both continuity and change (Faulkner 1991). The generation of penal administrators who learnt their trade in the1960s would have recognized many of the central concerns of criminal justice in the early twenty-first century. However, there is also little doubt that the profound re-configuration of criminal justice has been deeply troubling for many of those who served their apprenticeships at the height of the 'rehabilitative ideal' and were active, if reluctant, participants in the emergence of a more muscular brand of penal populism (Pratt 2007). This complex dialectic requires careful exploration and invites greater scrutiny of four dimensions of policy change that provide an essential backdrop to the events described in this book.

Crime control

The first, and arguably most striking feature of policy change, has been the shift towards a 'high crime society' and the steady erosion, either real or perceived, of the liberal democratic state as the pre-eminent guarantor of social order (Garland 1996). These changes remain highly contested, but drawing upon evidence from police recorded crime figures and the Crime Survey of England and Wales[1] (CSEW) it is possible to trace the rough edges of this historical shift. There has been a tendency amongst politicians and other commentators to treat historic crime data as an objectively 'true' or 'real' picture of crime, but in reality, all sources of evidence offer a partial perspective that can both illuminate and obscure our analysis of this complex social phenomena (Maguire 2007 pp.253–254; Reiner 2016). Recorded crime statistics have been collected since 1851 and allow for a broad historical survey of the incidence of crime made known to the police. However, these figures are limited in scope to 'notifiable offences' and do not take into account the prevalence of less serious, 'summary offences'. They are also subject to significant variations in police accounting (Newburn 2007b) and in January 2014 recorded crime figures lost their status as

[1] Previously known as the British Crime Survey (BCS).

'official statistics' due to ongoing concerns over reliability in data collection (UK Statistics Authority 2014). In comparison, the CSEW is generally seen as a more reliable measure of many categories of criminal activity but the survey does not encompass some of the most serious crimes, such as murder, or so-called 'victimless crimes' like drug abuse or environmental damage. Moreover, the recent origins of the crime survey can make longer-term historical comparisons difficult (Maguire 2007 pp.241–301).

Extrapolating long-term historical trends from these sources is therefore value-laden, but there does appear to be a degree of convergence in the data, at least for the period 1960 to 1993. The recorded crime statistics suggest that the incidence of crime increased markedly in the post-war era before beginning to fall after 1995. As Figure 1.2 reveals, a total of 743,713 crimes were reported to police in England and Wales in 1960, a figure that grew steadily through the 1970s before accelerating to 5,100,241 in 1995.

Over time, the steep rise in recorded crime has become highly contested and a significant focus of political debate, but the headline figures can obscure important differences in the incidence of crime over time, variations between offence categories as well as the individualized, lived experiences of crime in many communities (Maguire 2007 pp.253–254). More difficult to quantify is the relationship between recorded crime rates and the so-called 'dark

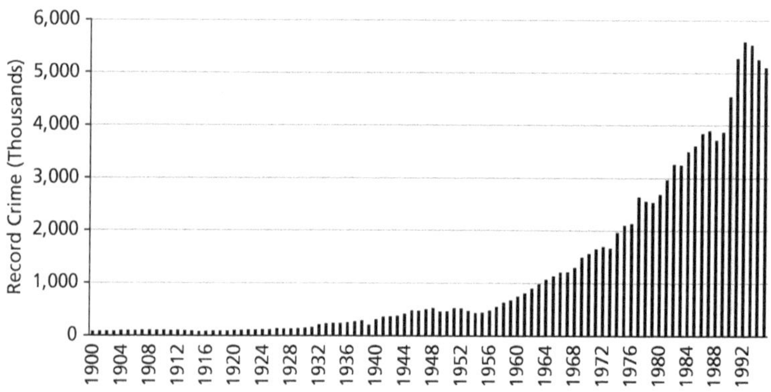

Figure 1.2 Total recorded crime, England and Wales, 1900–1995

Source: Home Office (2012)

figure' of crime (Biderman and Reiss 1967). For example, Reiner (2010; 2016) has argued that it is possible to distinguish a number of distinct phases within the recorded crime rise. Drawing on evidence from the General Household Survey (GHS), Reiner argues that between 1955 and 1983 much of the rise in recorded crime, particularly in relation to property offences, can be attributed to the increasing propensity of victims to report crimes to the police (2010 p.254). Thereafter, reporting rates began to stabilize, and the available evidence does confirm that crime grew at an unprecedented rate between 1983 and 1992, before beginning to fall after 1993.

A broadly comparable picture can be found in the CSEW. Established in 1981 as the British Crime Survey (BCS), the survey indicates that recorded crime statistics consistently underestimate the incidence of overall crime whilst also appearing to reinforce the conclusion that crime increased markedly in the 1980s before beginning to plateau and subsequently fall in the mid-1990s (see Figure 1.3). Total reported crime increased from 11,066,000 in 1981 to a peak of 19,109,000 in 1995 before falling thereafter.

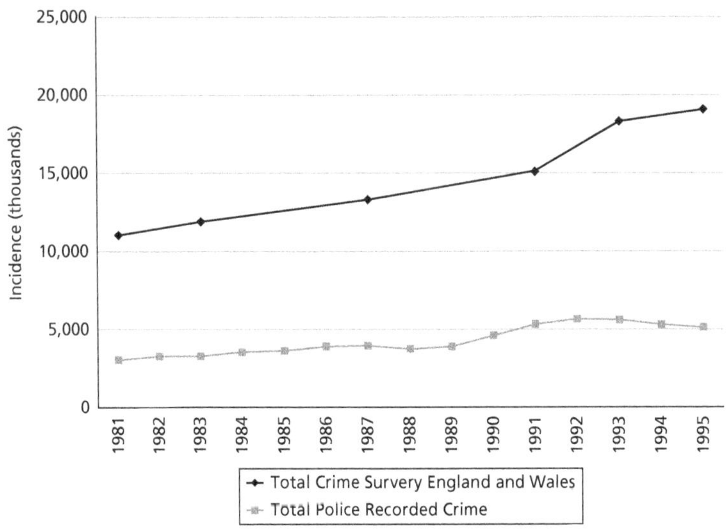

Figure 1.3 Crime survey for England and Wales estimate of overall crime, 1981–1995

Source: ONS (2013)

Allied to this was a worrying increase in the risk of victimization. The percentage of households that reported they had been victims of crime once or more in 1981 was 27.7 per cent, a figure that would increase to 39.7 per cent in 1996 before beginning to fall.

The impact of this transformation in the basic conditions of social life led the sociologist Jock Young to describe rising crime rates as 'the major motor in the transformation of public behaviour and attitudes, in the development of the crime control apparatus ...' (1999 p.17). It was also a key driver of new public policy responses to crime. Reflecting on the development of crime and criminal justice in Britain since 1945, Morris has argued that governmental responses to crime progressed through a number of distinct phases as policymakers sought to deal with the inexorable rise in recorded crime, especially amongst young people (1989 p.93). In the immediate aftermath of World War Two, the police were widely seen as the primary agents of crime control but this gradually gave way to a mixed economy of penal responses as policymakers embraced the prevailing penal optimism of the 1960s and the basic premise that prison could help to rehabilitate offenders prior to their re-integration back into the community (Morris 1989 p.106). Ultimately, this proved short-lived and the 1970s ushered in a period of scepticism about 'rehabilitation' defined by a belief that 'nothing works' (often attributed to the much-misquoted Martinson 1974). Stripped of these penal shibboleths, a more pragmatic focus emerged with growing interest in situational crime control and a 'just deserts' sentencing philosophy premised upon the belief that punishment should be proportionate to the harm caused by the offence (von Hirsh 1976 and 1985; von Hirsh and Ashworth 1998).

The politicization of criminal justice

For much of the period after the Second World War crime control was viewed as a bi-partisan matter to be administered by experts away from the glare of party politics (Windlesham 1987, 1993, 1996, 2001). This consensus undoubtedly yielded political benefits for politicians so long as the equilibrium was maintained but it also reflected a strong civilizing impulse to manage such an emotive issue in the right and proper way (Loader 2006). As Roy

Jenkins made clear in his maiden speech as Home Secretary to the House of Commons on 2 February 1966:

In my view crime is a most unsuitable subject for strict party conflict, and as long as I am Home Secretary I hope that we can prevent it from becoming a subject for strict party conflict. It is a most unsuitable subject because it is one in which, more than most, passion and emotion are very bad counsellors. We all have a duty to encourage the nation to look objectively at the facts and to see which reasoned conclusions about prevention and punishment can be drawn from them. It would be most unwise to introduce politics into the question of crime to the extent of suggesting that this most difficult situation was the fault of this Government. (HC Deb 2 February 1966 vol 723 c1121)

This worldview began to unravel in the 1970s. Shaken by continued rises in recorded crime and declining levels of public trust in government, criminal justice emerged as a more contested electoral issue. Downes and Morgan have traced the development of law and order in this less certain world through successive editions of the *Oxford Handbook of Criminology* (2002; 2007; 2012). They argue that the politicization of law and order was shaped by 'the perceived need to respond to the almost continued rise in recorded crime, the reduced potency of certain informal controls, the growth of illicit drug taking, and the threat of politically inspired terrorism' (2007 p.234). In the period immediately after 1945, law and order had been relatively insulated from party politics by a cross-party liberal ideology. This spirit of bipartisanship and the central planks of the post-war consensus, often referred to 'Butskillism' (Marsh et al. 1999), began to break down in the 1970s as the main political parties began to fight for control of the law and order terrain. At first, this was a rather asymmetric divide. While the Labour Party remained wedded to an orthodox social democratic understanding of crime (Young 1988), the Conservative Party were successful in developing a law and order proposition that linked public fear of crime and insecurity to a wider political narrative:

The Conservatives fused the issues of law-breaking and order defiance. They attacked not just the policies but the integrity of Labour. They refashioned their traditional claim to be the natural party of government, representing the order of established authority. They successfully pointed to Labour's responsibility for the alleged 'ungovernability' of Britain. They capitalized on widespread public fears about: national

> decline; loss of economic competitiveness and bad industrial relations; the growth of permissiveness and declining public morals; fear of crime, inner city decay, and the extravagances of youth fashion and street protests. They made restoring the 'rule of law', which they claimed Labour had undermined, one of their five major tasks .... (Downes and Morgan 2007 p.204)

For those on both the right and the left of the political spectrum it has become common to interpret the development of penal policy during Thatcher's years in office through the prism of contemporary events and political discussion. As the historian Eric Hobsbawm once noted, 'all history is contemporary history in fancy dress' (1997 p.228). In reality, the picture was far more complex than this simple picture might suggest. The 1979 general election was won, in part, on 'the most radically tough law and order ticket the Conservatives had ever produced' (Downes and Morgan 2007 p.213), but away from the rhetoric, government policy continued to rest upon a complex blend of classic liberalism and one nation conservatism, infused with the ideas of an ascendant 'new right' agenda (O'Malley 2000). Reiner (2010) has described law and order in the 1980s as a rather phoney 'war on crime' and suggests that, with the notable exception of public order, there was a systematic attempt by the Conservative Government to make greater use of non-custodial sentences, implement insights from the nascent field of situational crime control and recast crime control as a social issue for which everybody must take a share of the responsibility (2010 pp.8–9). This supposed 'Indian summer' (Windlesham 1993) came to an end following the 1992 General Election as the Major government grappled with mass unemployment associated with the 'Lawson boom', the destabilizing effects of 'Black Wednesday' and a concerted effort re-energize the Conservative Party by, in part, moving government policy in a more punitive direction (Downes and Morgan 2007 p.258). There is also some evidence to suggest that the 'clear blue water' established by the Conservatives contributed to the diminishing electoral prospects of the Labour Party, at least in the short term (Downes and Morgan 2007 p.204). Whether this resonance with the electorate was real or perceived the Labour Party responded to Conservative pressure with a gradual toughening of its law and order platform (Tonry 2003), a process that accelerated under Shadow Home Secretary Tony Blair. Crime was recast as the unacceptable social cost of Conservative economic mismanagement, the Criminal Justice Act 1991 was heavily condemned for focusing on the offence rather than the offender and the now famous 'tough on crime, tough on the causes of crime' slogan, coined by Gordon Brown but popularized by Tony Blair, came to signify New Labour's embrace of a more muscular approach to law and order. So much so that by the mid-1990s the main political parties were converging around a more punitive law and order agenda and, 'a new second order consensus emerged. No party could any longer afford to cede the law and order ground to the opposition: all parties felt obliged to address it in some way' (Downes and Morgan 2007 p.204).

The breakdown of the rehabilitative ideal

The decline of the 'rehabilitative ideal' (Allen 1981) and subsequent politicization of law and order had a profound impact upon the emotional tone of penal policy and justifications for punishment (Garland 2001; Pratt 2007). As policymakers embraced a mixed economy of crime control measures (Morris 1989) punishment became increasingly rehabilitative in focus and orientated towards the successful integration of offenders back into society. Perhaps the archetypal expression of this policy position can be found in the 1959 White Paper *Penal Practice in a Changing Society*:

> The constructive function of our prisons is to prevent the largest possible number of those committed to their care from offending again. Since the report of the Gladstone Committee in 1895, it has been accepted that this end will not be reached by a regime designed simply to deter through fear. The object should be, in the words of that Committee, to send the prisoners out 'better men and women, physically and morally, than when they came in'. (Home Office 1959 p.11)

This optimism began to evaporate as policymakers came to terms with the emergence of a high crime society, a series of negative research findings and the perception amongst many politicians that they needed to establish their 'tough' on crime credentials with an ostensibly punitive electorate (Downes and Morgan 2007). This 'punitive turn' was multifaceted and over time saw the development of an extensive crime control apparatus encompassing civil enforcement, penal supervision, and financial penalties, but it is the impact upon national incarceration rates that has arguably been most prominent (for a contrary view see Matthews 2005). Between 1960 and 1995, the courts demonstrated a growing propensity to sentence offenders to custody and for longer periods of time. Figure 1.4 reveals that in 1965 approximately 40,000 persons found guilty of criminal offences were sentenced to immediate custody. By 1985 this figure had doubled to more than 80,000 before concerted effort by the Home Office, the Lord Chief Justice, and the Magistrates' Courts resulted in year-on-year reductions in the use of custody between 1985 and 1994 (Home Office 2002a) at which point the use of immediate custody began to rise sharply.

Greater use of immediate custody was compounded by a gradual shift towards longer prison sentences. In 1969, the average sentence length for males aged seventeen or over was eleven and a half months. By 1986 this had increased to thirteen months cementing the position of England and Wales as one of Europe's most prolific incarcerators (see the Home Office Criminal Statistics England and Wales series, 1960–1995). The causal relationship between crime rates and imprisonment remains fiercely contested and largely outside the scope of this book, but there does appear to be some support for the conclusion that sentencing

Figure 1.4 Persons sentenced to immediate custody in England and Wales, 1950–2001

Source: Home Office (2002a p.18)
(Contains public sector information licensed under the Open Government Licence v3.0.)

trends are anchored within wider social attitudes towards crime (see Roberts and Hough 2002). As Newburn has noted, there is 'growing evidence that sentences are affected not only by the legislative context in which they work but also by the general mood, or what Tonry refers to as "sensibilities"—the penal zeitgeist' (2007b p.459). As the penal zeitgeist toughened the prison population increased from 30,421 in 1965 to 49,471 in 1995 (see Figure 1.5). Over time, the cumulative through-flow of prisoners into the prison system generated significant overcrowding within a predominantly Victorian prison estate that had been built to service a very different penal regime. Figure 1.5 tracks the average prison population in relation to the Certified Normal Accommodation (CNA) of the prison estate, defined as the Prison Service's own measure of how many prisoners can be held in 'decent and safe accommodation' (Jewkes and Bennett 2008 p.38). This reveals that the CNA of the prison estate rose from 25,354 in 1960 to 48,291 in 1995, a rate of growth that was rarely

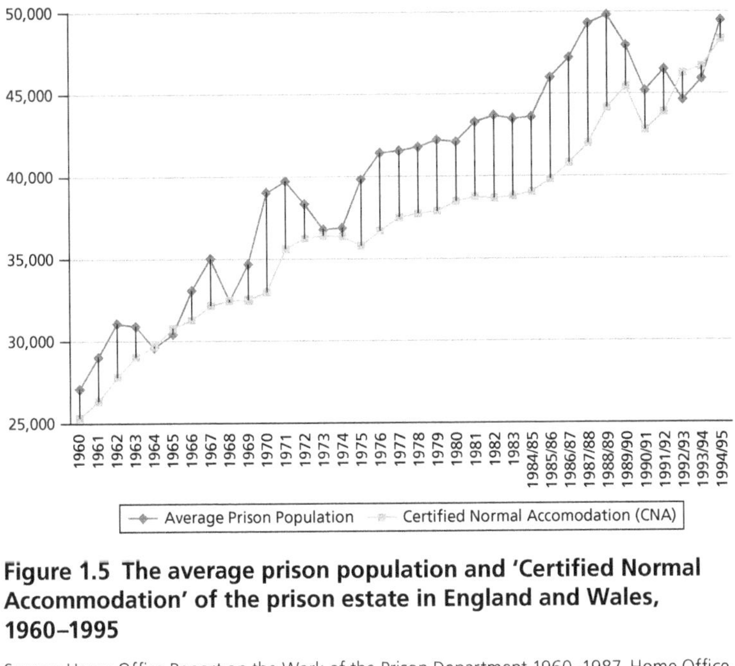

Figure 1.5 The average prison population and 'Certified Normal Accommodation' of the prison estate in England and Wales, 1960–1995

Source: Home Office Report on the Work of the Prison Department 1960–1987. Home Office, Report on the Work of the Prison Service 1988–1991, HMPS Report on the Work of the Prison Service, 1992–1996

adequate to meet the needs of the average prison population in the intervening years.

For the majority of the period in question there was a significant shortfall in prison capacity and the Prison Service was forced to rely upon cell sharing to accommodate more and more prisoners. In 1965, a total of 5,485 prisoners were held either two or three to a cell and this reached a high of 18,983 in 1987/88 before declining thereafter. A rising population and historic under investment in the prison estate saw the emergence of new forms of 'tactical management' as the Home Office sought to maximize the use of accommodation within the prison estate (Faulkner 2014 p.41). At a strategic level, this logic was understandable but in practice, the efforts made by the Prison Service to even out the distribution of prisoners within the estate presented a series of operational challenges. Tactical management of the prison estate saw the regular use of 'overcrowding drafts' to transfer prisoners to less overcrowded prisons. These drafts often saw prison inmates moved far away from their families and quickly emerged as a major contributor to prison disorder (Faulkner 2014 p.41). Conditions in local prisons were particularly poor while the landmark Mountbatten Report (Home Office 1966) into prison security and the Prison Department's subsequent adoption of a policy of dispersal served to promote a focus on control and risk management to the detriment of the rehabilitative programmes that were the centrepiece of government policy (Ryan 2003 p.28). Over time these pressures upon the prison system would intensify and the operational failure to address these deep rooted issues was identified by the Woolf Report (Home Office 1991) as contributory factors in the riot at HMP Strangeways in April 1990, and the prison disturbances that followed.

The mediating role of the Home Office

The American political scientist Theda Skocpol once remarked that 'as politics create policies, policies also remake politics' (1992 p.58). This cyclical relationship remains a rather unknown quantity within the criminal justice sphere (Barker 2009 p.89). While there has been considerable criminological discussion of the politics of law and order and the operational challenges of a high prison population (Howard League 2009; Mathiesen 2006) comparatively little is known about the role of the Home

Office at the intersection between these countervailing forces, or how the department shaped, and was in turn shaped by these dynamics over time. This is to be regretted. As we will see, the internal division of the Home Office, the allocation of funding between its various functional responsibilities and the deeply embedded hierarchies of power that shaped departmental decision-making have exerted a profound influence over the trajectory of early release in England and Wales.

The Home Office was established on the 27 March 1782 when the responsibilities of the anachronistic Northern and Southern Departments were rationalized and transferred to the newly created Foreign and Home Offices. Under these arrangements the Home Office became responsible for all domestic and colonial affairs (RIPA 1982) and this unique constitutional position at the frontier between state and citizen came to define the work of the department (Faulkner 2014). Reflecting the growth of modern government, administration of this eclectic departmental portfolio required a large executive. Total staff numbers (industrial and non-industrial) within the Home Office and its various subsidiaries increased from 21,743 in 1970 to 42,721 in 1990 (Butler and Butler 2000 p.309). During this time, the junior ministerial team also grew in size and stature. In 1970, the Home Secretary could call upon the services of one Minister of State and two Parliamentary Under-Secretaries, but by 1995 this had expanded to three Ministers of State and one Parliamentary Under-Secretary supported by a team of special advisors. Despite almost continual growth in the size and complexity of government the internal structure of the Home Office was slow to adapt and throughout the period in question officials continued to be organized around the core departmental responsibilities of Immigration and Nationality, Criminal and Probation, Children, Prisons, Police, Civil Defence and Fire, General Matters, Establishment, and Organization and Finance (TNA: HO 223/4). As the 'organization chart' set out in Figure 1.6 makes clear, neither the policy nor the practice of 'early release' mapped neatly onto this departmental structure and as we shall see in Chapter 4 this often inhibited the development of policy and the implementation of new working arrangements.

Despite a reputation as one of the Great Offices of State the influence of the Home Office cannot be reduced to spending power alone. Figures from the 'UK public spending website' indicate

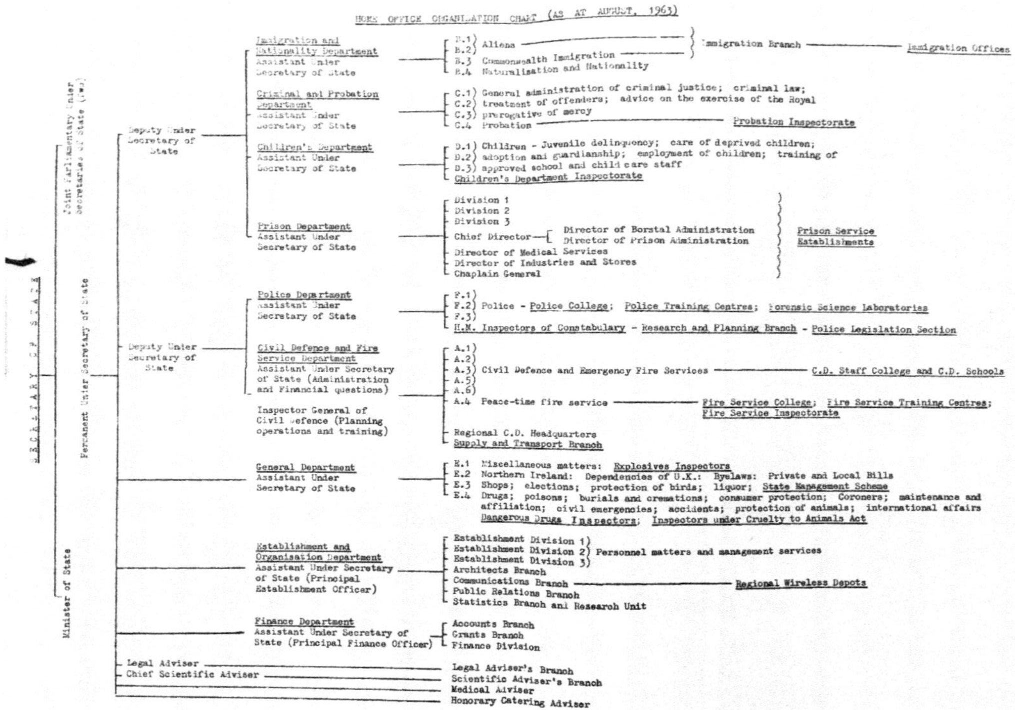

Figure 1.6 Home Office 'organizational chart', August 1963

Source: TNA: HO 223/4 © The National Archives, 1963

that investment in 'protection' which includes the police, prisons and the courts grew from approximately £5.6bn in 1960 to £23.1bn in 1995 (at 2017 prices), a budgetary increase that represented comparable real term growth to investment in Education, Health, and Welfare, albeit from a lower baseline. While the overall budget was modest in Whitehall terms it is perhaps more significant that some elements of Home Office expenditure were protected from austerity measures and political interference. The 1979 Conservative Party Manifesto declared that 'we will spend more on fighting crime, while we economize elsewhere', and to an extent this commitment was honoured while in government creating winners and losers within the various Departments of the Home Office (McLaughlin 1994 p.115). Historically the Home Office was an asymmetric department and the Police Service dominated in terms of power, resources, and influence (see Figure 1.7).

This reveals that the lion share of Home Office funding was allocated to the Police Service who saw investment rise from approximately £4 billion in 1968/69 to £7.7 billion in 1989/90 (2017 prices). During this time, total police strength in England and Wales grew from 83,296 in 1965 to 127,222 in 1995 (Home Office

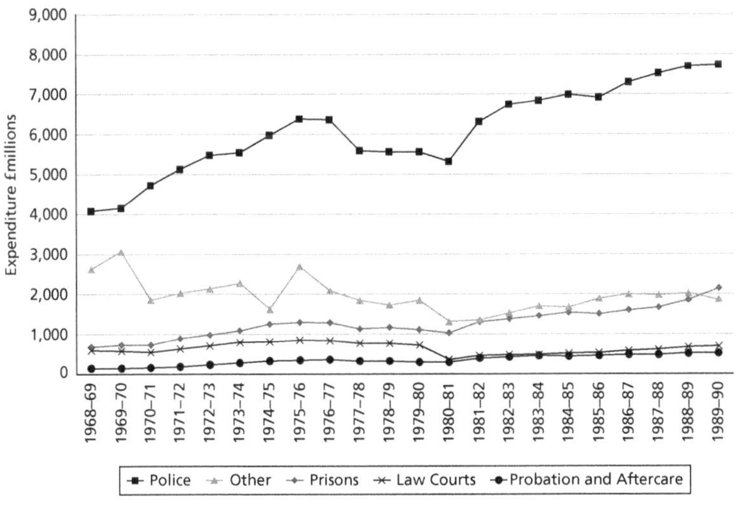

Figure 1.7 Functional breakdown of Home Office expenditure, 1968–1990 (2017 prices)

Source: Various, HMSO Government Expenditure Plans 1968–1991

2000). In contrast, investment in the Probation and Aftercare Department was marginal, while the Prison Service budget grew from £684 million in 1968/69 to £.2.7 billion (2017 prices) as additional investment came on stream in the 1980s. In the early years of the Thatcher government the Home Office enjoyed considerable financial and political autonomy, but it was not immune from outside influence. As the 1980s progressed the department was heavily, albeit reluctantly, influenced by the administrative changes associated with 'new public management' (Faulkner 2006; McLaughlin 1994). A cornerstone of the Thatcher project, new public management was predicated upon the belief that public administration could be improved by applying the techniques and expertise of the private sector. In 1979 the Rayner Efficiency Unit had been set up with a view to generating improved efficiency within Whitehall (Jones 1993 p.187). This was followed by the Audit Commission (1984) handbook, *Improving Economy, Efficiency and Effectiveness in Local Government in England and Wales* and a series of initiatives including the Next Steps Agencies and Citizens Charter intended to open up public administration to private sector discipline and rigour (Jones 1993). As McLaughlin has noted, the Home Office was one of a few Departments that 'steadfastly refused to publish an annual report, set targets or construct benchmarks against which its performance could be measured' (1994 p.118). But this began to change as the financial outlook for the United Kingdom deteriorated and it became clear that the government's financial commitment to law and order was not delivering substantive reductions in recorded crime, re-offending, or increases in police clear-up rates (McLaughlin 1994 p.115). Faced with the inability or unwillingness of various criminal justice agencies to respond to increasing criticism and 'put their houses in order' (McLaughlin 1994 p.115) the government responded in the late 1980s by opening up the criminal justice system to investigation from the Public Accounts Committee, the National Audit Office and Audit Commission (Jones 1993 p.198). This process began to fundamentally re-shape the department leading to the establishment of the Prison Service as an Executive Agency in 1993 and the appointment of Derek Lewis, a former chief executive of Granada Television, as Director General, the first non-career civil servant to hold the post.

Case Studies: Three Defining Moments of Reform

Through careful excavation of the archival record this book will explore the capillaries of power that connect this 'big picture' of criminal justice change with the unique developmental trajectory of early release in England and Wales. Aspects of this history have been surveyed within the literature. In one of the first systematic reviews of the parole system in England and Wales, the contributors to Donald West's (1972) edited collection *The Future of Parole* explored the practical application of risk management and penal supervision, and built the case for a 'therapeutic approach' to parole decision-making. More recently, Stephen Shute has traced the origins of the modern parole system from the 'ticket of leave system' for transportees to the penal colonies through to the debates that raged around the abolition of the death penalty and the growing influence of indeterminate sentencing in Great Britain and overseas (Shute 2003 pp.377–387). But these accounts remain the exception to the rule. There have been few, if any, systematic historical studies that draw together these various strands of thought together to provide a detailed analysis of the key moments of reform and controversy in England and Wales (Maguire 1992). Moreover, the early release literature has tended to eschew historical study in favour of analytical snapshots that have gravitated towards such questions as the quasi-legal status of the Parole Board (Padfield 2007), the legitimacy of executive action (Hood 1974a, 1974b) and the growing influence of human rights legislation (Nichol 2007 pp.1–19; Padfield et al. 2012a).

We will draw upon each of these insights, but it is the interaction and opposition between these various pressures and how they coalesced to shape the development of early release as a public policy concern over time that is of most interest here. By examining early release through a public policy lens, we will signify a broader focus on operational concerns, resource allocation and stakeholder management as well as the more widely discussed ideational and political dimensions of policy-making. In this more holistic sense public policy can be seen as 'an assertion of the will, an attempt to exercise control, to shape the world' (Moran et al. 2006 p.3) and our interest here is how policymakers have sought to administer, modify, and reform the operation of early release over time.

Addressing the 1976 Cropwood Round-Table Conference *Penal Policy-Making in England*, Michael Moriarty, then Assistant Under-Secretary of State at the Home Office, helpfully drew attention to three primary levers by which policy-makers in the Department have sought to exercise control and shape criminal justice, '... changes in the legal framework; qualitative decisions about the way in which the penal system is run within the legal framework; and the securing of resources for maintaining the system' (Moriarty 1977 p.129). The density of reform associated with these policy levers, coupled with the relative lack of existing historical study, ensures there are no shortage of historical events that demonstrate the challenge of shaping the policy and practice of early release. Rather than attempt a comprehensive narrative history of the entire period, a task that would require a much larger volume than is possible here, this book adopts a case-study approach that will draw attention to three critical junctures or 'signal events' that came to define the historical evolution of early release in England Wales between 1960 and 1995 (Loader and Sparks 2004 p.14). As Amenta (2009) has argued, the practicalities of historical research rule out many prospective research designs and demand a greater immersion in the historical records:

> ... acting more like historians makes historical sociology more time consuming and difficult. There are no shortcuts to mastering historiography or engaging in archival work. More significantly, these structures tend to force historical social scientist deeper into their cases and tend towards case study. That is to say, social scientists seeking deep historical knowledge will be pushed towards studies of developments in fewer countries or places within a country over briefer periods of time. (Amenta 2009 p.354)

In the first case study (Chapters 3 and 4), we examine the period 1960 to 1968 and the events that led to the introduction of a modern system of parole in the Criminal Justice Act 1967, a period of policy development that is absolutely fundamental to an understanding of how early release developed in England and Wales in the decades that followed. The second case study (Chapters 4 and 5) encompasses the period 1975 to 1982 and the steps taken to extend a system of parole to short sentence prisoners. This was a particularly turbulent period in the history of criminal justice, characterized by the gradual erosion of the rehabilitative ideal, a rising prison population, and growing concern about the procedural weaknesses inherent in a system of executive release. The third and final case study (Chapters 7 and 8) explores the period from 1987 to 1995 and the decision to undertake a root and branch review of parole following the 1987 General Election. Here we focus on the proceedings of the Carlisle Committee and the radical overhaul of early release policy and practice enshrined in the Criminal Justice Act 1991. An extended timeline of key events is set out at Appendix 1 along with background information on the key individuals that feature in this book at Appendix 2. These appendices are intended as an aide mémoire to guide the reader through the occasionally dense web of events and key individuals that feature in this book.

By focusing on a small number of cases it will be possible to achieve a far greater degree of immersion in the historical records than would have been possible with a broad historical chronology of the period. As Pierson has noted, 'choices about the scope of time covered in a particular analysis have profound effects. They lead to substantial shifts in the kinds of theories we employ, the methods we use, the kinds of causal forces we are likely to see at work, and the even the outcomes of interest that we come to identify in the first place' (2003 p.199). A case study approach is well suited to the complex, often messy interactions that defined these key moments of reform. It encourages a greater sensitivity to the watershed moments policy-makers themselves considered significant and it open up new vistas from which to observe the profound reconfiguration in criminal justice as a public policy concern in England and Wales between 1960 and 1995. The 1960s in particular have often been reduced to little more than a 'golden age' of penal policy or a blank canvas onto which post 1970s anxieties could be projected (Loader and Sparks 2004 p.14). As a result, there has been little discussion of the debates, disagreements, and political configurations that marked the pre-1970s world of criminal justice. Likewise, we cannot understand the events that followed in the mid-1990s and beyond without adequate discussion of their historical antecedents. As Downes and Morgan (2007) have noted the mid-1990s was a key turning point in the emergence of a more populist penal policy and considerable attention has been paid to pivotal events such as the murder of James Bulger (Green 2008), Michael Howard's infamous 'Prison Works' speech, and the appointment of Tony Blair as Shadow Home Secretary, which signalled the arrival of a 'race to the bottom' as the main political parties battled for control of the law and order agenda (Anderson and Mann 1997; Downes and Morgan 2007). There is no doubting the importance of these events, but they did not happen in a historical vacuum; contemporary policy-making depends to an important degree on the legacy of past decisions.

Conclusion

In this introductory chapter, we have built the case for the study of early release in comparative historical perspective. This has revealed that unlike policing and sentencing practice, or what might be described as the 'front end' crime control capabilities of the liberal democratic state, early release has been subject to comparatively little sustained attention. There has been scant exploration of the key periods of reform, crisis, and public policy debate. Nor has there been sustained analytical interest in the various ways in which policy-makers have sought to shape this area of criminal justice administration. We went on to situate early release within a wider picture of criminal justice change and identified three case studies that will form the substantive focus of this book: The Criminal Justice Act 1967; the steps taken to extend a system of parole to short sentence prisoners in the mid-1980s; and the decision to undertake a root and branch review of parole following the 1987 General Election.

2

Conceptualizing Policy Change

This chapter sets out a theoretical framework for the systematic and historically grounded analysis of early release in England and Wales between 1960 and 1995. It reviews the existing criminological literature on the history of criminal justice in England and Wales and reflects upon the tendency to conceptualize policy change as the product of individual action or the broad socio-economic shifts associated with late twentieth-century modernity. It goes on to consider the mediating role of political institutions in shaping complex policy outcomes and presents a theoretical framework for the analysis of early release based upon the building blocks of historical institutionalism. The chapter concludes with an honest appraisal of the challenges facing a criminologist doing historical study and reflects upon the largely untapped potential of archival research as a criminological and social science methodology.

Beyond Structure and Agency: The Mediating Role of Political Institutions

> A way of seeing is a way of not seeing. (Poggi 1965 p.284)

In Chapter 1 we outlined the central concerns of this book and advanced the case for the study of early release in comparative historical perspective. But this is only half the story. How do we begin to make sense of the complex chain of events that shaped the evolution of early release in England and Wales between 1960 and 1991? Even the most straightforward historical events can belie simple explanation and 'distilling the frenzy' of actors, political conflicts, and compromise agreements that marked the development of early release between 1960 and 1995 is a formidable task (Hennessey 2012). As Poggi (1965) reminds us, the analytical

Getting Out: Early Release in England and Wales, 1960–1995. First Edition. Thomas C. Guiney. © Thomas C. Guiney 2018. Published 2018 by Oxford University Press.

choices we make inevitably illuminate some elements of the political world and obscure others. While a focus on individual agents may yield a dynamic narrative history, this often lacks analytical rigour when events are viewed over a longer time frame. In contrast, a focus on the underlying structures of power that shape the contemporary world may offer a deeper understanding of policy change but this will inevitably sacrifice a degree of granularity in favour of broader explanatory power (Hay 2002 pp.100–110). As students of history we cannot escape from these difficult choices, nor can we ignore our own embeddedness within these historical processes. Complex historical phenomena demand reflexive research strategies that are clear, transparent, and precise about the ontological as well as the epistemological and methodological assumptions that guide our work (Hay 2002 p.64). Given the focus here is on a relatively narrow area of public policy over a thirty-five year period, this chapter builds the case for a 'theory of the middle range' that seeks to: (a) explain a limited aspect of political life, and (b) occupy an epistemological position that is 'intermediate to general theories of social systems which are too remote from particular classes of social behaviour, organization and change to account for what is observed and to those detailed orderly descriptions of particulars that are not generalized at all' (Merton 1967 p.39). There is growing criminological interest in the mediating role of political institutions within the broader political economy of crime and in this chapter, we locate our analysis within the broad tradition of historical institutionalism, a well-established theory of the middle range that adopts an intermediary position between structure and agency and offers the analytical tools to develop an empirically rich account of early release in England and Wales between 1960 and 1995.

This preference for a theory of the middle range represents something of a departure from the existing criminological literature. Many of the most influential historical accounts of criminal justice change have focused on the role of individuals and political elites as key engines of policy change (see e.g. Faulkner 2006, 2014; Ryan 2003; West 1972). Arguably, the most influential contribution within this tradition can be found in Lord Windlesham's study, *Responses to Crime* (1987, 1993, 1996, 2001). Across these four volumes Windlesham traces the evolution of governmental responses to crime from the 'gentler age' of 1947 to 1965, through to the reactive, piecemeal legislative proposals of the mid-to-late 1990s. For much of the post-war period criminal justice was the preserve of a small yet influential group of policymakers that took an enlightened and dispassionate approach to questions of crime. For better, or worse, this milieu did not last. The paternalistic approach to crime and disorder established by R.A. Butler and successive Home Secretaries was gradually eroded by the rise in recorded crime and growing public appetite, either real or perceived, for retribution and 'just deserts'. In Windlesham's diagnosis 'Pandora's Box' has been opened leaving criminal justice exposed to the winds of populism and the insecurities of the general public (1987 p.20). The picture of contemporary criminal justice history that emerges here is permeated by a strongly agent-orientated or 'intentionalist' lexicon, from the meticulous scrutiny of the 'movers and shakers' within the criminal justice system and the power dynamics within the party-political system, to the influence of academics and the personalities within the 'penal lobby'. This constellation of factors undoubtedly captures something of the realignment of criminal justice in England and Wales, but it fails to account for the wider socio-economic context in which such decisions were taken. The detail and richness of Windlesham's depiction of criminal justice policy are to be commended and provide an invaluable secondary source of information for this study, but they also highlight many of the limitations of intentionalist accounts. While praising the comprehensiveness of Windlesham's study, Loader and Sparks (2004) ultimately find it unsatisfactory for providing a rather:

> ... internal, Westminster-centric treatment of political events and processes with scant reference to either the economic, social and cultural contexts within which they are played out, or to the criminological and political ideas that relevant actors implicitly or expressly mobilise and tussle over. One is left in little doubt that the liberal, elitist paradigm for governing crime has collapsed, but with few sociological clues as to why. (Loader and Sparks 2004 p.11)

While agent-orientated studies may be well calibrated to the detail of everyday policy-making these causal dynamics often melt away when policy change is located within a broader comparative or historical perspective. Why, for example, has the United Kingdom proved so susceptible to the allure of penal populism? Why should these changes emerge so forcefully in the 1970s and

1980s? It is impossible to answer these questions without some reference to the broader social, political, and economic structures that reshaped Western liberal democracies in the latter half of the twentieth century. These shifts have generated a burgeoning research literature. Wacquant (2005, 2009b) has examined how the breakdown of the post-war 'Fordist-Keynesian' settlement gave rise to mass incarceration in many Western countries, while in *Governing through Crime* Simon (2007) documents how crime became the 'axis' around which a new civil and political order was created. In his pioneering work *The Culture of Control* David Garland (2001) reflects upon the broad organizing principles that structure the ways in which contemporary societies think and act around criminal justice. In so doing, Garland offers a 'history of the present' that traces the decline of the 'rehabilitative ideal' and a post-war political settlement that pursued inclusionary and welfare-orientated penal policies (2001 p.1). The rehabilitative mentality has not disappeared entirely, but since the 1970s it has given way to a largely retributive discourse which has crystallized around the centrality of the victim and protection of the public (2001 p.9). Seeking an explanation for these phenomena, Garland stresses the importance of the economic, social, cultural, and political changes associated with the transition to late twentieth-century modernity. The key point being that policymakers have struggled to come to terms with profound shifts in the dynamics of capitalist production, the restructuring of the family and household changes in the social ecology of the city and suburb, the rise of electronic mass media, and the democratization of contemporary culture (2001 p.78). This has seen successive generations of policymakers gravitate towards a stratified criminal justice policy that undulates between an expressive 'criminology of the other' and a 'criminology of everyday life' that seeks to control crime through the application of managerialism techniques (2001 p.185). Over time, this policy response has fuelled the public's appetite for 'tough' crime measures and a race to the bottom as the political parties have converged around a law and order agenda characterized by a populist punitiveness. As Newburn has argued, 'recent trends in liberal democracies such as America, Britain, and elsewhere suggest that there is something of an elective affinity between neoliberal economic and social policies and populist punitiveness and cognate adaptations in the penal sphere.' (2007b p.461).

The *Culture of Control* has rightly emerged as one of the leading contributions to Western criminological thought (Newburn 2007a p.330), but it is not without limitations. Many have commented upon a tendency to paint with broad brush strokes and construct a picture of historical change that leaves little room for the variability and contingency that characterize national responses to crime across both time and space. Nelken (2009) has argued that in common with several other accounts of the 'punitive turn' the *Culture of Control* suffers from a mistaken ethnocentrism that assumes that the ways in which we think about and respond to crime are universally shared. Similarly, Sparks and Loader (2004) have criticized the *Culture of Control* for failing to adequately account for the pre-1970s world of crime control and the stresses, disagreements, and conflicts that marked the development of penal policy at this time. The sociology of punishment literature continues to evolve and the evident contingency of liberal democratic responses to crime has provoked a renewed interest in meso-level analyses of political culture and institutions (Baker 2009; Cavadino and Dignan 2006b; Green 2008). David Downes once described criminology as a 'rendezvous subject' (cited in Garland and Sparks 2000 p.7) in response to the high degree of intellectual cross-pollination he observed between criminology and the neighbouring disciplines of sociology, psychology, law, and philosophy (Young 2003 p.97). As criminology adapts to these new analytical challenges it has seen the emergence of a strong inter-disciplinary research agenda which has sought to traverse traditional criminological interest in deviancy, imprisonment, and the legitimacy of punishment with a political science literature attuned to the political process, policy formulation, and the application of power. In their ground-breaking study *Penal Systems: A Comparative Approach* Cavadino and Dignan (2006b) conducted a wide-ranging comparative analysis of global penal systems. Far from confirming a ubiquitous trend towards penal convergence across the globe, their analysis demonstrates a more complex picture of similarity and difference, both in national incarceration rates and public discourses around crime more generally. Similarly, Loader has examined the influence of 'liberal elitism' in shaping governmental attitudes towards crime in post-war Britain (Loader 2006 p.561). Informed by extensive interviews with senior policymakers, Loader argues that for much of the post-war period, criminal justice policy was the preserve of a small metropolitan elite of 'platonic guardians' bound together by 'liberal elitism,' a governmentality characterized by 'a set of express and implied values and beliefs about the proper conduct of government towards crime' (Loader 2006 p.562). Critically, this belief system was only possible within a socio-political context where the general public were more deferential to government, crime was less common, and society demonstrated higher levels of equality and social solidarity. As the socio-economic conditions of British society began to change, the political settlement marked by liberal elitism began to break down. More recently, Barker (2009) has documented how variations in the democratic traditions of the US federal states have exerted a strong influence over the developmental trajectory of criminal justice policy and the treatment of offenders. At the heart of Barker's explanatory account are the concepts of 'political structure' and 'collective agency'. While the latter relates to how people take action in the political arena, interact in the public sphere, and engage with policymakers the former concerns the 'rules of the game' (North 1990) and 'legitimate channels of action' (2009 pp.25–46). As Barker notes, institutional structures have a powerful influence on the temper of criminal justice policy that is worthy of further research:

> This study shows how contemporary American penal regimes were shaped by the legacies of past practices and institutions.... These findings suggest that certain kinds of institutional configurations were more likely to deepen demands for retribution as well as provide their legal and political expression, while others were more likely to bring about more conciliatory measures. (Barker 2009 p.180)

In each of these contributions, institutional and cultural factors can be seen to play an important mediating role between structure and agency with important implications for how the liberal democratic state seeks to justify, and in turn administer an effective criminal justice system. As Karstedt (2010) has noted, institutional analysis has enjoyed something of a renaissance in contemporary criminology, re-entering scholarly debate via the pathways of the 'old institutionalism', as anomie theory, collective efficacy, and a renewed interest in the political economy of punishment. For example, Zimring and Johnson (2006) have argued that contemporary crime control responses depend to a considerable degree upon its institutional design and level of insulation from other pressures.

While 'less insulation' is likely to make the criminal justice system more receptive to populist demands for punishment the existence of a professional body of judges and a system that encourages 'principle and individualised punishment decisions' can provide the necessary degree of insulation to restrict popular impulses towards harsher punishment (2006 pp.266–280). Perhaps, the most influential contribution to this debate can be found in Nicola Lacey's (2008) *The Prisoners' Dilemma*. Reflecting upon variations in penal practice across time and place, Lacey counsels against reading the drift towards 'penal populism' as an inevitable corollary of global forces that will eventually engulf all liberal democratic systems. The relationships between political economy and punishment do not operate in simple input-output terms but are mediated instead through a range of economic, political, and social institutions (2008 pp.55–62). It is through this mediating process and the ensuing impact of institutional stabilization and path dependence that commonalities and discontinuities occur within national penal systems. Once these arrangements begin to crystallize they create powerful institutional incentives for particular political choices over others. The analytical tools developed in *The Prisoners' Dilemma* offer a powerful insight into the various ways in which liberal democratic states respond to the problem of crime. It opens up new possibilities for thinking about policy change and draws attention to the little understood role of political institutions in shaping criminal justice responses between countries and more importantly for our purposes, over time within the liberal democratic state. As Reiner has argued, a broader conception of political economy that attends to the intersection between 'civil society', 'the state', 'the economy', and 'the polity' is an essential component of a fully social theory of crime and criminal justice that recognizes the 'dialectical complexity of mediations and interactions between macro-structures and individual actions' (Reiner 2007 p.373). We are only just beginning to explore the role political institutions play within this dialectical complexity (Lacey 2013) and *The Prisoner's Dilemma* should be seen as a call to arms for further research in this area. It is therefore necessary to engage with the political science literature if we are to develop a robust theoretical framework to guide our analysis of how political institutions have shaped the trajectory of early release in England and Wales over time.

Historical Institutionalism: Organizational Factors in Political Life

Scholarly interest in institutions is enduring. Their presence within the political landscape has long been recognized within the traditions of public law and political science but this tended towards a rather static, monolithic view of institutional structures (Lowndes 2010 p.60). In their now classic article *Rediscovering Institutions: The Organizational Basis of Politics*, March and Olsen (1984) explicitly sought to transcend the traditional political science concern for the concrete institutions of the executive, the legislature, or the electoral system in order to build a richer understanding of how politics 'really works' within institutional settings (March and Olsen 1984 p.6). The key point being that institutions are not simply bricks and mortar, constitutional constructs or transaction points for calculating individuals but complex networks of rules, norms, and behaviours that mediate between individual actors and broader structural pressures:

> An institution is a relatively enduring collection of rules and organized practices, embedded in structures of meaning and resources that are relatively invariant in the face of turnover of individuals and relatively resilient to the idiosyncratic preferences and expectations of individuals and changing external circumstances. (March and Olsen 2006 p.1)

This insight has stimulated a very different research agenda from what is now considered the 'old institutionalism'. Where once political scientists focused on the formal constitutional responsibilities of institutions like the Ministry of Defence or Home Office the 'new institutionalism' has shifted the locus of enquiry towards the less well-understood decision-making, budgetary, and procurement procedures that define the day-to-day business of government (Lowndes 2010 p.67). This 'institutional turn' (Jessop 2000) has seen many political scientists reject long-held assumptions about change in the political world. Chief amongst them, the tendency to view political outcomes as the result of rational 'equilibrium contracts' between self-interested individuals, a Whiggish faith in progress, and a belief in efficient historical processes that provide unique solutions appropriate to that time limited context (March and Olsen 1984 p.735). As March and Olsen argued in their defining overview of the new institutionalist critique:

> Although the concept of institutionalism has never disappeared from theoretical political science, the basic vision that has characterized theories of politics since about 1950 is (a) contextual, inclined to see politics as an integral part of society, less inclined to differentiate the polity from the rest of society; (b) reductionist, inclined to see political phenomena as the aggregate consequences of individual behavior, less inclined to ascribe the outcomes of politics to organizational structures and rules of appropriate behavior; (c) utilitarian, inclined to see action as the product of calculated self-interest, less inclined to see political actors as responding to obligations and duties; (d) functionalist, inclined to see history as an efficient mechanism for reaching uniquely appropriate equilibria, less concerned with the possibilities for maladaptation and non-uniqueness in historical development; and (e) instrumentalist, inclined to define decision making and the allocation of resources as the central concerns of political life, less attentive to the ways in which political life is organized around the development of meaning through symbols, rituals, and ceremonies. (March and Olsen 1984 p.735)

Given the power of this critique, the 'new institutionalism' has inspired a burgeoning literature that is well beyond the scope of this book (for a useful overview of the literature see Peters 2005). Fortunately, Hall and Taylor (1996) provide an invaluable roadmap for the inter-disciplinary traveller. In their article *Political Science and the Three New Institutionalisms* Hall and Taylor argue that the 'new institutionalism' should not be interpreted as a unified body of thought but a number of distinct approaches to political analyses that developed in reaction to the positivist accounts of political behaviour that dominated, particularly in American political science, during the 1960s and 1970s (2006 p.936). Three broad schools of thought have developed within this intellectual tradition each of which makes differing ontological assumptions about the political world; a rational choice institutionalism, a sociological institutionalism, and a historical institutionalism that draws upon both of these perspectives (see also Marsh and Stoker 2010 pp.184–210; Hay and Wincott 1998). Where rational choice institutionalism has tended to view politics as a series of 'collective action dilemmas' between rational actors with fixed preferences, sociological institutionalism has posited a very broad definition of institutions as a series of 'symbol systems, cognitive scripts, and moral templates that provide the "frames of meaning" guiding human action' (Hall and Taylor 1996 p.947). In contrast, historical institutionalism has centred upon the various ways in which political struggles are mediated over time by the institutional settings in which they take place. This is ultimately concerned with revealing how 'institutions, understood as sets of regularized practices with a rule-like quality, structure the behaviour of political and economic actors' (Hall 2009 p.2). In this sense, historical institutionalism is neither a particular theory nor a specific method. Rather, it is best understood as an approach to political analysis which can be distinguished from other social science perspectives by its emphasis upon conceptualizing public policy as life is lived rather than taking a snapshot of those interactions at one point in time. As Steinmo would put it in a leading text:

> Historical institutionalism is neither a particular theory nor a specific method. It is best understood as an approach to studying politics. This approach is distinguished from other social science approaches by its attention to real world empirical questions, its historical orientation and its attention to the ways in which institutions structure and shape political behavior and outcomes. (Steinmo 2008 p.118)

This attentiveness to history and real world empirical questions is particularly well suited to our focus on a relatively narrow area of public policy over a forty-year time horizon. Unsurprisingly, given the burgeoning literature within this transition, historical institutionalism has taken many forms, but it is possible to identify four central planks or building blocks of historical institutionalist research within Hall and Taylor's review (1996) which provide a useful analytical framework for thinking about the evolution of early release in England and Wales. Namely, the relationship between institutions and individuals, the distribution of political power, the role of ideas, and the importance of history in shaping political outcomes. These building blocks are discussed below in turn.

Institutions and individuals

Historical institutionalism starts from the premise that it is more enlightening to study human interactions in the context of rule structures that are themselves human creations. While political institutions and the organizational environments they produce are often taken for granted or seen as bureaucratic impediments to be overcome, government would be almost impossible (and highly inefficient) without them. March and Olsen express this in the following terms:

> Institutions simplify political life by ensuring that some things are taken as given. Institutions provide codes of appropriate behaviours, affective ties, and a belief in legitimate order. Rules and practices specify what is normal, what must be expected, what can be relied upon, and what makes sense in the community; that is, what a normal, reasonable, and responsible (yet fallible) citizen, elected representative, administrator or judge, can be expected to do in various situations. (March and Olsen 2006 p.9)

In this sense, institutions help to impose order upon uncertainty and translate an overabundance of external inputs into manageable information that can inform decision-making. Invariably, some political institutions perform these functions better than others, but the key point is that this utility comes at a price. The basic logic of action within institutional milieus is one of rule following which is continually reinforced through a suite of behavioural norms and practices that reduce flexibility and variability amongst individuals (see Hay 2002 pp.103; March and Olsen 1989). Over time, such structures can prove extremely resistant to change and exert a significant influence over the trajectory of public policy. It is important not to overstate this point. Institutions are resilient to the turnover of individuals but in a very important sense, they are human creations that cannot operate independently of them. As Steinmo et al. (1992) remind us, institutions constrain and refract politics, but they are never the sole cause of political outcomes. For this reason, historical institutionalism represents a powerful theory of the middle range that is well calibrated to the analysis of historical contingency and stability over time. This also hints at some limitations of institutional analysis. By very definition, institutional analysis implies a structuralist focus and Colin Hay has helpfully summarized five ways in which institutions are seen to structure individual action:

1. The 'density' of the existing institutional fabric in any given context renders established practices, processes and tendencies difficult to reform and steer.
2. Institutions are normalising in that they tend to embody shared codes, rules and conventions, thereby imposing value systems that constrain behaviour.

3. Institutions define logics of appropriate behaviour to which actors conform in expectation of the likely sanctions for non-compliance.
4. Institutions embody sets of ideas about that which is possible, feasible, and desirable and the means, tools and techniques appropriate to realise policy goals.
5. Creation may be constrained by a reliance upon existing institutional templates. (Hay 2002 p.105)

Applied in a rigid fashion there is a danger that historical institutionalism crowds out individual agency and leaves very little analytical space for the various ways in which individuals and coalitions of interest can influence the trajectory of public policy. Recognizing this tendency means it can be mitigated to a degree by the adoption of a research strategy that is, to borrow a phrase from historian Christopher Clark, saturated with agency (2014 p. xxix). However, there is ultimately no getting away from this structuralist tendency and that is not necessarily a bad thing. As Hall and Taylor observe, '"institutionalists" must remain structuralist at least in the sense that they seek to reveal how institutions shape social and political life. Otherwise, much of the analytical distinctiveness of institutionalism will be lost' (Hall and Taylor 1998 p.959).

The distribution of political power

Unlike rational choice theory, which has tended to conceptualize policy-making as a process of collective bargaining between broadly equal actors, historical institutionalism has paid greater attention to the uneven distribution of political power between social groups (Hall and Taylor 1996 p.941). This might include the degree of access actors have to the decision-making process, the institutional tools available to outsiders agitating for change, or the cumulative effect of policy pronouncements for the distribution of political and economic power over time. Hall describes this in the following terms:

> Institutional factors play two fundamental roles in this model. On the one hand, the organization of policy-making affects the degree of power that any one set of actors has over the policy outcomes ... On the other hand, organizational position also influences an actor's definition of his own interests, by establishing his institutional responsibilities and

relationships to others. In this way, organizational factors affect both the degree of pressure an actor can bring to bear on policy and the likely direction of that pressure. (Hall 1986 p.19)

This raises some fundamental questions about the nature of political power. The 'community power debate' has attracted heated discussion between those who view power in classical terms as control over decision-making (Dahl 1961), the highly influential work of Bachrach and Baratz (1962; 1970) who understood power as the second-order ability to set the agenda for the decision-making process and scholars like Steven Lukes (1974; 1978) who have championed preference shaping as the 'third dimension' of political power. These concerns are largely outside the scope of this book but suffice it to say here that the ways in which we view and interpret the exercise of political power can have a very real bearing on how we perceive the policy-making process. In general, historical institutionalism is more sympathetic to the second and third faces of political power and this requires us to go further in understanding how institutions distribute power, not just in relation to key decisions, but also to shape the political agenda and influence the preferences of actors working within these structures. Moreover, historical institutionalism demands greater attentiveness to the distribution of power between social groups and the feedback loops generated by political choices which by their very nature alter the legal, financial, and political balance of power between parties. This dynamic process creates winners and losers within our political systems, which can in turn, have a significant effect on access to decision-making structures, the types of arguments that are likely to be successful and the ability of groups to form coalitions of interest or exert sustained institutional pressure (Weir 1992).

The role of ideas

In recent years' considerable attention has been paid to the role of ideas in driving the complex interplay between institutional stability and renewal (Hay 2006). Much of this interest can be traced back to Hall's seminal article *Policy Paradigms, Social Learning, and the State* (1993). Therein Hall draws attention to the ideational dimensions of public policy and advanced the view that policymakers operate within 'policy paradigms' that provide an interpretative framework for the understanding and realization of political aims. Two elements of this analysis are particularly noteworthy. Hall offers a powerful conceptual model for accounting for both similarity and difference within public policy approaches over time. For Hall policy change can occur at three levels of abstraction. 'First order' change refers to the often-incremental refinement of policy on particular subject areas. While the ultimate goals of policy remain steady, their application evolves to reflect new experience and knowledge. 'Second order' change may occur when the targets of a particular policy are changed, or the underlying method is refined to take account of new externalities (Hall 1993 p.279). While the overall hierarchy of policy objectives remains, the basic techniques of policy are re-invented. 'Third order' change in comparison is a far rarer occurrence and is said to occur when there are, 'simultaneous changes in all three components of policy: the instrument settings, the instruments themselves, and the hierarchy of goals behind policy' (1993 p.279). Drawing heavily upon Kuhn's (1962) work on the sociology of scientific knowledge, Hall argues that while first and second order change are best understood as examples of 'business as usual' policy making, third order change represents, a 'paradigm shift' in both the means and ends of policy development.

Hall calls for a greater emphasis upon the role ideas play within policy development:

> Politicians, officials, the spokesman for social interests and policy experts all operate within the terms of political discourse that are current in the nation at a given time, and the terms of political discourse generally have a specific configuration that lends representative legitimacy to some social interests more than others, delineates the accepted boundaries of state action, associates contemporary political developments with particular interpretations of national history and defines the context on which issues will be understood. (Hall 1993 p.289)

For much of the post-war period Keynesianism provided a settled interpretative framework for the identification and resolution of fiscal concerns. In the 1970s, however, cracks began to emerge in the Keynesian armour and monetarism emerged as a coherent and ideologically attractive alternative. This set in train a period of first and second order re-alignment in British economic policy but it was not until the election of the Conservative Party in 1979 that a radical re-formulation of the goals and techniques of economic policy occurred. The result was a 'paradigm shift' that saw monetarism emerge as the accepted economic paradigm amongst Treasury officials and financial regulators.

History matters

As the name suggests, historical institutionalism departs most markedly from other forms of institutional analysis in the emphasis it places upon the temporal as well as the spatial elements of policy development. As Pierson argues in *Politics in Time*, the study of politics in historical perspective can greatly enrich our understanding of complex social dynamics and argues the case for shifting from 'snapshots' to 'moving pictures' (2004 p.1). History matters but this implies more than a simple linear, cause and effect model of historical development. Historical institutionalism posits a more sophisticated picture of how history shapes the policy-making process through the countervailing forces of 'path dependence' and 'timing and sequence'. In recent years these terms have proliferated in use and are now deployed to support of a variety of conclusions:

> Social scientists generally invoke the notion of path dependence to support a few key claims: Specific patterns of timing and sequence matter; starting from similar conditions, a wide range of social outcomes may be possible; large consequences may result from relatively 'small' or contingent events; particular courses of action, once introduced, can be virtually impossible to reverse; and consequently, political development is often punctuated by critical moments or junctures that shape the basic contours of social life. All these features stand in sharp contrast to prominent modes of argument and explanation in political science, which attribute 'large' outcomes to 'large' causes and emphasize the prevalence of unique, predictable political outcomes, the irrelevance of timing and sequence, and the capacity of rational actors to design and implement optimal solutions (given their resources and constraints) to the problems that confront them. (Pierson 2004 pp.18–19)

Path dependence has been particularly susceptible to so-called 'concept stretching' (Sartori 1970). Used in a narrow sense it has come to mean little more than an appreciation of how events at an earlier point in time will influence the possible outcomes of a sequence of events occurring at a later point in time (Sewell 1996 p.262). But applied in a more expansive sense path dependence emerges as a 'dynamic process involving positive feedback, which generates multiple possible outcomes depending on the particular sequence in which events unfold' (Pierson 2004 p.20). At the core of this process is the role of positive reinforcement. As Levi has observed, positive feedback creates developmental trajectories that are hard to reverse once in motion (1997 p.28). Once institutions are created they become resilient to change and this 'stickiness' can close off some policy avenues while encouraging others. This can be a significant impediment to 'root and branch' reform of political systems, even for those who command substantial financial and political capital. Applying these tools to historical study, Pierson (1994) has demonstrated how the systematic attempts by both the Thatcher and Reagan governments to 'roll back the frontiers of the welfare state' were catalysed and frustrated by institutional structures. This was particularly apparent in respect of public housing reform. In England and Wales, the relative fragmentation of the tenants' lobby coupled with the overall quality of the housing estate allowed the Thatcher government to pursue a far more effective policy of privatization than was possible in the United States where the unified nature of the US Social Security System made it far easier for critics to mobilize opposition amongst those who would be affected by the cuts (Pierson 1994 pp.74–100). Within the social sciences there has been a tendency to attribute 'large' historical effects to 'large' historical causes and scholars working within the historical institutionalist tradition have demonstrated how seemingly minor decisions at the right point in time can generate substantial political outcomes at a later point in a causal sequence (Pierson 2000).

The Criminologist as Historian

As this review suggests, historical institutionalism provides a 'way of seeing' the political world (Poggi 1965) and a guide to empirical enquiry but it does not provide a ready-made framework or research design, 'for the generation of evidence that is suited both to a certain set of criteria and to the research question in which the investigator is interested' (Bryman 2008 p.31). Unlike experimental, longitudinal, and ethnographic approaches that offer extensive methodological guidance (Bryman 2008 p.62) the path from criminology to historian is not so well signposted. As Sewell has argued, social scientists and historians have tended to talk past one another and a more constructive dialogue between the disciplines is long overdue. For while social scientists have been pre-occupied with formal methodologies and generalizable claims, historians have tended to emphasize descriptive rigour with a less privileged position afforded to theory and methodology:

> Theory has a strikingly less central place in history than in the social science disciplines. From the beginning of the systematic differentiation of disciplines in the late nineteenth century, historians and social scientists alike have contrasted the 'ideographic' or 'descriptive' research of historians—which attempts to capture the uniqueness and particularity of it object—with the 'nomothetic' or 'explanatory' research of social scientists—which aims to establish general laws or at least valid generalizations. Social science fields might be said to be defined by their theories and formal methodologies; history is more informally (but no less effectively) defined by its careful use of 'primary' sources, its insistence on meticulously accurate chronology, and its mastery of narrative. (Sewell 2006 p.3)

As we have already seen, many recent studies of historical change in the criminal justice sphere have demonstrated a strong preference for 'nomothetic' or 'explanatory' research associated with the broad social, political, and economic shifts of late twentieth-century modernity. Once again, the *Culture of Control* offers a useful case-study in this regard, not least because Garland is so open about his methodological choices. From the outset Garland recognizes the inevitable costs of abstraction but ultimately deems this an epistemological price worth paying in order to alight upon a level of analysis capable of yielding an explanatory account of the broad social structures that shape the causes of crime and our responses to it (2001 p.viii), not just in Britain, but across the Western world. For this reason, Garland's historical analysis gravitates towards a traditional social science concern for parsimony and generalizability rather than a historical research agenda that has tended towards complexity. Heavily influenced by Foucault's genealogical method, Garland describes his approach as 'analytical rather than archival' (2001 p.2) and offers a 'history of the present' (2001 p.1) that attempts to distance the analysis offered in the 'Culture of Control', from the 'conventions of narrative history and above all from any expectation of a comprehensive history of the recent period' (2001 p.2). Similar analytical choices can be found in other leading texts.

Reflecting upon the influence of Young's *The Exclusive Society* (1999) and Wacquant's *Punishing the Poor* (2009a), Farrall et al. (2014) have argued that in giving preference to the 'big picture' of penal change the criminological literature has tended to favour macro-level analyses which can underplay subtle differences between administrations and countries over time (2014 p.3). More persuasively perhaps, the authors argue that this picture 'gives primacy to theoretical rather than empirical considerations to the extent that few claims are subjected to rigorous data analyses' (2014 p.3). A distinct approach is needed if we are to achieve an empirically grounded narrative history of 'early release' that fills a significant gap in our knowledge while also arriving at a theoretically rich account of policy development that explains why certain developmental trajectories took hold and not others. Reflecting upon this epistemological challenge, Loader and Sparks (2004) advocate a 'historical sociology' of criminal justice characterised by a 'more quizzical historical sensibility that is attuned to the trajectories of competing practices, ideologies and ideas and the legacy of particular signal events and conflicts bequeath us today' (2004 p.14). In practice this requires greater emphasis upon how relevant actors interpret the political and institutional settings they find themselves operating in, the competing meanings in-use of relevant legal, criminological, and political categories and sensitivity to the interconnections between crime related demands, rationalities, and the wider terrain of political ideas—notably liberalism (2004 p.13). Perhaps more importantly, a truly authentic historical sociology requires a far greater degree of historical contextualization than is common on much contemporary scholarship (Simon 2007; Wacquant 2009a, 2009b; Young 1999, 2007).

This rebalancing of the applied and the analytical implies an approach that is closer in spirit to that taken by historians than by social scientists. As Gunn and Faire have noted, it remains the case that, 'in large swathes of social, cultural and political history ... dissertations, theses and books are written with barely a nod towards methodology' (Gunn and Faire 2012 p.3). This tendency to confer a less central role to theory and formal methodology can be unsettling for many social scientists, including criminologists (Sewell 2006). Where the social sciences have dedicated considerable attention to reliability, replication, and validity, both internal and external (Bryman 2008 p.30), historical research has tended to focus on chronology and mastery of narrative. As a result, the historian must hone a rather more informal, and applied research craft that is sensitive to 'social temporality' or what might be described as the timing, order, and sequencing of events (Amenta 2009). The level of detail and contextualization associated with a grounded and applied historical institutionalism is resource intensive and time consuming. It favours depth over breadth and demands extensive archival research and the triangulation of the evidence to build a comprehensive chronology of events. Historical research places a strong focus on practice, immersion, and real-time decisions taken in the archive:

> Historical training routinely includes an introduction to archives and sources ... But it is rare to find any explicit discussion of what choices might be made in the archive, what strategies pursued or how different types of sources might be interpreted. It is assumed that these skills will be absorbed by students or historians through a form of immersion, time and practice providing eventual mastery. Despite burgeoning interest in the history of the archive over the last decade, there has been remarkably little discussion of the actual process of archival research, or what the historian and theorist Michael de Certeau termed the 'historiographical operation' by which the 'past', or its documentary traces, are turned into 'history' defined as a specific form of writing. (Gunn and Faire 2012 p.5)

De Certeau's (1988) notion of the 'historiographical operation' captures something of the challenge of a criminologist doing historical study. The researcher can never be an objective or neutral arbiter in the historical operation. Difficult decisions must be made about the relevant importance of parsimony and complexity, and the competing claims of the historical and social scientific method (Loader and Sparks 2004). In this context it has demanded a research design and methodology that reflects the more time consuming and resource intensive nature of historical research. It has required heavy engagement with the archival record and it has encouraged a 'snowballing' approach to data-collection and analysis (Robson 2013) that places a strong emphasis upon experience, instinct and real-time decision making in the archives. With this in mind, the case studies set out in Parts II to IV of this book draw upon a wide range of archival material, complimented, where possible by extant secondary sources. Records were drawn from a number of archives in England and Wales, most notably the National Archives at Kew. This has proved a hugely productive source of information and the key file series used by this study are set out below at Table 2.1.

Table 2.1 National Archives, key file series

File Series	Department	Original Series Number
BV3	Parole Board	/
CAB 128 CAB 129	Cabinet Office: Cabinet Minutes Cabinet Office: Memoranda	CM and CC file series
CAB 134	Cabinet Office: Home and Social Affairs Committee	/
CAB 165	Cabinet Office: Legislation Committee	/
HO 223	Home Office: Establishments	ESG (Establishments, General Matters)
HO 263	Home Office: May Committee	/
HO 291	Home Office: Criminal	CRI and CCS Symbol file series
HO 303	Home Office: Publicity and Public Relations	PTY Symbol file series
HO 317	Home Office: Private Office Papers	/
HO 318	Committee on the Prison Disciplinary System: Report and Papers	/
HO 330	Home Office: Probation	PBN Symbol Series
HO 336	Prison Commission and Home Office Prison Department	PCOM
HO 383	Home Office: After-care	AFC Symbol file series
HO 391	Home Office: Prison Department	PDG Symbol file series
HO 495	Home Office: Criminal Policy	CP series
CM 46/13	National Audit Office	FPE 16/29 PART 2
PCOM 9	Prison Commission and Home Office, Prison Department:	/
PCOM 14	Prison Commission and Home Office, Prison Department:	/
PREM	Records of the Prime Minister's Office	/
T-Series	Treasury	/

To support detailed contextualization of the events described in this book it has also been possible to draw widely upon the special collections at the Churchill Archive University of Cambridge, the British Library, and the London School of Economics. Party-political records are drawn from the Conservative Party Archive housed at the Bodleian Library, University of Oxford, along with party manifestos and conference reports for the major political parties, many of which are now available online. Where documents were identified as significant, the relevant pages were photographed using a smartphone making sure to include the file cover, name, and archival reference number. These images were then uploaded to a laptop computer and 'optical character recognition' software was used to collate and convert these images into searchable, fully interactive PDF documents. Using this bespoke approach to data collection, made possible by advancements in smartphone technology, it has been possible to develop a substantial library of digitized archival records. The records were subsequently uploaded to the NVivo qualitative data analysis (QDA) software package to assist with management, coding, and analysis of the data.

A key limitation of archival research is that public access to public records in the United Kingdom has historically been subject to a 'thirty-year rule'. Section 5(1) of the *Public Records Act* (1958) states that, 'Public records ... shall not be available for public inspection until they have been in existence for [thirty] years or such other period .... as the Lord Chancellor may ... for the time being prescribe as respects any particular class of public records.' This was amended by the Constitutional Reform and Governance Act 2010 and the UK Government is currently migrating to a 'twenty-year rule' whereby there will be two document releases per year until 2022 when the National Archives will receive the files from 2001 and 2002. The implication being that at the time of writing (January 2018) records up to and including 1991 had been transferred to the National Archives and made available to the general public. To overcome this difficulty, significant use was made of the Freedom of Information Act 2000. In total, ten Freedom of Information (FOI) requests were submitted to the Home Office, Ministry of Justice, and Parole Board on topics as diverse as sentencing practice, internal Home Office reviews of parole, and the 'integrated resource and policy planning documents' prepared for Ministers each spring in advance of the annual Public Expenditure Survey (PES). This yielded 689 pages of documentation, much of which was reviewed when exercising the statutory right to view files in person at the Ministry of Justice.

The author is also very grateful to David Faulkner who made a substantial number of his own personal papers available to this study. This has made it possible to achieve a far greater degree of triangulation in the data for the events post-1987 than would otherwise have been possible. However, this has not entirely addressed gaps in the archival record, and in some cases it has been necessary to make difficult choices about how to present historical events where there is insufficient evidence to interpret these data with any degree of confidence. While it would have been desirable to explore some of the events described in this book in greater detail, for example the decision to introduce a system of 50 per cent remission in 1987, it has not been possible given the scarcity of archival records and the inventible gaps in the memory of those reflecting on events that occurred over thirty years ago.

Alongside these primary sources, this book has made extensive use of secondary sources to ground the data analysis and triangulate the available evidence. It has drawn heavily upon a series of Government publications including Command Papers (Green and White), statistical bulletins, and parliamentary papers. It has also made full use of Departmental Annual Reports that often provide a range of qualitative and quantitative evidence pertaining to financial accounts, workforce numbers, and key indices of change within the prison estate. Where possible these official sources have been complemented by a range of supporting materials that add colour and context to the data. The book has drawn upon the insights contained in a range of political diaries, memoirs, autobiographies, and the various pamphlets, briefings, and events produced by penal reform organizations like the Howard League of Penal Reform, Prison Reform Trust, and the National Association for the Care and Resettlement of Offenders (NACRO). As the data-collection phase of this study drew to a close eight in-depth exploratory interviews were conducted with senior decision-makers offering differing experiences and vantage points within the criminal justice system. This included; two senior Home Office Officials, a Parliamentarian, a Deputy High Court Judge, a Former Chief Probation Officer, an Academic, a Prison Governor, and a prominent Penal Reformer.

Conclusion

This chapter has developed a theoretical framework to guide our analysis of early release in England and Wales between 1960 and 1995. Our interest in a relatively narrow area of public policy over a forty-year time horizon led us to favour a 'theory of the middle range' which seeks to achieve an empirically grounded narrative history of 'early release' while also arriving at a theoretically informed explanation for why certain developmental trajectories took hold and not others. Having reviewed the existing criminological literature, we sought to locate this analysis within the broad tradition of 'historical institutionalism' and outlined the core 'building blocks' of this approach to policy analysis. We advanced a view of policy change that is built upon a dialectic relationship between structure and agency, and sympathetic to the second and third faces of political power. We went on to posit a central role for ideas as a driver of policy change and embedded this within a dynamic view of history based upon the interaction between path dependence, and timing and sequence. Finally, we reflected upon the challenges facing a criminologist doing historical research and advanced the case for a quizzical and historically grounded institutional analysis of early release that eschews a 'big picture' view of policy change in favour of detailed contextualization. In so doing, this book reconnects with a longstanding criminological tradition of inquiry into the historical development of the liberal democratic state and penal policy—e.g. Sir Leon Radzinowicz's five-volume study *History of the English Criminal Law and Its Administration*, the fifth volume of which was co-authored with Roger Hood (1986), Bailey's (1981) *Policing and Punishment in Nineteenth Century Britain*, and Scull's (2015) more recent study *Madness in Civilization: A Cultural History of Insanity*.

PART II

Penal Optimism, 1960–1968

3

An Idea Whose Time Had Come

Parole, Indeterminacy, and the Personalization of Punishment

In Part II we trace the emergence of parole onto the policy agenda in England and Wales between 1960 and 1968. The chapter begins with an examination of the long-term historical trends in early release administration and how this gave rise to a reform agenda that was shaped by the prevailing optimism and confidence of the 1960s. It goes on to consider growing criminological support for indeterminate sentencing and the influence of the landmark Longford Committee Report *Crime: A Challenge to Us All* (Labour Party 1964a). Here it will argue that the initial policy scoping for a parole system in England and Wales was heavily influenced by the 'rehabilitative ideal' and a desire to give administrative expression to prevailing support for indeterminate sentencing and the personalization of punishment. The chapter concludes with an overview of the intense policy discussion that gave rise to the parole framework articulated in *The Adult Offender* White Paper (Home Office 1965).

A Brief History of Early Release in England and Wales

It is one of the more reliable pieces of criminological knowledge that in contemporary Western societies the vast majority of men and women sentenced to imprisonment will be released before the end of their sentence. Across time and place there have been no shortage of administrative mechanisms to realize this objective (see Padfield et al. 2012b) but it is striking just how quickly 'parole'—a framework that integrated discretionary release, active supervision, and threat of recall to prison—crystallized as the favoured option for reform in England and Wales. Why should this be the case? Within the archival record (TNA: CAB 129/123; HO 383/219) and associated literature (Home Office 1989 p.7) there has been a tendency to describe the emergence of parole in the 1960s as 'an idea whose time had come'. The prevalence of this explanation is intriguing, not least because it is notable by its absence from later periods of reform discussed in this book. At first sight, it may appear to offer little more than a teleological shorthand for a series of complex events that belie simple explanation, but on closer inspection, it hints at a number of more tantalizing possibilities. That policymakers and practitioners viewed parole in pragmatic terms as the 'right' technocratic response to the challenges they were facing. Or perhaps, that parole was the natural extension of an unfolding project to rehabilitate and integrate offenders back into society. To understand these claims, it is necessary to locate the emergence of parole within a wider social and historical context.

While it is tempting to scour the historical records in search of the aetiological 'smoking gun' that signalled the arrival of a modern system of parole in England and Wales, the historical antecedents of parole, remission, and release on licence are, in reality, far more diffuse (Home Office 1989 pp.3–13; Radzinowicz and Hood 1986 pp.465–596). As far back as the seventeenth century, the Privy Council had authorized the granting of reprieves and stays of execution to those convicted of serious crimes (Bottomley 1990 p.326). But it is arguably not until the advent of penal transportation and the power of the Crown to grant convicts of good character a 'ticket of leave' providing limited rights to live and work within the colonies that a formalized administrative system of early release began to take shape in Great Britain (McConville 1981). As a manifestation of the prerogative of mercy, the ticket of leave system was inexorably linked to a fledgling interest in the art of government and the maintenance of order in the penal colonies (Bottomley 1990). Captain Philip Gidley King, the third Governor of the New South Wales penal colony, is said to have laid the foundations for the ticket of leave system when in 1801 he granted the first 'annual certificates' that allowed convicts to work within the New South Wales territory (Macintyre 1999 p.43). In part, this was a pragmatic step to satisfy growing labour demands and relieve pressure on scarce resources, such as fresh drinking water, but it also reflected a growing awareness of the role hope and incentive played in maintaining social order in such remote corners of the Empire. Over time the ticket of leave system was codified and became a central feature of penal transportation, described by the Select Committee on Transportation 1837–1838 in the following terms:

> A convict, transported for seven years, obtains, at the end of four years; for fourteen years, at the end of six years; and for life, at the end of eight years, as a matter of course, unless his conduct has been very bad, a ticket of leave, which enables him, according to certain regulations, to work on his own account. This indulgence on the whole has a very useful effect, as it holds out hope to a convict if he behaves well, and is liable to be re-assumed in case of misconduct. (Molesworth 1838: xvii)

Conditions in the penal colonies were often intolerable and many convicts, as well as the indigenous peoples they encountered, suffered appalling brutality, but as the Carlisle Committee would note in their 1989 report *The Parole System in England and Wales*, the ticket of leave framework did at least provide a template, 'for some of the most innovative and influential penal projects of the day' (Home Office 1989 p.3). In the 1840s, the modernizer Captain Alexander Maconochie was widely lauded for transforming the fortunes of the notorious Norfolk Island penal colony by introducing a marks system that placed greater trust in convicts and rewarded good behaviour with better conditions and eventual release (Bottomley 1990 p.323; Home Office 1989 p.3). Equally significant was the work of Sir Walter Crofton, a future Director of the Irish Prison System, who developed 'a system of graded progression through a program of education and training' that would prove highly influential in the US penal code (Bottomley 1990 p.323). Growing scepticism about the deterrent effect of transportation and its negative impact upon the fledgling colonies saw transportation fall into disuse in the mid-1850s and the practice was abolished following the arrival of the convict ship Hougoumont at the port of Fremantle, Western Australia on the 9 January 1868 (McConville 1981 p.381). With the abolition of transportation, the punishment of criminals could no longer be outsourced to the new world. In the late 1850s the government embarked upon a major prison-building programme and moved to introduce a new sentence of penal servitude blending elements of imprisonment and hard labour (McConville 1981). By this time the underlying rationale for the ticket of leave system was firmly established within British penal practice (Shute 2003 p.379) and the idea was imported into the new regime with those sentenced to penal servitude becoming eligible for release on licence at the discretion of prison authorities (McConville 1989 p.403). This nascent system of release on licence was eventually placed on a statutory footing in 1863 following a critical report of the *Royal Commission on Transportation and Penal Servitude* (1863) which recommended the establishment of a formalized version of the 'marks system' first pioneered in Western Australia (see Radzinowicz and Hood 1986 p.501; Shute 2003 p.379). Two features of the regulatory structure established by the Penal Servitude Act 1853 are worthy of note here. First, while the Penal Servitude Act established a system of release on licence, there was no accompanying provision for the active supervision of convicts while on release. The deficiencies of this arrangement were exposed in 1863 following an outbreak of lawlessness and violent robberies which were widely attributed in Parliament to a group of convicts recently released on licence (Radzinowicz and Hood 1986 p.524). Second, penal servitude sat uneasily alongside a system of locally administered justice (Home Office 1989 p.4). While minor misdemeanours were typically served in local prisons under the control of Local Authorities, serious offenders sentenced to penal servitude were classed as 'convicts' and managed centrally by the Home Office (Home Office 1989 p.4). This dichotomy introduced a number of anomalies into British penal administration. While males serving sentences of penal servitude were eligible for release on licence of up to one quarter of their sentence, no formalized arrangements existed for those serving their sentences in local prisons. In practical terms, this meant that while early release was at least a theoretical possibility for some of the most serious convicts, local prisoners convicted of less serious offences, were expected to serve their sentence in its entirety (Home Office 1989 p.4). The Prison Act 1878 brought all prisons in England and Wales under the control of the Home Secretary, with responsibility for administration and inspection delegated to a newly established Board of Prison Commissioners. However, the differential treatment of convicts and prisoners continued under these new governance arrangements, a situation widely condemned by the 1895 Gladstone Committee which recommended that eligibility for early release should be extended to ordinary prisoners (HMSO 1895 para.44). The Government accepted this recommendation, but rather than place all prisoners on the same legal footing The Prison Act 1898 reinforced this dichotomy by introducing a distinct system of what became known as 'remission' for local prisoners. The Act empowered the Home Secretary to introduce Prison Rules setting out the treatment of those in custody and in 1907 the rules were settled to the effect that men and women held in local prisons could, 'by special industry and good conduct', earn remission of up to one-sixth of their sentence (Freedom of Information/ FOI: HO 291/2138). This marked a step forward in the treatment of local prisoners but at an administrative level, the twin-track approach merely compounded the variable treatment of 'convicts' and 'prisoners'. While convicts continued to be released on licence and remained at risk of recall for the remainder of their sentence, local prisoners who earned remission time were released unconditionally (Home Office 1989 p.5). Of perhaps greater significance was the fact that remission was automatic. Owing to the difficulties prison administrators faced in undertaking real time assessments of prisoner conduct the marks system had fallen into disuse and was gradually replaced by a presumption in favour of release (an excellent account of which can be found in TNA: HO 263/148). Disparities in the quantum of early release that could be earned by various categories of offender remained for much of the early twentieth century, a situation finally brought to an end in August 1940 when a pressing need for accommodation to house those detained under wartime regulations forced the Home Secretary to increase early release for prisoners and male convicts to one-third of their sentence (Home Office 1989 p.4). This framework was subsequently codified in 1949, shortly after the Criminal Justice Act 1948 had abolished the use of penal servitude, hard labour, and flogging in England and Wales.

While brief, this abridged history provides an important backdrop to the events of the early 1960s. Many of the themes that we will explore in this book from the confused normative basis of early release, the interaction of parole and remission, and the operational tension between early release as a right and a privilege were already firmly established within British penal policy and practice by the 1960s. It is also clear that many of the administrative components of an integrated early release system had been tested within British prisons. Administrators were aware of the logistical difficulty (and perceived unfairness) of placing discretion in the hands of prison authorities, the merits of unconditional release vis-à-vis release on licence with liability for recall had been scrutinized by several learned committees and the Home Office had been publicly criticized for its failure to provide adequate aftercare and supervision arrangements. This is critical to understanding the debates that surrounded the introduction of a modern system of parole in 1967. The events of the 1960s were not *sui generis* but an attempt to adapt long-standing questions about the management of incarcerated populations and operationalize a defensible system of early release to the particular concerns of the period. Moreover, this short history draws attention to one further, often neglected feature of the penal landscape in the early 1960s. Namely, that with the abolition of penal servitude and convict licences, the Home Office was left with an early release toolbox for adults that was manifestly unfit for purpose at a time when the effective rehabilitation of prisoners back into the community was a central policy objective of the penal system. A system of remission based upon automatic and unconditional release with no continuing liability for recall was about as far away from the spirit of the 'rehabilitative ideal' as it is possible to imagine and contrasted particularly unfavourably with the borstal system, widely regarded at this time as the 'jewel in the crown' of British penal policy, which provided for a comprehensive system of supervision for borstal trainees while on licence (Faulkner 2014 p.26; Hood 1965). One gets a sense of this 'policy problem' from the author's interview with a former Chief Probation Officer, invited to reflect upon the formative stages of his career in the 1960s:

But, I mean throughout the service I think this [parole] was seen as a really good useful, positive development. Because what we had before then was approved school after care, borstal after care and that's another word you don't hear any more, isn't it, Borstal.

The young offender institutions. Borstal aftercare and then something called voluntary aftercare, right. Not taken up very much actually.

...

And it was seen as a good thing but prisoners wouldn't take it up, well you can understand it. It's such an admission of inadequacy to say I'm being voluntarily helped by a probation officer. But here, that [parole] legitimized the whole process in a sense because they were released on parole and all prisoners would take advantage of that because you know it got them out. So it was very ... but we in probation took it ... I mean I think it's fair to say that most probation officers would put those cases ... they put them as a top priority. (Interview E: 15 September 2014)

Faced with these challenges policymakers looked to cognate areas of criminal justice for inspiration, a process Mary Douglas has referred to as policy or intellectual bricolage (Douglas 1986 p.66). The Home Office was keen to learn lessons from the borstal system which continued to exert a strong, albeit faltering, influence over penal policy in England and Wales (TNA: PCOM 9/665; PCOM 9/2248). The Prison Commissioners were merged into the Prison Department in 1963 bringing a great deal of institutional memory in relation to the operation of both borstal and convict licences into the Home Office (Faulkner 2014; Windlesham 1993 p.79). Many senior officials who had served their apprenticeships in the Prison Commission would go on to be closely involved in the creation of the modern parole system (for example Sir Philip Allen and Norman Storr who would reach the ranks of Permanent Secretary and Assistant Secretary respectively). The key point being that the reforming project ushered in by the Gladstone Committee (HMSO 1895) and the entirely justifiable decision to abolish penal servitude served to highlight the variable treatment of prisoners and convicts as well as adults and adolescents who were subject to the more developed licence arrangements of the Borstal system. In time, these administrative concerns would prompt a problem-solving process infused with the prevailing culture and values of the 1960s.

Criminal Justice in an Age of Optimism

At the 1964 general election, the Labour Party was returned to power after thirteen years of Conservative government. At one time, the outgoing Prime Minister Harold Macmillan had enjoyed high levels of public approval but by the early 1960s, the political landscape was shifting. The government had struggled to address a deteriorating economic situation, Britain's place in a changing world, and the fallout from the 1963 Profumo affair that had rocked the political establishment and challenged the hierarchical nature of British society (Dutton 1997 pp.68–74). In contrast, Labour had enjoyed considerable success by positioning itself as the party of renewal, a narrative that resonated with the prevailing optimism of the times, the growing affluence of the British middle classes and a post-war desire to build a better future (Labour Party 1964b; Seale 1995 p.230). This worldview came to infuse a number of public policy areas including criminal justice. As Morris has noted:

> The public mood was again one of expectation, not so much for 'reform' in the traditional sense, but of new and exciting innovation. The Robbins Committee on Higher Education, which was to oversee the greatest period of university expansion that the country had ever known, had been appointed early in 1961. In the United States John F. Kennedy had been elected the youngest ever President and was seen as a symbol of hope and progress by young people in the West .... In various subtle ways the Labour Party under Wilson's leadership capitalized on many of these hopes and emotions and presented the possibility of a society in which the quality of life would continue to be enriched for everyone, this time by the conscious exploitation of the new technologies that were emerging in what was to become known as the 'post-industrial society'. (1989 p.110)

In practice, there was considerable policy convergence between the two main political parties and Dutton has argued that 'Labour probably won in 1964 on the successful projection of an image rather than an alternative set of policies' (Dutton 1997 p.75). Despite a 3.5 per cent swing towards the Labour Party in October 1964, the first-past-the-post electoral system yielded a slender parliamentary majority of just five MPs and it was immediately evident that the government of Harold Wilson would have to return to the polls sooner rather than later to build a credible political mandate. Parliamentary realpolitik therefore had a significant impact upon the trajectory of public policy between 1964 and 1966. Unable to rely upon a significant parliamentary majority the Labour government was modest in its aims and limited in its impact. While there were some successes in relation to pensions and housing (McKie and Cook 1972 p.42) the rhetoric did not always match the reality, leading the historian Sir Robert James to describe the first Wilson government as a 'cautious, conservative, tentative government, deeply suspicious of truly radical departures' (1972 p.81). Where the Wilson government did flex its muscles, it was often to help 'pump prime' a stuttering economy. In part, this reflected the economic paradox of post-war Britain.

The 1960s were a time of prosperity that transformed the fortunes of many middle-class families who had 'never had it so good', but it was also the case that the rising affluence and consumerism of British society took place against a backdrop of relative economic decline (Marsh et al. 1999 p.43). Labour inherited a sizeable trade deficit from the Conservatives and the annual average GDP growth rate in Britain fluctuated around 3 per cent between 1950 and 1973, far below the economic performance achieved in France (5.1 per cent), Japan (9.7 per cent), and Germany (6.0 per cent) over a comparable period (Marsh et al. 1999 p.45). Successive post-war governments struggled to close this gap without overheating the economy and risking the devaluation of sterling. At its core was a fundamental dilemma; attempts to accelerate growth resulted in higher imports, a balance of payments deficit, and a crisis of confidence in sterling which necessitated 'stop-go' periods of austerity (Dutton 1997 p.78). In July 1961, the Chancellor of the Exchequer Selwyn Lloyd introduced a series of deflationary measures intended to cool down the British economy including tax increases, cuts to public expenditure, and a public sector pay pause. This difficulty was compounded in 1963 when Charles De Gaulle vetoed Britain's application for membership of the EEC thereby undermining the governments' attempts to grow a trade surplus (Marsh et al. 1999 p.106). Economic uncertainty had a cooling effect upon budgets across Whitehall. As Figure 3.1 below reveals government expenditure as a percentage of GDP went through cyclical periods of growth and contraction, which saw expenditure peak and trough throughout the 1960s, 1970s, and 1980s.

This may seem somewhat removed from the everyday concerns of prisoners and penal administrators, but it had a huge impact upon Departmental planning throughout the period examined in this book (a theme we return to in more detail in Chapter 5). As Michael Moriarty, a senior Home Office official noted in *Penal Policy-Making in England* (Moriarty 1977) the stop-go nature of government spending set the tone for negotiations between HM Treasury and the Home Office and the expenditure decisions, both capital and revenue, taken within the Department. Given the long lead-in times typically associated with building works and refurbishments, capital expenditure was particularly vulnerable to austerity measures and often scaled back during periods

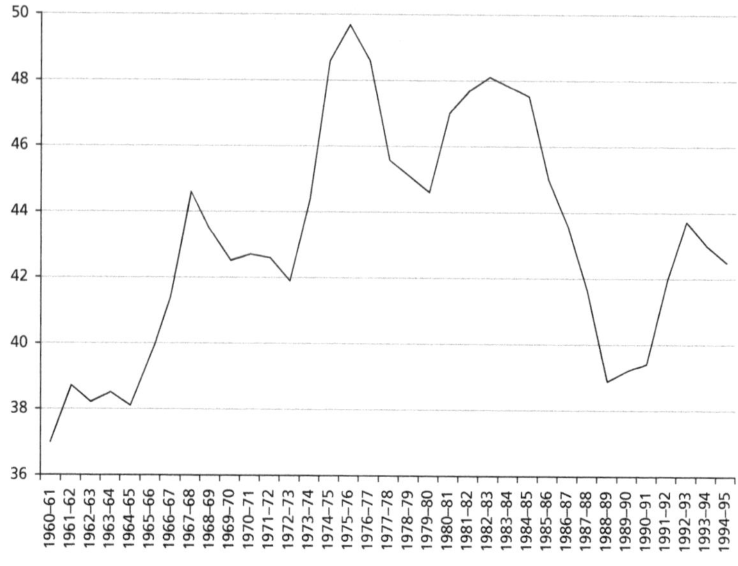

Figure 3.1 Government spending as a percentage of gross domestic product, 1960–1995

Source: Office for Budget Responsibility (2015)

of fiscal retrenchment. In contrast, revenue costs were bound up with wages, redundancy, and recruitment, issues that were politically sensitive and difficult to cut back in the short term.

Within the budget for Home Office services, there are decisions regarding the allocation of resources between capital and current expenditure; between buildings, equipment of various kinds and staff (and, within staff, between grades or functions); and among the different services. Two particular characteristics of this kind of policy-making are the speed at which the decisions often have to be taken, and the limited room for manoeuvre. The basic time-scale is the annual preparation of estimates and the annual public expenditure survey (PES) in which public expenditure needs are forecast for the ensuing five-year period. In orderly times these procedures should afford adequate scope for the underlying policy issues to be worked through. In practice, the economic problems of recent years have frequently required the downward revision of estimates and forecasts at short notice. Room for manoeuvre is limited by the manpower-intensive character of penal services and indeed all Home Office services: what is seen as an overriding need to maintain existing staff levels, and where possible to make good deficiencies and leave some margin for growth to meet demand, means that suddenly-demanded cuts tend to fall largely on capital spending programmes and other non-staff items. (Moriarty 1977 p.130)

As a result, penal administrators were stymied in terms of the quantum of resources that would be made available to the Home Office, as well as the consistency of future expenditure commitments needed to make long-term strategic decisions about the administration of the penal system. Moreover, this occurred at a time when rising crime rates and sentencing practices were already putting increasing strain on the prison estate. Recorded crime had risen from 478,394 in 1945 to 1,133,882 in 1965, an increase of 137 per cent in just twenty years. There was also some evidence to suggest that sentencing practices were hardening in light of a perceived crime wave driven, in part, by the growing affluence of the middle classes, the proliferation of marketable goods like cars, and inter-generational shifts in youth culture (Morris 1989 pp.93–103). This had a direct impact on the operation of the penal system. During the 1960s the prison population increased from a yearly average of 27,099 in 1960 to 39,028 in 1970, a rise of 44 per cent in just under a decade (see Figure 1.5). Mirroring the sentencing behaviour of the courts this general trend was punctuated by periods of retrenchment and expansion. Between 1962 and 1964 the prison population decreased before rising significantly between 1964 and 1967 leading to a 'prison population boom' that had a significant influence upon the final shape of the Criminal Justice Act 1967 (Morgan 1983). As the prison population increased prison governors were forced to make greater use of cell sharing. In 1965, a total of 5,337 prisoners were held in three-man cells with a further 148 accommodated two to a cell. By 1970, this figure had increased dramatically with 9,288 held three to a cell and 4,886 in two-man cells (see Figure 3.2).

It can be difficult to build an objective picture of prison conditions in England and Wales, prior to the creation of Her Majesty's Chief Inspector of Prisons in 1981. The Gaol Act 1835 did empower the Home Secretary to establish a Prison Inspectorate, but, in reality, this office lacked any real authority; the inspectorate consisted of only five full-time inspectors and they possessed limited powers of inspection over local prisons that were subject to little central government oversight. A Chief Inspector of Prisons was appointed in 1971 to bring greater consistency to

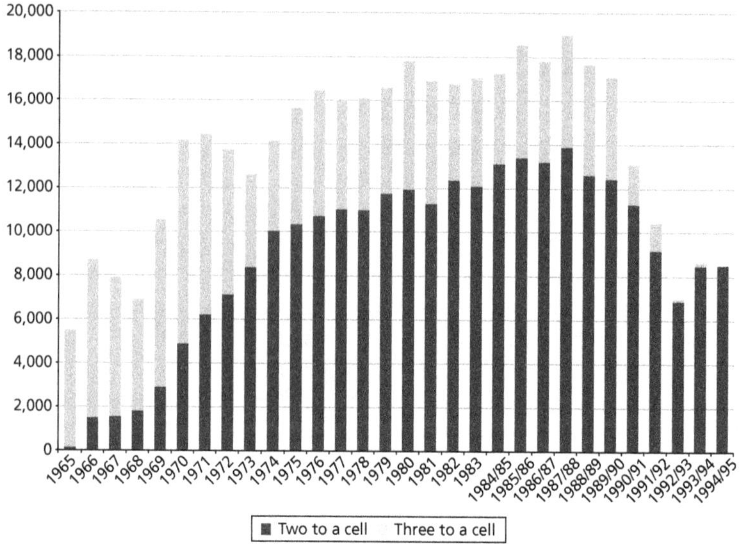

Figure 3.2 Number of persons held either two or three to a cell, 1965–1995

Source: Home Office Report on the Work of the Prison Department, 1965–1987. Home Office Report on the Work of the Prison Service, 1988–1991. HMPS Report on the work of the Prison Service, 1992–1996

prison inspection but without adequate resources to inspect the several hundred prisons in England and Wales it can be difficult to build a national picture from the available reports (Shute 2013 p.501). Nonetheless, the available evidence does suggest that conditions in the prison estate were not conducive to the lofty goals espoused in the Prison Rules. Sir Lionel Fox famously described Britain's ageing Victorian prisons as 'monuments in stone to the ideas of a century ago' (cited in LSE Archive and Special Collections: Morris T/6) and a dire picture of these penal artefacts was offered by the Prison Commissioners in a surprisingly candid commentary from their Report for the Year 1962.

Despite some increase in accommodation provided by the opening or development of new establishments, overcrowding has persisted in the local prisons and its attendant evils, so often described in previous reports, have again hampered efforts to establish a longer working week and modern training techniques. The staff, happily not now so thin on the ground as in recent years, has, as always, coped valiantly and cheerfully with the recurrent problems, and morale has remained high. The halcyon days between the wars, when no cell contained more than one prisoner, seem unreal now to those who remember them, but as the extensive building programme now in progress gathers pace there is hope they might one day return. (Home Office 1962 p.12)

Against this backdrop it is reasonable to conclude that Home Office policymakers were predisposed to any policy innovations that were likely to encourage the rehabilitation of offenders, facilitate the integration of prisoners back into the community, and in time help reduce the prison population.

A Recognizable Peak: The Coupling of Parole and Indeterminacy

Much penal policy debate in the early 1960s crystallized around the need for a clearer criminal justice pathway starting with the sentence of the court and extending out to a period of intensive treatment while in custody and effective aftercare to support the integration of offenders back into the community on release (TNA: HO 383/219; PCOM 9/665). In their Report *The After-Care and Supervision of Discharged Prisoners* (Home Office 1958) the Advisory Council on the Treatment of Offenders recommended the introduction of compulsory after-care and supervision for long-term prisoners. This was based upon a longstanding belief that this cohort of offenders had a special need for 'guidance and help on release' to reverse the ill effects of prison institutionalization. This logic was widely accepted and provision for compulsory after-care was included in the *Criminal Justice Act 1961* but never activated owing to a lack of resources. Instead the focus of attention shifted back to voluntary aftercare arrangements and the Advisory Council for the Treatment of Offenders report *The Organisation of After-Care* (Home Office 1963b) broke new ground in calling for the reorganization of probation and aftercare services in England and Wales (Newburn 2003a p.133). At the same time, the growing use of parole in America, Canada, and Australia had not gone unnoticed by British policymakers and the issue of aftercare remained stubbornly on the political agenda for much of the 1960s. On the 28 October 1963 the Chairman of the Howard League of Penal Reform, Kenneth Younger, wrote to the Home Secretary Henry Brooke to draw his attention to demeaning prison conditions and called upon the Home Office to embrace 'an "open door" policy in the penal field. By this we mean the release on licence and under supervision of prisoners serving 12 months or over at a time which might be determined by the penal authorities but might, in suitable cases, be quite early' (as cited in LSE Archive and Special Collections: Morris T/6). A short while later the Murder (Abolition of Death Penalty) Act 1965 would help to focus attention on the treatment of prisoners serving long determinate sentences and mandatory life sentences. During the passage of the Bill, Lord Dilhorne, a former Lord Chancellor and Lord Parker, the sitting Lord Chief Justice, moved an amendment to the Bill seeking to grant the Home Secretary new powers to release prisoners serving long determinate sentences once they had spent five years in custody (Hansard: HL Deb 05 August 1965 vol269 cc405–425). While these amendments never made it onto the statute book, the government did commit to a review of long-term, determinate sentence prisoners with a view to returning to Parliament with proposals in the not too distant future.

Each of these concerns must be considered contributory factors in the emergence of parole in England and Wales but what is particularly striking is the extent to which these considerations were located within a wider narrative bound up with prevailing justifications for punishment, particularly the therapeutic methods associated with the rehabilitative ideal. Since the late nineteenth century, the arc of penal policy had been towards the rehabilitation and treatment of the offender and this was reflected in the highly influential statement of purpose included in the Gladstone Committee report.

> We think that the system should be made more elastic, more capable of being adapted to the special cases of individual prisoners; that prison discipline and treatment should be more effectually designed to maintain, stimulate or awaken the higher susceptibilities of prisoners to develop their moral instincts, to train them in 'orderly and industrial' [sic] habits, and whenever possible to turn them out of prison better men and women, both physically and morally, than when they came in ... It may be true that some criminals are irreclaimable ... but ... the great majority of prisoners are ordinary men and women amenable, more or less, to all those influences which affect persons outside. (HMSO 1895, para.25)

Over time this rehabilitative focus had become increasingly modernist in its orientation and infused with the prevailing belief that science and technology could improve the delivery of public services (see Home Office 1959; Radzinowicz 1999). Perhaps the leading exponent of this view was the sociologist and parliamentarian, Baroness Barbara Wootton. In the nineteenth Clarke Hall lecture, *Contemporary Trends in Crime and its Treatment*, Baroness Wootton (1959) set out the case for a 'forward looking' approach to punishment in the following terms, 'the treatment of offenders thus enters the category of human actions which are at least potentially rational and scientific. By careful observation of past experience, empirical generalisations can be formulated which become themselves the basis for more successful future action' (1959 p.19). Parole was attractive within this context because it gave administrative expression to high-level normative ideals that favoured indeterminate sentences and the personalization of punishment. Put another way, one can see this as a mutually reinforcing methodology that linked high-level policy goals to administrative action; inmates differed in their response to 'treatment' and this necessitated individualized doses of incarceration. This personalization of punishment required that a degree of indeterminacy was built into custodial sentences (both determinate and indeterminate) to allow for the early release of suitable candidates and extended periods of detention for those requiring more intensive 'support'. What is more, an expertly administered system of release on licence, premised upon rigorous selection, had the potential to reinforce the reformative value of prison and guard against executive abuse of absolute indeterminacy.

One can trace the development of this line of reasoning through a series of highly influential commentaries on crime and punishment in the early 1960s. In a radio broadcast on 15 February 1962, and subsequently published by *The Listener* under the title *Indeterminate Prison Sentences,* Rupert Cross, then a Lecturer in Law at Oxford University, called for reform of prison sentences along the following lines:

> I want to suggest that every sentence of imprisonment for more than six months should be indeterminate. My suggestion is that ... the Prison Commissioners (or some body of persons acting on their behalf) should have power to release the prisoner after a much shorter period if they consider the case to be a suitable one for an early release'. (Cross 1962 p.289)

Cross explicitly noted that the 'individualization of punishment is the current demand' (1962 p.289) and questioned the ability of the sentencing judge to adequately predict a prisoner's response to rehabilitation while in prison. Surely it was better, Cross argued, that the executive with access to real time information on a prisoner's progress and prospects on release should be able to vary the sentence accordingly? Nigel Walker, then a Reader in Criminology at Oxford, expanded further upon this theme in a broadcast on the 28 June 1962. A lifelong supporter of indeterminate sentencing Walker was particularly critical of a sentencing regime he perceived as making it, 'as difficult as possible for methods of disposal to be reviewed and corrected in the light of the offenders reactions to his treatment' (Walker 1962 p.1100). In its place Walker endorsed the creation of a 'Supervision and Custody Board' with the power to grant, 'earlier release under supervision to those who seem ready for it' (1962 p.1100). Finally, in his article *Alternatives to Definite Sentences*, Eryl Hall-Williams (1964), then a Reader in Criminology at the London Scholl of Economics (LSE), traced the emergence of indeterminacy in British penal policy and reflected upon the sentencing reforms advocated by Walker (1962), and Cross (1962). Of particular note, Hall Williams questioned the practicability of the schemes outlined above and cast doubt on the track record of the Home Office in identifying the 'right moment' for release. Accordingly, Hall Williams favoured a rather more modest package of reform based upon the creation of a 'Sentence Review Board' able to review and amend the original sentence of the court as new information came to light.

> Under the system proposed, it would be open to the Home Secretary to apply to the Sentence Review Board for the review of the sentence of anyone detained in custody before two-thirds of the sentence had expired. The Review Board would be able to alter the sentence so as to permit earlier release. This might obviate the necessity to change the two-thirds rule [remission]. But the appropriateness of the rule should certainly be reviewed in any general reorganisation. (1964 p.60)

In each of these contributions, one can detect a clear nervousness about the introduction of 'absolute indeterminacy' into British law and a desire to establish a flexible system of punishment consistent with the principles of individual liberty and the rule of law. Commentators differed on how best to achieve these objectives, but it is clear that by 1964 support for a limited system of indeterminate sentencing was gaining traction within penological circles.

However, it was not until the work of the Longford Committee that these various policy prescriptions began to coalesce into a workable programme of reform with political impetus (Labour Party 1964a). The Study Group, chaired by Lord Longford, was one of several policy reviews established to prepare the Labour Party for government and enjoyed a broad term of reference, 'to advise the Labour Party on the recent increase in recorded crime, the present treatment of offenders, and the new measures, penal or social, required both to assist in the prevention of crime and to improve and modernise our penal practices' (Labour Party 1964a p.1). Published on 15 July 1964, their landmark report, *Crime: A Challenge to Us All* made sixty-six recommendations on issues as varied as the re-organization of the Home Office, the demolition of Victorian prisons, and transfer of responsibility for juvenile offenders to the Family Courts (Labour Party 1964a). Critically, the Committee would also advocate the introduction of a system of parole for prisoners serving determinate sentences. The personal papers of the late Professor Terrance Morris, now held at the LSE, offer a fascinating insight into the development of parole within the Longford Committee's deliberations (LSE Archive and Special Collections: Morris T/6; T/7). The records reveal that parole emerged relatively late in the Committee's proceedings. In March 1964, four months prior to publication, Dr Morris (as he then was) circulated a memorandum entitled *Ten Points* to the study group calling, amongst other things, for the introduction of parole as part of 'the progressive introduction of the indeterminate sentence, and the ultimate abolition of the determinate sentence' (LSE Archive and Special Collections: Morris T/6). This was discussed at a meeting of the Committee on 10 March 1964 prompting a wide-ranging debate on the political merits of indeterminate sentencing. It was agreed that Lord Gardiner would prepare a positioning piece on parole for further discussion by the Committee and a note entitled *A Parole System* was drafted later that same month (LSE Archive and Special Collections: Morris T/6: RD.733/March 1964). For completeness, this note can be found in full below at Figure 3.3.

The language and rationale articulated by Lord Gardiner was adopted almost wholesale in the final report. In *Crime: A Challenge to Us All,* the Longford Committee argued that, '[p]rison, in short, should always be the last resort' (Labour Party Study Group 1964a p.47) and since its use should be consistent

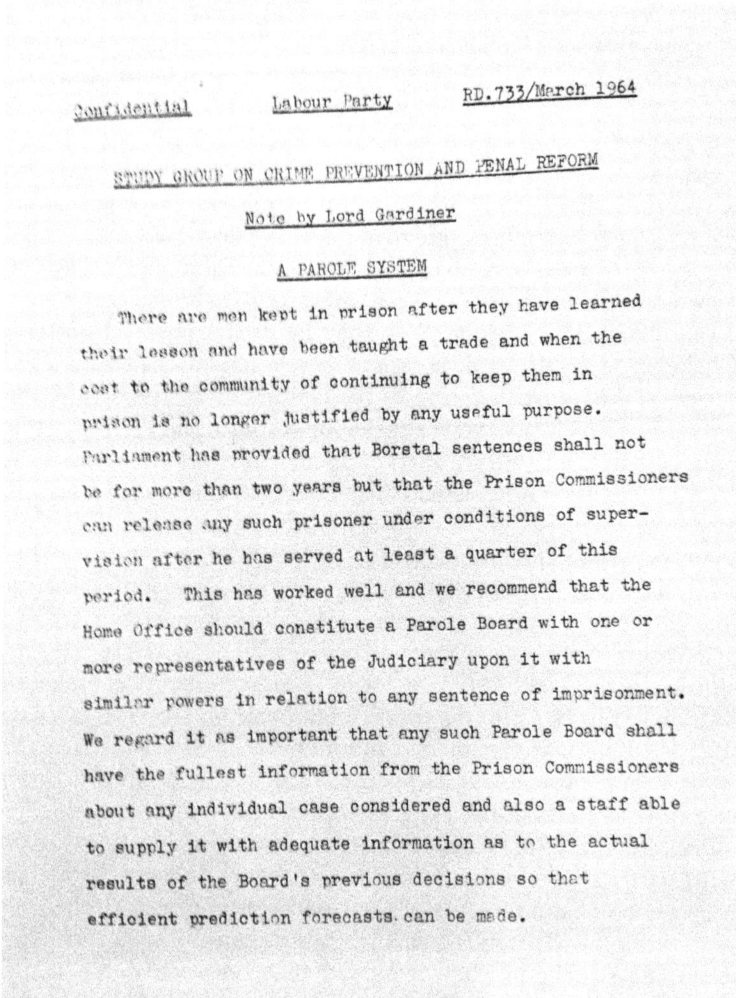

Confidential Labour Party RD.733/March 1964

STUDY GROUP ON CRIME PREVENTION AND PENAL REFORM

Note by Lord Gardiner

A PAROLE SYSTEM

There are men kept in prison after they have learned their lesson and have been taught a trade and when the cost to the community of continuing to keep them in prison is no longer justified by any useful purpose. Parliament has provided that Borstal sentences shall not be for more than two years but that the Prison Commissioners can release any such prisoner under conditions of supervision after he has served at least a quarter of this period. This has worked well and we recommend that the Home Office should constitute a Parole Board with one or more representatives of the Judiciary upon it with similar powers in relation to any sentence of imprisonment. We regard it as important that any such Parole Board shall have the fullest information from the Prison Commissioners about any individual case considered and also a staff able to supply it with adequate information as to the actual results of the Board's previous decisions so that efficient prediction forecasts can be made.

Figure 3.3 Lord Gardiner's note 'A Parole System' to the study group on crime prevention and penal reform, March 1964

Source: LSE Archive and Special Collections: Morris T/6 © Estate of Lord Gardiner, 1964

with the aims of rehabilitation, 'we doubt the value of keeping men in prison after they have learned their lesson; at this point the cost of continuing to keep them in prison is no longer justified' (Labour Party Study Group 1964a p.43). Accordingly, the

Committee encouraged a future Labour government to establish a Parole Board with the power to release suitable prisoners on licence before the end of their prison sentence.

> Parliament has provided that borstal sentences shall not be for more than two years but that the Prison Department may release any Borstal trainee after he has served at least a quarter of this period. We recommend that the Home Secretary should appoint a Parole Board with two or more representatives of the judiciary upon it with similar powers in relation to any sentence of imprisonment. (Labour Party Study Group 1964a p.43)

The Report is significant for a number of reasons. One can see the genesis of what has often been described as the 'recognisable peak' argument (Hood and Shute 2002; Shute 2003), a rhetorical device deployed by policymakers throughout the passage of the Criminal Justice Bill 1966/1967 to justify a parole system premised upon individualized treatment. Moreover, many members of the Longford Committee would go on to hold senior positions within the Wilson Government following Labour's victory at the 1964 General Election. Lord Longford served as the Lord Privy Seal, a position that enjoyed Cabinet rank. Gerald Gardiner was appointed Lord Chancellor in 1964; Sir Frederick Elwyn Jones would serve as Attorney General and latterly Lord Chancellor, while Alice Bacon joined the Home Office as Minister of State and sat on the Labour Party National Executive (Windlesham 1989 p.106).

A System of Parole Takes Shape: *The Adult Offender* White Paper

On 1 July 1965 the Cabinet of the new Labour Government met to agree the legislative programme for the 1965/66 parliamentary session (TNA: CAB 134/2001). Amongst the beneficiaries of this planning meeting was Sir Frank Soskice. The Home Secretary was authorized to introduce a Criminal Justice Bill in the next parliamentary session giving legal effect to various initiatives inherited from the outgoing Conservative government (TNA: CAB 134/2001). This was quickly supplemented by a number of Labour initiatives developed while in opposition. Cabinet Office records indicate that on 2 August 1965 Soskice wrote to the Cabinet Home Affairs Committee seeking approval to augment the Bill with measures to abolish preventative detention and introduce a system of parole for medium to long-term adult prisoners (TNA: CAB 134/1997; CAB 134/2001). The Home Secretary's memorandum explained his intentions in the following terms with more than a sprinkling of Longford Committee vernacular thrown in for good measure:

> Experience has shown that many long term prisoners reach a peak in their training, at which they are likely to respond to generous treatment, but may go downhill if kept in prison for the full term of the sentence. I propose, therefore, to institute a parole system permitting early release, subject to conditions and to liability to recall to prison, for selected medium and long-term prisoners. Apart from the benefit to the public which should ensue from enabling these prisoners to lead a more useful life while on parole, the system should also result in some saving of money, prison staff and space. (TNA: CAB 134/1997)

The paper trail emerging from the Home Affairs Committee provides a rich and fascinating insight into the chronology of policy development at this time. The Home Office had originally intended to introduce a rather modest Criminal Justice Bill in the 1965/66 parliamentary session without the publication of a White Paper (CAB 134/1997; TNA: CAB 134/2001). Parole was to be the centrepiece of this Bill but a final decision was deferred until September 1965 while the Home Office consulted the Lord Chief Justice and Scotland Office. When the issue returned to the Home Affairs Committee on 22 September 1965, Soskice was able to update the Committee and strengthen his case for reform. Consultation with the formative Royal Commission on the Penal System and senior judiciary was encouraging (TNA: CAB 134/2001). Moreover, a national conference with Prison Governors in August 1965 had indicated strong support for the initiative as a useful tool of discipline and control, 'every Governor I have consulted has emphasised that if he could hold out to prisoners in his charge the hope of an earlier release on parole, subject to licence, it would very greatly strengthen his hand in influencing them towards improved behaviour and in conducting his prison' (TNA: CAB 134/2001). The Home Affairs Committee duly granted policy approval for the introduction of a system of release on licence, but by November 1965 it was clear that the Criminal Justice Bill had lost its place within the Parliamentary timetable and would be held over to a future session (TNA: CAB

134/1997). The political and economic context was simply not conducive to the wide-ranging legislative programme Labour had intended to implement while in opposition and criminal justice reform was a significant casualty of wider power dynamics. The Wilson government commanded a wafer-thin majority in the Commons and this precarious position sapped Labour's reforming zeal, stifled ambition, and necessitated prioritization. In particular, the early years of the Wilson government were dominated by efforts to avert the devaluation of sterling (Pimlott 1992). As the diaries of Crossman and others reveal this single issue consumed more of the government's time and political capital than any other issues (Crossman 1976). Bogged down in the Commons and exposed on a variety of economic flanks, criminal justice reform was low down the list of government priorities. As the prospects of a Criminal Justice Bill dimmed the Home Office changed tack and sought permission first from the Cabinet Home Affairs Sub-Committee in November 1965 (TNA: CAB 134/1997) and then from Cabinet to publish a new White Paper (TNA: CAB 128/39/83). In the minutes from Cabinet it was noted that:

> The Home Secretary said that the Government might be liable to incur criticism from liberal opinion if they did not soon make a distinctive contribution to the reform of the penal system; and, since there was no immediate prospect of introducing a Criminal Justice Bill, it was proposed that a White Paper on the Adult Offender should be published as a counterpart to the White Paper on young offenders which had been published in August. The new White Paper should set the government's main proposals for legislation against the background of current thinking and action on penal problems. The central feature of these proposals was the introduction of a system of parole which would enable long-term prisoners whom there seemed to be some prospect of reclaiming to return to society after they had served a third of their sentences, but subject to recall to prison for a further third if they misbehaved. (TNA: CAB 128/39/83)

The White Paper received full Cabinet approval on 2 December 1965 (TNA: CAB 128/39/83) and was published as *The Adult Offender* later that same month (Home Office 1965). The centrepiece of the government's plan was a commitment to introduce a system of parole for adult offenders. The Home Office described *The Adult Offender* as a publication 'for the purposes of discussion' (1965 p.3) and while the proposals for parole were generally well received the White Paper attracted some criticism for a conspicuous lack of detail. In a detailed response to the Home Office the Magistrates Association indicated that while they were broadly supportive of a system of parole, 'our chief criticism of the White Paper is that it is too vague' (TNA: PCOM 9/665) and called upon the government to provide more detail of how the scheme would work in practice. This probably reveals as much about the culture and character of the Home Office at this time as it does about the pace of policy development. While some elements of the proposal were open for discussion, in reality, the administrative framework for a system of parole was almost fully formed by December 1965 (see TNA: PCOM 9/665; PCOM 9/2248; HO 383/219). We know this because on 10 September 1965, Brian Cubbon, then Head of C1 Division in the Criminal Department, wrote to the Prison Department setting out a number of exploratory questions the Home Secretary would need clarity on in advance of any parliamentary statement on the White Paper (TNA: PCOM 9/665). This included the categories of offender who would be eligible for parole, the point within a sentence when parole would take place, the likely numbers on release, and the anticipated quota of probation staff required to administer the system. In a detailed response dated 1 October 1965, Norman Storr, an Assistant Secretary in the Prison Department, set out the present state of thinking (TNA: PCOM 9/665). This paper trail is significant because it represents one of the earliest surviving records that describes the proposed system in detail, but also because it is extremely close in form and substance to the proposals that were eventually included in the draft Criminal Justice Bill published in December 1966. First, Mr Storr confirmed that all prisoners serving determinate sentences would be eligible for parole after serving twelve months or one third of their sentence, whichever was the longer. An early attempt to map the prisoner journey from the PED (parole eligibility date) to EDR (earliest date of release) and LDR (latest day of release) is set out at Figure 3.4 below.

Second, civil servants were keen to impress upon the Home Secretary that eligibility for parole would not be synonymous with release. In other words, parole would not be automatic and all release decisions would be at the discretion of the Home Secretary:

> selection for parole, as contrasted with eligibility, will be on the positive qualification of a prisoner and this qualification will be acquired

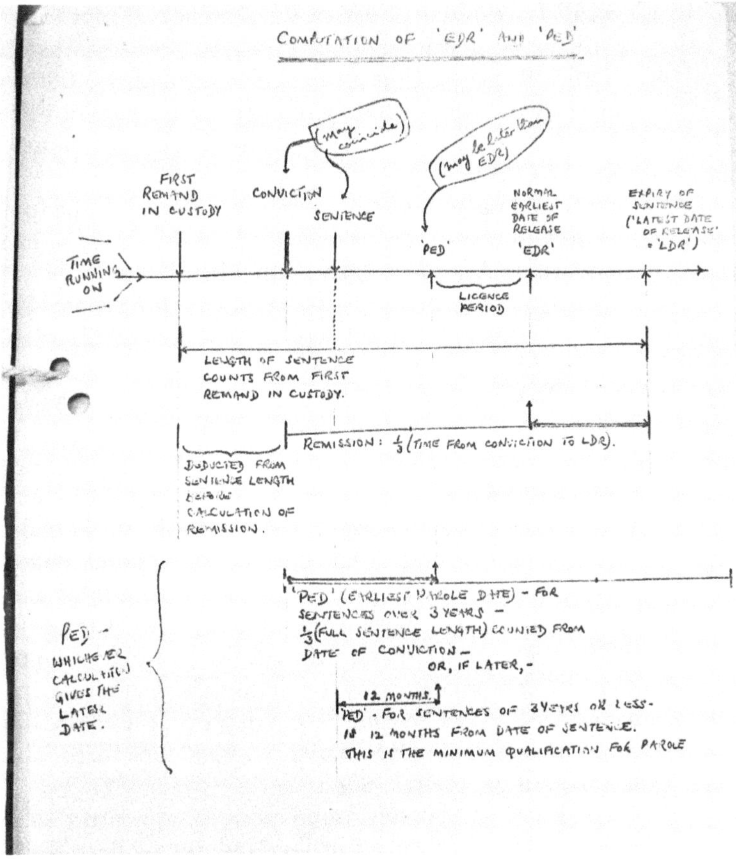

Figure 3.4 Home Office computation of parole release eligibility

Source: TNA: HO 391/432 © The National Archives, 1971

by his own conduct and attitude during the custodial part of his imprisonment. The criterion for selection will be the likelihood of his not resorting to further crime if released on parole. (TNA: PCOM 9/665)

More than any other issue the discretionary nature of parole was seen as central to retaining the support of the courts and general public who, it was assumed, would not look favourably upon the automatic release of thousands of prisoners each year. Third, prisoners would be released on licence under the supervision of a probation officer. Fourth, while on licence prisoners would be at risk of recall for the remainder of the sentence subject to remission. Fifth, while it was impossible to give precise statistics the Home Office Research Unit estimated that roughly 3,000 to 3,500 prisoners would immediately qualify for parole with approximately 400 expected receiving a positive release recommendation (TNA: PCOM 9/665).

To all intents and purposes, this memorandum set out the fundamental planks of the parole system that would be set out in the Criminal Justice Act 1967. Like many liberalizing measures from this era, parole is commonly associated with the progressive reforms of Roy Jenkins (Allen 2004 p.78; Williams 1972). Here we have clear evidence that its origins lay firmly in the Home Office of Frank Soskice and his Permanent Secretary Sir Charles Cunningham, enthusiastically supported, it must be said, by members of the Longford Committee like Alice Bacon and Lord Longford who had by now risen to key positions in government. Indeed, given the detail expressed in these records, it is almost certain that the proposed scheme had been in gestation far longer, perhaps in preparation for a likely Labour government or as part of ongoing policy thinking within the Home Office. Certainly, the Home Office Research Unit had already made several scoping studies of the factors related to reconviction along with an unpublished study, *First and Second Prison Sentences with Special Reference to Parole* (TNA: HO 291/727) which appears to have been undertaken in the early 1960s.

By the close of 1965, the policy foundations of a modern system of parole were firmly established in England and Wales (TNA: PCOM 9/665). The political, economic, and ideological case for a system of parole had been made out and the Home Office had largely negotiated the dense institutional fabric of rules, interest groups, checks, and balances that define the development of public policy (TNA: CAB 134/2001; HO 383/ 219; PCOM 9/665; PCOM 9/2248). With the publication of *The Adult Offender*, the locus of activity would shift from the internal machinations of the Home Office and Cabinet to the presentation and reception of these ideas outside of Whitehall.

4

A Very British Compromise

The Criminal Justice Act 1967

In this chapter, we explore the impact of Roy Jenkins' appointment as Home Secretary and the detailed legislative planning that resulted in the complex system of parole given legal effect by the Criminal Justice Act 1967. It goes on to examine the administrative steps taken in 1968 to establish the new parole system and limit the damage of a small number of high profile crimes committed by the first cohort of parolees. The chapter concludes by reflecting on the idiosyncratic operation of parole in England and Wales at this time; a very British compromise that would exert a significant influence over the trajectory of early release policy and practice in the subsequent thirty years.

A Change at the Top

Shortly after the publication of *The Adult Offender*, the Prime Minister Harold Wilson announced a Cabinet re-shuffle in anticipation of a likely General Election in the summer of 1966. As is so often the case, political forces entirely unconnected to the criminal justice system would have a significant impact upon the subsequent trajectory of penal policy. Soskice, who was suffering from ill health, was appointed Lord Privy Seal and recommended for a peerage (the government's parliamentary majority was too precarious to risk a by-election in the short term). In turn, Roy Jenkins who had recently turned down the role of Secretary of State in the Department of Education and Science was appointed Home Secretary in recognition of, 'his administrative ability and courage in one of the most difficult

Getting Out: Early Release in England and Wales, 1960–1995. First Edition. Thomas C. Guiney. © Thomas C. Guiney 2018. Published 2018 by Oxford University Press.

departments (Aviation)' (Pimlott 1992 p.191). This was by no means a simple assignment for the inexperienced Jenkins who had literally been a high flyer as Minister for Aviation. While considered one of the top jobs in the Cabinet the Home Office had sunk many political reputations. Famously, when asked to reflect upon his time as Home Secretary during the Second World War, Herbert Morrison MP is said to have responded with a warning that 'the corridors of the Home Office are paved with dynamite' (as cited by Callaghan 1982 p.12). Jenkins was about to experience this combustibility first hand and spent much of his early tenure trying to transform the working culture within the Department. Led by the 'formidable' Permanent Secretary Sir Charles Cunningham (Jenkins 1991 p.182), the Home Office of the 1960s was a highly centralized and hierarchical organization. Jenkins would later describe a working culture based upon 'the most centralised system of submissions to the Secretary of State which can ever have been seen in Whitehall' (1991 p.182). Echoing this sentiment in *The Home Office: Perspectives on Policy and Administration* Jim Callaghan, described an esoteric department characterized by high staff turnover, most notably in the Prison Department where the Director General rarely stayed in post for more than three years, and a Byzantine distribution of responsibility between the Home Secretary, the Lord Chancellor, and the Law Officers (Callaghan 1982 pp.12–16). Above all else, Callaghan was struck by the autonomous workings of each division within the Home Office at this time:

> It is obvious that, at the practical working level, the linkages between the different aspects of Home Office work are not very strong ... Policy issues do not sweep across whole areas of the Home Office in a single tide. On the contrary, each part has its own expertise and, more often than not, its own legal code. Whilst there may be an abstract similarity between certain Home Office problems, this often disappears in the management of the problems themselves. (Callaghan 1982 p.14)

Jenkins was determined to break this culture. In his memoir *A Life at the Centre* he describes a strained and turbulent relationship with Sir Charles which came to a head in late January 1966 (1991 p.181). In what he describes as one of the most difficult and defining meetings of his career, Jenkins met with Sir Charles on 10 January 1966 and insisted upon wholesale reform of the department intended to foster a more collegiate atmosphere and external facing approach. Following an extended power battle between the two most senior figures in the department these changes were reluctantly implemented by officials and just a short while later a pre-agreed extension to Sir Charles's tenure as Permanent Secretary was withdrawn, and he was replaced by Sir Philip Allen (later Lord Allen of Abbeydale). A career civil servant, Phillip Allen had joined the Home Office in 1934 rising to the rank of Deputy Chairman of the Prison Commission for England and Wales in 1952. Allen subsequently joined the Treasury as Second Permanent Secretary from 1963 to 1966 before returning to the Home Office as a Permanent Under-Secretary in 1966. Seen as part of a 'new breed' of more politically astute civil servants this change of leadership helped to unlock a period of unparalleled productivity within the department (*The Telegraph*, 29 November 2007). Reflecting on his return to the Home Office, Lord Allen recalls that 'morale in the Home Office had sunk quite low in Frank Soskice's time' (Allen 2004 p.63), a state of affairs that quickly gave way to a period of unprecedented excitement and creativity within the Home Office.

> On a personal note though, I think that one of the most exhilarating times I ever spent was my first month back in the Home Office from the Treasury in 1966. We had a series of meetings with the Home Secretary, Mr Jenkins, to come to decisions on various propositions for inclusion in the Criminal Justice Bill which was being prepared for introduction that autumn. Among others things, we discussed aspects of the proposed new parole system, and introducing suspended sentences and majority verdicts of juries; and it was fascinating to see how, under the leadership of the Home Secretary, the various experts—prisons, police, criminal department specialists, lawyers and the rest—chipped in with their own thoughts and their own experience. I think that Mr Jenkins would agree that although he was in full charge of the pattern of the Bill, what finally emerged on particular issues was not the policy laid down in detail by any one individual, but was rather the result of an interchange of views and experience between people with differing professional interests in the same problem. (Allen 2004 p.29)

A further transfusion of political capital came in March 1966 when the Labour government was re-elected with a significantly increased political majority. When asked by James Margach of *The Sunday Times* what he intended to achieve as Home Secretary during Labour's second term in office, Jenkins replied 'I would like to turn back this mounting crime wave. I would like to take some major steps forward in the reform of our penal system. And I would like also to see at any rate two or three liberal measures on the statute book' (cited in the Oxford, Bodleian Library Conservative Party Archive: LCC 1/2/7). This set the tone for what followed. The administrative framework for parole changed remarkably little during this time but it is clear that with Jenkins's arrival at the Home Office the Criminal Justice Bill was re-packaged as a far more ambitious and tightly defined package of reform. It is at this point that the Home Office brought forward plans to introduce the mandatory suspended sentence, streamline court proceedings with the introduction of majority verdicts, and regulate the possession of shotguns (TNA: CAB 134/2956). Similarly, officials continued to ruminate over the one outstanding issue in relation to parole; the 'wicked problem' of who should be responsible for governance of the system, the Home Secretary, an independent board, or tribunal (TNA: HO 383/219). In a memorandum to the Secretary of State and Minister of State Lord Stonham dated 20 June 1966 (TNA: HO 384/99) senior officials set out their formal advice for governance of the proposed parole system. In their view, parole should operate on the basis of, 'a continuous process of assessment within the prison machine and that S. of S. should have the final responsibility for selecting prisoners for release' (TNA: HO 384/99). Accordingly, the Home Secretary was invited to resist the creation of an independent parole board on the grounds that the Home Secretary already enjoyed considerable discretion to determine whether a sentence was served in an open or closed prison, that such a move would weaken the Home Secretary's accountability to Parliament and an overly judicial body may bring unnecessary formality to proceedings (TNA: HO 384/99). Moreover, it was noted that the equivalent Preventive Detention Advisory Board had proved entirely unsuccessful in assessing preventive detainees' prospects on release (TNA: HO 384/99). With the benefit of hindsight, the advice given to Ministers poses more questions than it answers. If the Preventative Detention Advisory Board had proved so unable to adequately judge the right moment to release adults serving extended sentences of preventive detention and officials anticipated similar difficulties with an independent Parole Board, it is not entirely clear why the Home Office machine would fare any better. Not least when the Advisory Council on the Treatment of Offenders had been extremely critical of the entire exercise of discretionary selection in their Report on Preventive Detention:

> It thus seems true to say that the Boards are unable to differentiate a good risk from a bad one. This was confirmed to us by the Chairman of the Board who told us 'we can never form a reliable opinion about a prisoner's prospects on release, and fortified though we are by almost exhaustive information, our decision at the end is basically a hunch, and often a majority hunch at that'. (Home Office 1963a p.37)

The most likely explanation is that the desire to keep selection of parole 'in house' reflected the centralizing tendencies of the Home Office and a desire to resist any fragmentation of power that might frustrate the Department's policy objectives in the medium-to-long-term. Evidence for this can be found in a subsequent memorandum to the Home Secretary, who had instructed his officials to explore ways to further reduce the prison population. Officials noted that any moves to create an independent parole board may frustrate the Home Secretary's efforts to reduce the prison population, 'everything turns on the way in which the discretion is exercised, (and if we were to have an independent parole board deciding who should be licensed, you would largely lose control of the way in which the power is used)' (TNA: HO 291/1246). At an even more fundamental level, it is probably true to say that if the Home Office had taken the recommendations of the Advisory Council at face value the whole edifice of a system of parole premised upon meticulous selection of suitable candidates would have been left in serious jeopardy. Not for the first time perhaps the emerging evidence did not fit the politics and the Home Office pushed on undeterred by this inconvenient truth.

Managing the Crisis: A Home Office on the Back Foot

On 3 August 1966 the Home Secretary wrote to the Prime Minister setting out his proposals for a Criminal Justice Bill in the next Parliamentary session (TNA: PREM 13/999). This was then discussed at Cabinet on 4 August 1966 (TNA: CAB 129/24). The Cabinet had previously approved plans for a parole system (without the establishment of a Parole Board) and the Home Office now sought approval to supplement the Bill with a package of measures intended to reduce the prison population including the introduction of a mandatory suspended sentence for all sentences of imprisonment for six months or less (Bottoms 1981 p.2), plans to tackle drunkenness, and limitations on the use of remand (TNA: CAB 128/41). This was followed by further scrutiny by the Home Affairs Committee (H-Committee) on 5 August 1966 and final clearance from the 'Legislation Committee' (known as 'L Committee') on 22 November (TNA: CAB 134/2956). If, as Harold Wilson once said, 'a week is a long time in politics', three months can be considered a political eternity. Between his appearance at 'H Committee' and 'L Committee' the authority of Roy Jenkins as Home Secretary was severely tested by a series of events that served to highlight the ideological distance that had opened up between the Labour government (as well as the liberal wing of the Conservative frontbench) and the general public. On Friday 12 August, three policemen were shot dead in Shepherd's Bush by gunmen Harry Roberts and his two accomplices who fled the scene prompting a nationwide manhunt. The pictures shocked a nation (see Figure 4.1 below) and led to an immediate backlash against a Labour government that had recently placed a moratorium on the use of the death penalty and abolished the use of corporal punishment in prisons.

A growing sense of crisis was compounded at the annual general meeting of the Police Federation on the 20 October 1966 where it was reported that 300 policemen staged a walkout out during the Home Secretary's keynote speech citing no confidence in the government (*The Times*, October 1966). Two days after this walkout the inexperienced Home Secretary was plunged into a yet another crisis. This time the focus was not on the safety of the police but security arrangements within Britain's jails. On 22 October 1966 the spy George Blake escaped from Wormwood Scrubs prison where he was serving a forty-two-year sentence for multiple offences related to spying for the Soviet Union. The audacity of the escape, coupled with the propaganda coup for the Soviet Union, proved inflammatory (a detailed account of these events can be found in Hermiston 2013). The stream of front-page headlines were a significant test of the government's political resolve and the Crossman diaries give an interesting insight into Jenkins' state of

DAILY EXPRESS

No. 20,589 SATURDAY AUGUST 13 1966 Weather: Sunny spells, cloudy later. Price 4d.

Armed police hunt killers of three detectives

THIS IS LONDON 1966

By JOHN BALL, MICHAEL BROWN, ROBIN TURNER

ARMED police, with tear-gas ready, mounted a huge hunt in London last night for a gang who murdered three detectives.

The three, the unarmed crew of a "Q" car, were shot down in Braybrook Street alongside Wormwood Scrubs prison near Shepherd's Bush.

As one lay still alive in the road one of the killers seized the police car and drove over him to eliminate the last witness.

THE NOTE

THE SHOTS

THE STORY

After the shooting: One detective (covered by eiderdown) lies in the road. Another body (also covered) is under police car GGW87C

THE HUNT

THE SQUAD

THE ALBUM

THESE THREE MEN

THE MEN

SERGEANT HEAD

CONSTABLE FOX

THE ENTERPRISE OF THE EXPRESS

IN THE KNOW

Test: Close takes over

Royal delay

Nurses attacked

Plane crashes

'Restore hanging' call

Pearson pays up

Trawler alert

Kiss killing

£10,000 gems raid

4 a.m.

9 hurt in hotel blaze

Wall Street up

LATEST

BOXING SILVER FOR ENGLAND

YOUTHS IN CLASH

Gold bars found

FLEet Street 8000

Figure 4.1 A 'Young Home Secretary' under pressure, 1966

Source: *Daily Express* 13 August 1966 © Daily Express/N&S Syndication, 1966

mind at this time. This reveals a less than supportive relationship with the Prime Minister, Harold Wilson, 'during our private talk Roy Jenkins rang up in a great stew about George Blake. When Harold put down the receiver he turned to me and said, that will do our Home Secretary a great deal of good. He was getting too complacent and he needs taking down a peg' (1977 p.87). In response to mounting media attention Jenkins announced on 24 October 1966 that an inquiry would be set up to examine prison security under the chairmanship of Lord Mountbatten (HC Deb 24 October 1966 vol 734 c649). Setting out the terms of reference for the inquiry in the Commons, Jenkins came under considerable pressure from all sides of the House and would later reflect in his memoirs that, '... the statement did not go at all well. The atmosphere was wrong before I came to the inquiry announcement, glacial on the opposition benches, uneasy on the Labour side, and Mountbatten appeared as more a gimmick than a coup' (Jenkins 1991 p.202). The Conservative opposition seized on the statement as an opportunity to embarrass the government and re-affirm their credentials as the natural party of law and order. Following 'scenes of uproar in the commons' (*The Daily Mirror*, 25 October 1966a) Edward Heath held an impromptu meeting of his Shadow Cabinet before submitting a motion of censure against Jenkins on that grounds that, 'this House deplores the refusal of the Secretary of State for the Home Department to set up a specific inquiry to report as a matter of urgency on the escape of George Blake from Wormwood Scrubs Prison' (HC Deb 31 October 1966 vol 735 c115). The Motion was heard on Monday 31 October 1966 and is often cited as one of the finest moments of Jenkins' parliamentary career. As Crossman noted contemporaneously, if in somewhat partisan terms:

> Then we went back to hear Roy Jenkins wind up with a tremendous annihilating attack which completely destroyed the Opposition. Before he got up he sat there next to me rubbing his hands and looking as nervous as hell but the moment he started one realized that he'd prepared that speech with tremendous care. He demolished Quintin's case and demonstrated that no special precautions had been taken by Henry Brooke [background on Quintin Hogg and Henry Brooke can be found at Appendix 1]. The demolition job was so total that when the vote came many of the Tories just weren't there. It was a tremendous reversal achieved by sheer debating skill—the first really good evening the Party has had since we came back from the recess. It did a lot to change the atmosphere. (Crossman 1977 p.100)

The issue of prison security would return to the front pages of the media in December 1966. Just weeks before the publication of the Mountbatten Report the 'Mad Axeman' Frank Mitchell, escaped from Dartmoor prison with the alleged assistance of the Kray Twins. The escape served to reinforce public fears of organized crime in England and Wales and many in the media drew comparisons with the Great Train Robbery and Ronnie Biggs' subsequent escape from HMP Wandsworth in July 1965. Nonetheless, the statement brought the government some valuable breathing space. Jenkins had pulled off a significant political reversal that bolstered the authority of the Home Secretary at a time when he was about to marshal a significant Criminal Justice Bill through Parliament. These events are significant from a historical perspective because they indicate just how contingent and sensitive to external forces the trajectory of criminal justice policy can be. Roy Jenkins was rocked by the Shepherd's Bush murders and the escape of George Blake. He could easily have lost control of the situation and his job given the lukewarm support of Harold Wilson who was increasingly suspicious of his young rival. Instead, a solid Parliamentary performance helped to change the mood music, at least within Parliament, and cemented Jenkins' reputation for competence in times of crisis. This series of events had little if anything to do with the political merits of parole or the provisions contained in the Criminal Justice Bill 1966/1967 and yet these events and the government's response to them would arguably hold more sway over the fortunes of the Bill than any of the points of finer detail. A case in point of why Harold MacMillan is said to have feared 'events, dear boy, events' above all else.

The Criminal Justice Act 1967

Buoyed by his handling of the Blake affair, Jenkins used a BBC party political broadcast that aired on 1 December 1966 to set out his plans for criminal justice reform, a package of measures the Home Secretary lauded as the most significant reform of the system since the Second World War:

> At first sight this may appear to be a random mixture of a Bill including proposals on such diverse subjects as juries, parole for prisoners, and the control of shotguns. But in fact it has running through it a single clear thread of purpose. The aim is to strengthen the hand of those engaged directly in the war against crime. All the main reforms included in this Bill contribute to that objective. They will make more effective the various agencies concerned in combating crime—the police, the criminal courts, and the Prison Service. (cited in Lester 1967 p.252)

The Criminal Justice Bill 1966/1967 received its Second Reading on 12 December 1966. Commending the Bill to the House the Home Secretary presented a rather different vision to his public broadcast. Gone was the rhetorical appeal to war and combat readiness, replaced instead with the altogether more restrained language of modernity and consensus, 'my object has been to construct a Bill which would be consistently liberal and rational in its approach to the difficult and emotional questions of crime and punishment' (HC Deb 12 December 1966 vol738 c52). Parole was presented alongside a package of reforms that 'revolve around the single theme, that of keeping out of prison those who need not be there' (HC Deb 12 December 1966 vol738 c1502). The proposals were warmly welcomed in Parliament. At this time, criminal justice was still largely insulated from party politics and the government's proposals commanded a level of bi-partisan support that is uncommon in contemporary discourse. Yes, there was discussion of recall arrangements and the powers conferred upon the Home Secretary, but the proceedings are notable for the absence of any steadfast ideological opposition. This was particularly true of the Conservative front bench led by Quintin Hogg (as he then was), the Shadow Home Affairs Spokesman. The Conservative Party had advocated the introduction of a parole system in their report *Crime Knows No Boundaries* (1966) and briefing the Shadow Cabinet at the Leader's consultative committee on 30 November 1966, Hogg reflected on the Bill in the following terms:

> There can be no question of a party attitude on the majority of these proposals. They are essentially matters on which experts differ, and individuals will not be dragooned into a common line. Personally I support the great majority of the changes, for what they are worth (as to which a certain degree of agnosticism is permissible). I am against entrusting the new Parole system to the Secretary of State, and would prefer a Parole Board on the Canadian model …
>
> Speaking generally the Bill itself is a potpourri of ideas (none, I think, original) which have been current for a long time. (Churchill/HLSM 2/42/2/16)

As Hogg had predicted the one area of contention concerned the governance arrangements for the new parole system. As originally introduced in the Commons, Clause 22 of the Criminal Justice Bill left the decision of whether to release a prisoner on licence wholly to the discretion of the Home Secretary. Home Office officials, particularly those likely to be involved in the on-going administration of the parole system, were wedded to an internalized decision-making structure but there is some evidence to suggest that Ministers and the 'bill team' charged with the safe passage of the legislation through Parliament were less willing to expend significant political capital in defence of this arrangement. Minutes from the Legislation Committee reveal that the Home Office was prepared to cede ground on this point and it was agreed in advance of the marshalling of the Bill that 'government spokesmen would not commit themselves firmly against it and if the case for a board was strongly argued when the Bill was under discussion in Parliament, policy could be reconsidered' (TNA: CAB 134/2956). As expected the merits of an independent parole board were debated at length during the passage of the Bill. At Second Reading Quintin Hogg set out the opposition's preference for an independent parole board, arguing that a strong judicial presence was critical to securing buy-in from the courts and ensuring that questions of liberty never became a matter for government ministers (Hansard: HC Deb 12 December 1966 vol 738 c76). When the Bill reached Committee, Sir John Hobson, the conservative member for Warwick and Leamington and a former Attorney General, moved a number of amendments designed to curtail executive control over the system by establishing an independent parole board (Hansard: Standing Committee A 7 March 1967 c704). The issue was considered at length in Committee and rather unusually for a Secretary of State; Roy Jenkins attended all Committee proceedings in person rather than delegate this responsibility to his junior ministerial team. While the Home Secretary was unable to accept the opposition's proposals, he was prepared to bring forward his own plans for a system of parole incorporating an independent parole board, 'the Government are disposed to consider a scheme on the lines I have put forward and would endeavour to put down amendments in this direction if they appealed to the Committee at the Report stage' (Hansard: Standing Committee A 7 March 1967 c743). The Home Office honoured this commitment at Report with a series of amendments intended to establish a 'Prison Licensing Board' a rather municipal name that was eventually changed to the Parole Board in the House of Lords. This exchange indicates that the government were willing to cede ground on points of substance, but it is surely revealing that parliamentary debate completely sidestepped the moral justifications for parole and focused narrowly on the quasi-legal basis of the board. Indeed, one of the defining features of the Criminal Justice Bill 1966/67 was the extent to which parliamentary debate was dominated by lawyers and legal argument. As Lord Brooke, the Leader of the Opposition in the Lords (and former Conservative Home Secretary) noted:

> I make no criticism, but the Bill seems to me to have been examined in another place predominantly from the point of view of lawyers. Indeed, the noble Lord, Lord Stonham, said that the Standing Committee was packed with legal luminaries. I trust, we shall have the full benefit of that in your Lordships' House, too, but I hope that we shall also look at it carefully and understandingly from the standpoint of magistrates, of the Probation Service and of other interests vitally concerned, to whom it is of very special importance. This is not a lawyers' Bill only; it is just as much a layman's Bill. You cannot be sure of getting justice by leaving it entirely to lawyers. (Hansard: HL Deb 10 May 1967 vol282 c1448)

The abundance of lawyers within Parliament is well documented (see House of Commons Library 2010 pp.5–6); but comparatively little research has explored the impact of this on both the style and substance of parliamentary debate (Howarth 2013 pp.41–63). We know that very few lay parliamentarians took an interest in criminal justice legislation at this time and were often highly deferential to legal professionals. It is plausible that the legal character of the debate, coupled with the number of senior lawyers on the Conservative benches, offered a more profitable avenue to scrutinize the Bill and influence its direction. What is clear is that most legislators, regardless of political party or profession were united in their support for a parole system premised upon the rehabilitative ideal and the personalization of punishment. Time and time again the Hansard record reveals that early release was justified on the grounds that it introduced a degree of indeterminacy into the penal system that would allow support of the effective personalization of punishment. Perhaps the most eloquent expression of this viewpoint was offered by Viscount Amory, a former Conservative Chancellor of the Exchequer and Chairman of the short-lived Royal Commission on the Penal System:

I now come to the joint questions of greater flexibility in sentencing and release on licence. It seems to me that if we take seriously that the object of treatment should be to turn the offender into a law-abiding and responsible citizen, then we must accept three conclusions. The first is that the treatment should be progressive—that is to say, graduated steps leading progressively back to full liberty—secondly, that the form of treatment must be tailored to the needs of the individual; and, thirdly, that these considerations will often involve modification of the original sentence in the light of the response of the individual to the treatment he has had. Therefore, one concludes that there must be a possibility of a greater element of indeterminacy in the original sentence. In that regard, some form of release or partial release under licence is highly desirable. (Hansard: HL Deb 10 May 1967 vol 282 c1489)

This passage beautifully captures the 'golden thread' of penal thought that linked Rupert Cross's early support for indeterminacy with the proposals of the Longford Committee, the White Paper, and the debates within Parliament. While policy-makers differed on the 'first order' design of the parole system and the 'second order' instruments of policy there was almost universal consensus on the 'third order' hierarchy of goals to be pursued by the penal system (Hall 1993 p.278). In this sense, the Criminal Justice Act 1967 can be considered an archetypal product of the rehabilitative paradigm that dominated penal policy in the 1960s.

Cautious First Steps for the Parole System in England and Wales

The Criminal Justice Act 1967 received Royal Assent in July 1967. It introduced a new legal framework for the 'release of prisoners on licence and supervision of prisoners after release' in England and Wales. Under the new arrangements a Parole Board was created to advise the Secretary of State on: (a) the release on licence and the recall of persons; (b) the conditions of such licences and the variation or cancellation of such conditions; and (c) any other matters pursuant to the operation of the new parole system.

Prisoners serving determinate sentences became eligible for parole once they had served either one-third, or twelve months of their sentence, whichever was the longer. Since all prisoners were entitled to unconditional release for the final third of their sentence, under remission arrangements, the new parole system only applied to prisoners serving sentences of eighteen months or over. In practice, this meant that a prisoner sentenced to three years imprisonment could expect to serve one year in custody, followed by eligibility for parole during the second year of their sentence and unconditional release in the final year subject to any time lost for bad behaviour. A distinct system was created for indeterminate sentences. Under the Act, the Home Secretary could authorize the release on licence of a person serving a life sentence, if recommended to do so by the Parole Board, and after consultation with the Lord Chief Justice and trial judge if available. The decision-making process was further clarified by the Parole Board in their 1968 Annual Report which made clear, that in most instances, the first review of lifer cases should take place after seven years had been served. To administer the new system Local Review Committees (LRCs) were established in prisons across England and Wales. Typically chaired by the Assistant Prison Governor the LRCs included representatives from the Board of Visitors, probation service, and lay members. In advance of a prisoner's parole eligibility date (PED) it was the duty of the LRC to review a prisoner's file and submit a dossier to the Home Office providing a reasoned opinion on whether parole should be granted. A new Parole Unit, housed within the Home Office Probation and Aftercare Department, was created to manage parole applications and prepare all suitable cases for review. Initially, all decisions were taken by the Parole Board 'on the papers', typically with a recommendation as to the prisoners' suitability for parole, the appropriate date of release (or next review date), and the conditions to be placed upon a licence. Since parole was positioned as a 'privilege and not a right' there were no oral hearings, prisoners were not informed of the reasons why their applications had been unsuccessful, and the Home Secretary reserved the right to overturn the recommendation of the Parole Board if it was deemed to be in the public interest.

Lord Hunt was appointed Chairman of the Parole Board in October 1967. The choice was symbolic. Jenkins was strongly opposed to a judicial chair and Lord Hunt, who led the 1953 British Expedition to Mount Everest, was a prominent public figure who commanded cross party support. As one former Prison Governor put it to me, 'I mean Hunt's appointment spoke volumes and this is the man who climbed Everest, who took risks. You know, he wasn't a bureaucrat ...' (Interview H: 20 January 2015). The Parole Board was originally comprised of seventeen members (one of whom resigned) and was required by the Act to include amongst its membership '(a) a person who holds or has held judicial office; (b) a registered medical practitioner who is a psychiatrist; (c) a person appearing ... to have knowledge and experience of the supervision or after-care of discharged prisoners; and (d) a person appearing ... to have made a study of the causes of delinquency or the treatment of offenders'. The first tranche of prisoner releases took place on 1 April 1968 to clear an administrative backlog of cases related to prisoners who became eligible for parole after the Criminal Justice 1967 received Royal Assent in July 1967, but before the administrative architecture of the parole system was established. A total of 406 prisons were recommended for parole by the Parole Board of which 350 cases were approved by the Home Secretary (HMSO 1969).

As Table 4.1 indicates, the total number of cases dealt with by the parole system subsequently increased to around 10,000 cases a year in the early 1970s, although a significant minority of eligible prisoners continued to exempt themselves from the parole process. In parallel, the number of prisoners recommended for parole by the Parole Board, and latterly by the LRCs under delegated powers, grew steadily thereafter from 1,835 in 1969 to 4,029 in 1975, representing an approval rate of approximately 40 per cent. This began to increase after 1975 when the reforms associated with the 'Jenkins initiative' began to take effect (a change we examine in more detail in Chapter 5).

Establishing an effective system of parole did not prove to be an easy task. The parole system in England and Wales had been premised upon expert assessment of prisoners and the provision of high quality paperwork that would enable the Board to operate a sophisticated system of discretionary release. In reality, administrative mismanagement and historic under-investment in prisoner case notes meant that prison records were often of poor quality, incomplete, and delivered late to the Parole Board. Reflecting on his time at the Parole Board some years later Lord Hunt was scathing about the state of affairs he discovered at the Home Office on his appointment in 1967, 'within a matter of months of the board being set up, we found a pretty scandalous state of affairs in the Home Office. We found a great pile of dossiers relating to forgotten men in the room of the then under-secretary. It was two High Court judges ... who cleared the backlog' (Hansard: HL Deb 03 July 1991 vol 530 c1030). This state of affairs was further compounded by the failure of

Table 4.1 The first ten years of operation, parole decisions made in determinate prisoner cases, 1968–1978

Year	Total cases dealt with	Total cases considered by Local Review Committees	Cases recommended for parole by the Local Review Committee or Parole Board	Percentage of all cases dealt with that were finally recommended for parole
pre 1968	4,764	4,347	406	9.3
1968	5,508	4,515	751	16.6
1969	7,264	6,774	1,835	27.1
1970	8,454	7,813	2,210	28.3
1971	10,338	8,653	2,971	30.8
1972	9,644	8,934	2,926	32.7
1973	10,614	9,846	3,344	31.5
1974	10,618	9,877	3,507	32.8
1975	10,154	9,455	4,029	39.7
1976	10,660	10,077	4,995	46.9
1977	10,989	10,074	5,218	47.5
1978	10,829	10,183	4,815	44.5

Source: HMSO Report of the Parole Board, 1968–1976

the various criminal justice agencies to communicate with one another effectively (Interview H: 20 January 2015). As one civil servant noted in September 1967:

If the secretariat is to be formed from within the Home Office, it would be administratively convenient if it could form part of the Probation and After-Care Department, but this may be politically unacceptable. Debates in both Houses on the Criminal Justice Bill suggest that the Prison Department would probably be unacceptable in some quarters. But wherever the staff is attached, I would hope that the secretariat could be located in the same building as the Probation and After-Care Department. We already face the daunting prospect of having the Criminal, Prison, and Probation and After-Care Departments and the Research Unit located in four separate buildings, and unless we can have ready and constant contact with the Board secretariat I fear that the scheme may well prove inoperable. (TNA: PCOM 9/2261)

In this context, it was perhaps inevitable then that the fledgling parole system soon began to court controversy. On 12 August 1968,

Sydney Williams made front-page news after shooting his wife and her new partner at their home in Four Ashes, Staffordshire before committing suicide. Williams had been amongst the first prisoners to be released on licence and it later emerged that neither the Parole Board nor the police had been informed of the repeated threats Williams had made against his wife or her partner. Given the damage caused by such adverse media publicity the new Home Secretary James Callaghan ordered an immediate review of the nascent parole system and issued revised guidance on the importance of data sharing between all criminal justice agencies (*Daily Mirror*, 12 August 1968).

Paradoxically it is these early failures that reveal something of the positive influence of parole and why it has proved such an enduring feature of the penological landscape. Following the introduction of parole, the quality of prison documentation improved significantly as prison authorities were forced to take prisoner's aftercare arrangements seriously. Yes, the architecture of the parole system was complex and unwieldy, but it also helped to insulate the fledgling system from criticism once the inevitable trickle of negative stories began with Sydney Williams (*Daily Mirror*, 12 August 1968). As one notable penal reformer put it to this author, this ornate decision-making structure was arguably a small price to pay for the reformative value of the new parole system and its sustainability in the medium to long-term (Interview C: 22 April 2014):

> I think there was a genuine rehabilitative streak in the notion of parole, both in the Crime: A Challenge to Us All type discussions prior to its introduction, but also in the design of it in the first place. There was a notion that prisoners could be rehabilitated and redeemed that was running through it that was genuine among those who designed it, and they were balancing it against the possibility of a backlash, the possibility of criticism but also the possibility that things could go drastically wrong. Hence it was so cautious and timid at the beginning but nevertheless I think it was a genuine rehabilitative notion that was reflected in the peak argument.
>
> So although despite the flaws in the peak argument as such the belief that people could change is a positive and a humane belief, and I think that was behind it.
>
> [*Author*: So something about checks and balances so that if it did go wrong they had plausible deniability ...]
>
> Yes ... .
>
> (Interview C: 22 April 2014)

As a result, parole enjoyed a degree of cross-party support that was absent from other penal reforms enshrined in the Criminal Justice Act 1967. While the mandatory suspended sentence was quickly abolished by the Conservative Party when they were elected in 1970 the parole system was expanded. The Criminal Justice Act 1972 empowered Local Review Committees (LRCs) to release certain categories of offender pre-agreed by the Parole Board, a move that reflected the growing public and political confidence in the system first introduced in 1967.

Conclusion: A Victory for Principle or Pragmatism?

The establishment of a modern system of parole in England and Wales has stimulated lively debate within the literature. In their conclusion to *On Licence* Morris and Beverley (1975) placed parole alongside the suspended sentence and limitations on the sentencing powers of magistrates as 'a piece of penal machinery designed to do little more than reduce the prison population and to negate the necessity for a large and expensive programme of prison building' (1975 p.159). Echoing these remarks Shute (2003) has suggested that the continued deployment of the empirically dubious 'recognisable peak argument' can be understood as 'a convenient way of providing a veneer of theoretical respectability to policies which were driven by other, more pragmatic concerns ... that parole would provide a quick and relatively inexpensive solution to the pressing problem of prison overcrowding' (2003 p.385). In contrast, Morgan (1983) has stated that the prison population thesis is unconvincing since the development of parole in England and Wales pre-dated the prison-overcrowding crisis of 1966/1967 and the parole eligibility guidelines outlined in the Criminal Justice Act 1967 related to only a small percentage of the prison population. On this issue, our analysis largely confirms Morgan's interpretation of the aetiology of parole. Part of the enduring interest of these events is the challenge of unpicking the rather 'nebulous consensus' (Tata 1990) that characterized the parole debate; the different views and agendas of those engaged in the policy-making process and the somewhat blurred lines between the underlying objectives of parole and its presentation to the public. Nonetheless, there are good reasons to conclude that parole was, at least initially, rooted in principle and inexorably bound up with the evolution of 'penal welfarism'. The likely impact upon the prison population and reductions in expenditure were undoubtedly important considerations and grew in significance when Jenkins was appointed Home Secretary in 1966 and the prison population began to rise at a concerning rate (TNA: HO 291/1246). However, these were secondary justifications that helped maintain the momentum for parole reform once the issue broke onto the political agenda. They were not, in and of themselves, the primary considerations. As we have seen, the debate that grew up around parole in the 1960s should not be considered *sui generis* but the latest contribution to a longstanding discourse about the appropriate aims and techniques of penal administration. Since the Gladstone Report, the arc of penal policy in England and Wales had been towards the rehabilitation and integration of offenders back into the community. It took time for this logic to build momentum and work its way into the institutional fabric of the criminal justice system to the extent that it provided a relatively stable set of rules, values, and norms of appropriate conduct for policymakers and administrators. Indeed, the 'rough edges' between classical notions of punishment and 'modern' forms of penal-welfarism were particularly noticeable with regards to early release arrangements. With the moratorium on capital punishment, the abolition of penal servitude, and the associated provision for the release of convicts on licence, prison authorities were left with a very limited early release toolkit based upon the unconditional release of offenders at the two-thirds point of the sentence with no continuing liability for recall, or supervision while in the community. A deficiency that was all the more marked given the considerable focus on aftercare for young people managed within the Borstal system, widely regarded at this time as the 'jewel in the crown' of the British penal system. Our analysis suggests that the dissonance created by prevailing penological support for indeterminacy and a remission framework that offered little more than automatic unconditional release unlocked a period of significant creativity inside the Home Office and the various external stakeholders with an interest in penal matters. Moreover, the available data does suggest that much of the debate around the establishment of a modern system of parole fails to account adequately for the different stress and nuance placed upon the scheme under the tenures of Frank Soskice and Roy Jenkins, and perhaps just as significantly by their Permanent

Secretaries, Sir Charles Cunningham and Sir Philip Allen. By 1966, the administrative framework for a system of parole was well established (TNA: CAB 134/2001; HO 383/219; PCOM 9/665; PCOM 9/2248) and owed a considerable intellectual debt to the Longford Committee recommendations first articulated by Lord Gardiner in his note *A Parole System* (LSE Archive and Special Collections: Morris T/6). With the appointment of Roy Jenkins as Home Secretary, the public presentation of parole began to shift (TNA: HO 291/1246). Parole was still linked to modernization of the penal system but from January 1966 it was integrated into a wider reform package including the suspended sentence that was orientated towards an overarching policy objective, 'that of keeping out of prison those who need not be there' (Hansard: HC Deb 12 December 1966 vol 738 c1502). No doubt this reflected the significant increase in the prison population between 1965 and 1967 but so far as parole is concerned this shift was as much a matter of presentation as substance. While recognizing the significant decision to establish an independent parole board during the passage of the Criminal Justice Bill, it is also the case that the fundamental administrative planks of the scheme first developed under Soskice remained intact.

Detailed contextualization of these events also suggests that longstanding interest in parole has served to divert our attention from the continued role of remission in the complex early release architecture that developed in England and Wales during the 1960s. If reductions in the prison population were the primary driver of penal reform the straightforward option would have been to extend remission up to 50 per cent of a prison sentence. Remission was inexpensive to administer, did not require a complex decision-making framework, and could be easily amended by statutory instrument. Conversely, if the reform agenda was purely driven by principle alone it would have been entirely understandable if the Home Office had taken the opportunity to abolish the outmoded system of remission altogether and replace it with a straightforward system of parole as was common in many other Western jurisdictions at this time. It is revealing that the Home Office rejected both of these options and elected instead for a compromise solution. Remission appears to have received remarkably little sustained attention within the Home Office, Parliament, or the subsequent literature. In part, this may have reflected the fact that few observers (or prisoners) really understood the distinction between parole and remission (see for example Bottomley's unpublished study of the operation of parole at Hull Prison). But it also suggests that pragmatic considerations like control, discipline, and reductions in the prison population were exerting an influence over the policy agenda, most notably within the Prison Department. By retaining a system of remission and the safety valve offered by the Prison Rules should the prison population reach crisis point, the Home Office remained true to an important rule of statecraft not to surrender powers that may prove difficult to reacquire at a later point in time. So long as remission was supported by Prison Governors (TNA: CAB 134/2001), provided an effective tool of prison discipline, and quietly expedited the early release of many thousands of prisoners every year, there was very little interest in opening up this aspect of the penal system to critical scrutiny. As a result, the Home Office and the various divisions with a stake in the parole system either ignored or closed down discussion of the paradoxes that would be unleashed by grafting parole onto the existing system of remission (some discussion can be found in TNA: HO 383/219). Chief amongst them the anomaly that high-risk offenders denied release by the Parole Board were subsequently released unconditionally under remission arrangements without any continuing liability for recall or supervision by a Probation Officer. This anomaly was the subject of scrutiny in the House of Lords, but largely downplayed by the Home Office during the passage of the Bill:

LORD HAMILTON OF DALZELLI wonder whether the noble Lord would be good enough to explain the purpose of subsection (5)(b), which I find rather difficult to understand. It says in effect that the licence of an ordinary prisoner will run from the date of his release to the end of two-thirds of the sentence. I understand that it is the intention to release the soonest the man with the best chance of success outside. He will be released after one-third of his sentence, and he will then have supervision and help for the whole of the second third. The man with the least chance of success will be released later and will have less supervision, until the man who is thought to have so little chance of success that he will not be released until the end of the normal two-thirds of his sentence will get no supervision at all.

Is it really the intention that the more help a man needs the less help he will get?

...

LORD STONHAMIt is a difficult point, and, frankly, I do not see at the moment any way of meeting it. But certainly I will look at it, and I will get in touch with the noble Lord between now and Report stage in case he wants to raise the matter again. (Hansard: HL Deb 12 June 1976 vol 283 c 761)

It may be that the Home Office Ministers had not been briefed on this question or did not want an official statement to be placed in Hansard. More likely is that the grafting of parole onto remission was seen as a necessary compromise solution. By retaining remission, the progressive, modern system of parole was unencumbered to focus on the important work of rehabilitation safe in the knowledge that remission would continue to keep the system ticking over in the shadow of the prison gates.

PART III

An Age of Uncertainty, 1975–1983

5

Squaring the Circle

Early Release and Short Sentence Prisoners

In Part III, we turn to the period 1975 to 1983 and the steps taken by government to extend a system of early release to short sentence prisoners. The Criminal Justice Act 1967 had demonstrated that it was possible to release a substantial number of determine sentence prisoners without significant risk to the public and in Chapter 5, we pick up the story in the mid-1970s as the Home Office began to explore options for extending the scale, scope, and reach of the parole system. The chapter examines the HM Treasury decision to disinvest from a significant prison-building programme in England and Wales following the 1973 Public Expenditure Survey, an outcome that cast a long shadow over criminal justice policy in the 1970s. It goes on to explore the delicate negotiations that led to the 'Jenkins initiative', a reform package that loosened the risk appetite of the Parole Board, before setting out a detailed history of the rise and fall of the 'partly suspended sentence', a policy innovation which empowered sentencers to reduce the custodial element of a short prison sentence in certain circumstances. The chapter concludes by examining the change of direction within the Home Office following William Whitelaw's appointment as Home Secretary in 1979.

The Long Shadow of Disinvestment

On 26 November 1971 the Director General of the Prison Service, Robert Cox, drafted an urgent memorandum for the attention of Secretary of State Reginald Maudling, the Permanent Secretary Sir Philip Allen, and Minister of State Mark Carlisle

Getting Out: Early Release in England and Wales, 1960–1995. First Edition. Thomas C. Guiney. © Thomas C. Guiney 2018. Published 2018 by Oxford University Press.

(TNA: PCOM 14/18). A serious problem was developing within the Home Office. On the basis of calculations from its Statistical Unit, the Home Office had released a series of troubling prison population projections suggesting the average prison population would rise to over 60,000 in England and Wales by 1980 (see TNA: PCOM 14/18, HO 291/1509). The annual prison population projections made in 1970 and 1971, set out at Figure 5.1 below, were significant for a number of reasons. Putting to one side the planning implications of such a steep rise in the prison population, the figures had been cited by the Home Secretary in Parliament and perhaps of most significance they were relied upon during the Departments' Public Expenditure Survey (PES) negotiations with HM Treasury. In large part on the basis of these projections the Home Office had secured approximately £1.6bn (2017 prices) in additional capital expenditure to undertake a prison-building programme intended to add 3,000 places a year and bring the Certified Normal Accommodation (CNA) of the prison estate up to 57,500 by 1979 (TNA: PCOM 14/18).

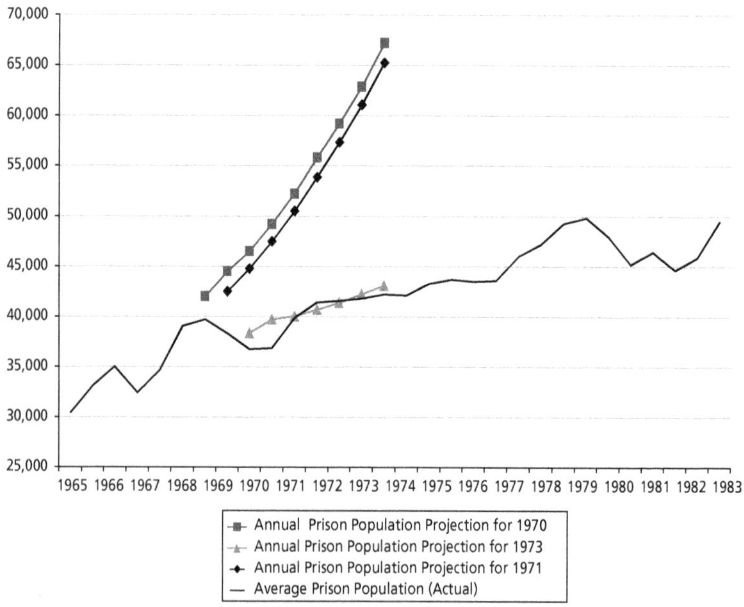

Figure 5.1 Home Office annual prison population projections 1970–1973

Source: TNA: PCOM 14/18

The credibility of this analysis was now being seriously questioned. The figures bore little resemblance to the Prison Departments annual outturn data and there were ominous signs that this variance had affected the Treasury's 'attitude to our proposals for new schemes, in particular their willingness to give early approval to standard design briefs for new establishments' (TNA: PCOM 14/18). Robert Cox invited the Home Secretary and the Permanent Secretary, whom as accounting officer was ultimately responsible to Parliament for Departmental expenditure, to reflect upon the presentational implications of rowing back on previous statements. While the figures were concerning, Robert Cox advised against a knee-jerk response given the long-term certainty of rising crime rates.

> It is difficult for us to put forward these estimates with complete confidence in the face of the stability of the figures over the last 15 months, and the Treasury may well challenge them. If the plateau continues into 1972 we may have to conclude that there has been some basic change that we have not so far identified. But it is wrong to make too much of short term fluctuations in considering long term trends. Unless and until there is much better evidence of a slowing down in the growth of criminality (which is the most important single factor) we think it right to assume that the prison population will continue to increase as it has done with some interruptions since the end of the war. (TNA: PCOM 14/18)

As a result of this exchange the Home Office slightly downgraded their population forecasts in 1972 and agreed to look again at the statistical assumptions underlying their prison population projections. But no substantive action was taken. So internalized was the assumption of rising crime rates at this time there seemed little reason to deviate too radically from the statistical forecasts when it was anticipated that the prison population would continue to rise in the medium to long term. This 'wait and see' approach bought the Home Office some time but over the course of the following year it became increasingly apparent that the Home Office methodology was flawed, an error bought into sharp relief by an unexpected reduction in the use of immediate custody by the courts (TNA: PCOM 14/18). The early 1970s are important in comparative historical perspective because for a number of years the criminal justice system challenged a simple, mechanistic reading of the relationship between rising crime rates, sentencing practice, and the prison population. The archival record reveals that despite increases in recorded crime fewer defendants standing trial for indictable offences were being found guilty by the courts (TNA: PCOM 14/18; Home Office 1973 p.2). It is also clear that the use of immediate custody by Magistrates and the Crown Courts had dropped by an order of magnitude entirely unpredicted by Home Office forecasters (Home Office 1973 p.2). As Figure 1.4 reveals, approximately 60,000 offenders were sentenced to immediate custody in 1970. By 1974, this had dropped to little over 50,000, a fall of 17 per cent in only four years that helped drive the prison population down from a post-war high of 39,708 in 1970 to 36,774 by 1973 (see Figure 1.5). In 1973, a revised methodology better attuned to demographic change and the differential treatment of various offence classes revealed the scale of the error (TNA: HO 291/1509). As a result, the predicted prison population in 1979 was revised down from the earlier estimate of 67,200 to the far more realistic figure of 43,120. On 26 June 1973 the new Permanent Secretary Sir Arthur Peterson wrote to the Home Secretary Robert Carr confirming that the forecasts relied upon in the annual PES negotiations had grossly overestimated the likely growth in the prison population (TNA: HO 291/1509). While noting the positive implications of current sentencing practice (a position relied upon heavily in external communications) it was clear that, 'the change in the projections will however put us in a difficult position with the Treasury in asking for resources for the building programme and for the prison service generally' (TNA: HO 291/1509). Carr's response gives some sense of what was at stake.

> I am nervous of using these new forecasts as a basis for discussion with the Treasury until we have had the chance to consider what they mean in terms of future policy. Unless we have a very clear idea of where we are going on penal policy the Treasury will simply leap on these figures in order to cut our expenditure. Once this happened it could take years to re-establish a proper capital programme again. We must have new prisons, even if the number of prisoners falls and we must also have some establishments of a different kind—e.g. hostels, etc. (TNA: HO 291/1509)

The Home Secretary was right to be cautious. The downward trend in sentencing practice did prove short-lived and the use of immediate custody began to rebound strongly after 1974. In 1973 a little over 30,000 persons aged seventeen and over were sentenced to immediate custody, a figure that had risen to 42,220 by the end of the decade (Home Office 1975; 1985). As it transpired, the revised 1973 projections provided a fairly reliable guide to the future growth of the prison population but by this stage the damage was done. On 15 August 1973, Home Office officials wrote to the Treasury confirming that, 'it no longer seems likely that the prison population will increase over the next 5 years at anything like the rate we had previously feared would be the case' (TNA: HO 291/1509). Accordingly, a meeting between the Home Secretary and the Chief Secretary to the Treasury, Patrick Jenkin MP was hastily arranged for 8 October 1973. There was only one item on the agenda; reductions in Home Office expenditure (TNA: HO 291/1509; T 353/104). These revelations were extremely embarrassing for the Home Office, but these underlying statistical and presentational errors may not have proved decisive were it not for wider structural weaknesses within the British economy. Timing, it seems, really is everything. But for the wider global economic insecurity or even the short-lived change in sentencing practice the trajectory of criminal justice policy may have been very different. Instead, these issues came to light at a time of considerable economic turbulence in England and Wales. The slow breakdown of the Bretton-Woods system between 1968 and 1973, compounded by geo-political tensions and the 1973 'Oil Crisis', created a global economic shock that hit Britain particularly hard (Sandbrook 2010 pp.10–12). The 1970s were a time of unprecedented cultural and social flux but economically it was also 'something of a reckoning for a country and a consensus that had been living on borrowed time' (Sandbrook 2010 p.12). Britain experienced power cuts, a three-day week and, on five separate occasions between 1970 and 1974, the Heath government felt it necessary to declare a state of emergency. Inflation was once again rising to dangerous levels, and in 1972 the Treasury introduced a suite of deflationary measures to control government expenditure (Sandbrook 2010). As we saw earlier, the criminal justice system was particularly vulnerable to the twin dangers of short-term disinvestment and long-term underinvestment. The democratic dividend of investing in the prison estate had always been marginal and proved to be a low priority as difficult decisions were made on how best to prioritize finite public funding between health, education, welfare, and defence. The Treasury was therefore predisposed to seek significant savings from the Home Office and as we noted in Chapter 3, the axe tended to fall on capital expenditure during periods of economic retrenchment (Moriarty 1977). Within this context, the revised figures were an open invitation for the Treasury to renegotiate the Public Expenditure Survey (PES) settlement agreed in 1971. The Home Secretary was advised by his officials that, 'the Chief Secretary will have been briefed to seek large reductions in the prison building programme as a consequence of the new and much lower population forecasts that have been accepted as a basis for planning since the Official 1973 PES Report was submitted' (TNA: HO 291/1509). In response, the Home Secretary was encouraged to adopt a strategy of damage limitation drawing attention to the preparatory work that had already been done, the high lead in costs associated with pre-construction planning, and the cost effectiveness of a modest prison-building programme with a stronger focus on refurbishment and renewal of Britain's ageing prison estate (TNA: HO 291/1509). As anticipated, the Chief Secretary began this high-stakes, inter-departmental meeting by confirming 'he was looking for reductions in forward estimates of expenditure in order to reconstitute the contingency reserve. In the Home Office expenditure there were two areas of potential reduction, namely police manpower and prison buildings' (TNA: T 353/104). Given the political sensitivity of cuts to police manpower the Chief Secretary indicated he was looking for reductions to the prison building programme in the region of £0.55bn (2017 prices) over the next three years. In response the Home Secretary:

> stressed his belief that it would be disastrous so to cut prison building as to appear to destroy the prison building programme. He welcomed a reduction in the prison population, which he regarded as in part at least the result of a policy of placing greater emphasis on non-custodial treatment, but there was a great need to take advantage of the situation to reduce overcrowding and replace antiquated prisons. (TNA: T 353/104)

However, as the meeting progressed it became clear that the savings the Home Office were prepared to countenance were far lower than those the Treasury were now seeking and the meeting closed in stalemate. It was agreed that further discussion at Ministerial level should be deferred while officials worked through the figures and calculated the likely savings at various levels of capital expenditure (TNA: T 353/104). There was, however a mood of inevitability about these discussions and in late 1973 the Treasury responded by making significant reductions to the Home Office budget once it became clear that the prison population forecasts were unduly pessimistic (see HMSO 1976b paras.65–72). The prison building programme was halved from a projected 17,000 additional places over a five-year period to approximately 8,700 over the same timeframe, a move that saw flagship projects mothballed in Lincolnshire, Surrey, East and West Riding, Berkshire, Kent, and Cambridgeshire (TNA: HO 291/1509). As Carr had feared, it would take years for this level of investment to be re-established and it was not until the mid-1980s that a prison-building programme of comparable ambition was finally implemented.

The sequence of events that culminated in the HM Treasury decision to disinvest from the prison-building programme cast a long shadow over penal policy in the 1970s. The Home Office was heavily criticised by the Public Accounts Committee (PAC) in their 1975/76 Report (HMSO 1976b paras.65–72). Internally, policymakers were forced to radically alter their plans for administration of the penal system (see also National Audit Office 1985 paras.3–6). When the prison population did subsequently begin to rise the prison estate was ill-equipped to cater for the increased flow of prisoners into the prison estate. Following rapid rises in the prison population between 1974 and 1976, the prison population rose steadily in the following decade from 39,820 in 1975 to 46,000 in 1984/85. This was a relatively modest rise when placed in a longer historical perspective, but it still represented a 15 per cent increase in little under a decade, placing further pressure upon a penal estate that was already struggling (see Figure 1.5). These year-on-year increases in the average prison population placed huge pressure on a prison estate that had seen little real terms growth following the challenging PES negotiations outline above (see Figure 1.5). As the gap to the CNA grew, the Prison Department began to make greater use of cell sharing. Prison overcrowding hit a peak in 1980 with 17,787 prisoners accommodated two or three to a cell, leading to serious industrial unrest, the publication of the 'May Report' (Home Office 1979) and the Prison Officers Association (POA) strike of 1980. While cell sharing would never return to the levels seen in 1980, the following decade saw more than 15,000 prisoners housed two or three to a cell, a practice that only began to fall into disuse in the 1990s. Prison authorities did reduce the number of prisoners held three to a cell from 9,288 in 1971 to 4,128 in 1984/85 but this was largely attributable to the refurbishment of larger Victorian prison cells and provided a small modicum of improvement within a system that was still overly familiar with cell sharing and prison overcrowding. The situation in local prisons was particularly acute and continued to deteriorate well into the 1980s as the remand population doubled from 5,100 in 1976 to 10,081 in 1986. In 1981 the newly established HM Chief Inspector of Prisons for England and Wales spoke candidly about the unfolding humanitarian crisis within local prisons:

> Our examination of six locals, which held 5,674 prisoners in accommodation intended for 3,548, brought home with great force the appalling conditions in which the inmates of these prisons are required to live, and the inadequacy of even the most basic facilities to cope with so many people. We are not just concerned at seeing two or three prisoners crammed into one cell, although that is unhealthy enough, but also with the dilution of the regime, the rapidly diminishing possibility of access to recreational, educational and other facilities and the inevitable preoccupation with the basic routines of bathing, feeding, exercise and slopping out, all because of the weight of numbers. (HM Inspector of Prisons 1982 p.11)

The 'Jenkins Initiative'

As the prison population started to rise after 1974, with no corresponding increase in the CNA of the prison estate (see Figure 1.5), the Home Office, to use its own words, became 'preoccupied' with measures intended to discourage the use of immediate custody, shorten prison sentences, and extend the scope of the parole system (see Home Office 1976 p.6). This gathered pace when Roy Jenkins returned to the Home Office in March 1974 and immediately vowed to take decisive steps to reduce prison overcrowding (*The Guardian*, 22 May 1974). This was easier said than done and Roy Jenkins would find it far harder to bend penal policy to his will during his second spell as Home Secretary. Years of economic stagnation meant the Home Office could no longer build their way out of trouble and the squeeze on Departmental budgets had prevented the Home Office from recruiting the additional probation officers needed to oversee greater use of non-custodial sentences

(TNA: HO 495/18). The Home Office therefore turned to early release in order to affect substantive reductions in the prison population at relatively low cost. By 1975, the parole system had been in operation for almost a decade and during that time had demonstrated that it was possible to release a significant number of prisoners on licence without seriously jeopardizing public safety. As detailed in Table 4.1 the number of prisoners released on licence by the Parole Board increased gradually in the first ten years of operation; in 1970 a total of 2,210 prisoners were recommended for parole, a figure that increased gradually to 3,507 in 1974, representing a release rate of around 32 per cent. Similarly, the number of releases made by Local Review Committees (LRCs) under the delegated powers contained in s35 of the Criminal Justice Act 1972 barely increased from 813 in 1973 to 923 in 1975.

As parole became a more accepted feature of the penal landscape many felt that the system could deliver a far higher volume of releases. As far back as October 1971 the Conservative Party had argued in their pamphlet *Crisis in Crime and Punishment* that, 'the parole system, due largely to the fine work of Lord Hunt and his colleagues on the Parole Board, has proved an outstanding success and there are good reasons for its extension' (1971 p.12). In the same year, five former members of the Board, including the influential academic Donald West, published a 'minority view' alongside the Parole Board's Annual Report for 1971, which criticized the Board in the strongest terms for what was considered an unacceptably low release rate (cited in Nuttall 1973 p.41). Similar views were gaining traction within the Home Office (Freedom of Information/FOI: HO 291/2138; TNA: HO 495/4: HO 495/18). On 15 May 1975, the then Head of the Crime Policy Planning Unit Michael Moriarty wrote to Neil Cairncross, Deputy Under-Secretary of State and Chair of the Criminal Policy Planning Committee, providing background information on the parole system for an upcoming strategy meeting (TNA: HO 495/25). Moriarty expressed his view that 'within the framework of the present scheme there may be some room for manoeuvre, with the object of making greater use of parole'. This conclusion led Moriarty to encourage senior Home Office decision makers to consider the merits of easing the risk appetite of the Parole Board and extending parole eligibility to new categories of prisoner (TNA: HO 495/25). Officials were aware of the developing academic literature on parole, most notably the concerns raised by Dr Roger Hood (as he then was) in his 1974 paper *Tolerance and the Tariff* (Hood 1974a). But while the Home Office was cognizant of these criticisms they were by and large secondary concerns when compared with the primary challenge of relieving pressure on the penal estate (TNA: HO 495/25).

Cairncross chaired a special meeting of the Criminal Policy Planning Committee on Thursday 15 May 1975 and this was followed by a Ministerial Presentation on 2 July 1975 to Lord Harris, the then Minister of State at the Home Office with responsibility for prisons (TNA: HO 495/25). On Friday 4 July the Home Secretary Roy Jenkins convened a meeting with Lord Harris, the Permanent Secretary Sir Arthur Peterson, and senior ranking Home Office officials to discuss 'penal policy' in greater detail (TNA: HO 303/98). Opening the meeting the Home Secretary stressed that the meeting should 'concentrate on measures which might be expected to provide some relief to the prison population' and went on to suggest that 'the main emphasis should be on measures concerning bail and parole' (TNA: HO 303/98). Following a wide-ranging discussion of parole procedure, governance, and the desirability of providing 'reject reasons' to unsuccessful parole applicants the Home Secretary directed his officials to work up detailed proposals for the expansion of the parole system. Since primary legislation would be needed to alter the legal basis of the parole system as set out in Part III of the Criminal Justice Act 1967, this largely consisted of softer changes to policy and guidance that could be expected to extend parole to prisoners previously deemed too risky, and improve the number of prisoners granted parole at their first hearing instead of waiting for a second or third case review. Interestingly, records also reveal that senior Home Office decision makers were extremely sceptical of the Parole Board's ability to drive these changes forward by their own volition. The Permanent Secretary drew attention to the rather conservative nature of the Parole Board; particularly the Chairman Sir Louis Petch, a former Second Permanent Secretary at HM Treasury, and suggested that the Home Office should take a lead on this issue. Accordingly, the upcoming NACRO Annual Conference was identified as an opportune moment to make a public statement of intent (TNA: HO 303/98). Thereafter, events moved quickly as the Home Office sought to negotiate the dense web of criminal justice stakeholders and secure buy-in to the government's reform proposals. The Home Secretary met with the Lord Chief Justice, Lord Widgery on 15 July 1975 to brief him on the growing pressure within the penal system and secure his approval for a series of measures intended to stimulate the increased use of parole (TNA: HO 495/25). The minutes indicate that the Lord Chief Justice expressed no objection to the proposals but took exception to any suggestion that the sentences of the court were too long (TNA: HO 495/25). The following day the Home Secretary met the Chairman and Vice-Chairman of the Parole Board to discuss his plans for the parole system. While the Home Secretary acknowledged the Chairman's concern about the risks of a higher parole rate, Jenkins was steadfast in his belief that the case for change was now irresistible.

> The Home Secretary said that the major problem which he faced at the present time is that of the recent upsurge in the prison population. The total prison population on 30th June was 40,577 which exceeded the previous highest population in June 1971. Even outside the present time of financial stringency it would not be possible to ease the impact of these numbers quickly; the present situation made it almost impossible to do so. The difference, however, between a tolerable and an intolerable situation in prison was a margin of a few thousand prisoners, and any improvements that could be made would be of great importance, parole, he said had worked well and he hoped that the ideas which he wished to suggest in the parole area would be seriously considered by the Board. (FOI: BV3/47)

Following this meeting Sir Arthur Peterson wrote formally to Sir Louis Petch summarizing the actions agreed with the Home Secretary and confirming his Departments intention to expand the operation of the parole system (FOI: BV3/47). The Parole Board was directed to take all necessary steps to grant earlier parole to prisoners who already received it, extend parole eligibility to categories of prisoner historically denied release on licence and make greater use of the s35 arrangements in the Criminal Justice Act 1972 to delegate decision making to prison-based LRCs. In his reply dated 30 July 1975 Sir Louis Petch confirmed that subject to a few drafting amendments the General Purpose Committee of the Parole Board were agreeable to the Home Secretary's reform package (FOI: BV3/47), an exchange of correspondence that bought to a close a period of intensive negotiation between the various actors with an interest in early release. On 31 July 1975 the Home Secretary delivered an eagerly awaited speech to the NACRO Annual Conference stating that, 'the prison population now stands at over 40,500 ... It has never been higher. If it should rise to, say, 42,000 conditions in the system would approach the intolerable and drastic action to relieve the position will be inescapable. We are perilously close to that position now' (as cited in Zander 1988 p.285). Urgent action was needed and the Home Office was now in a position to act. In response to an 'inspired parliamentary question'[1] from Ernest Perry MP a statement was made in Parliament on 4 August confirming the Home Secretary's intention to make greater use of parole:

> It is now over seven years since the principles of parole were explained in Parliament during Debates on what became the Criminal Justice Act 1967. The main criteria then laid down, which have been amplified in the independent Parole Board's annual reports have stood up well, and many thousands of prisoners have been parolees without appreciable increase in risk to the public.
>
> I am fully persuaded, however, that the use of parole can properly and safely be extended. I have therefore consulted the Parole Board and agreed with them new guidelines within which these basic principles can be interpreted to achieve this end without loss of public confidence in the scheme.
>
> There are two ways in which progress can be made; one is the granting of parole earlier to the kind of prisoners who already receive it. The other is to grant parole to more of the 60% of prisoners who are eligible but who do not receive it. (Hansard: HC Deb 04 August 1975 vol 897 c25W)

Following this statement, the Parole Board issued new guidance to LRCs and began to deliver against its new policy directions. With the benefit of hindsight the legacy of the Jenkins initiative can be seen as mixed. On the one hand, the proposals were received to near universal support in the media and resulted in a notable improvement in the parole rate in England and Wales. In 1975 a total of 10,154 determinate sentence prisoners were considered for parole, of which 4,029 were released by either the LRCs or Parole Board. This represented a release rate of 39.7 per cent (HMSO 1975). By 1977 the release rate had jumped to 47.5 per cent with 1,200 additional prisoners released on licence annually, a figure that remained fairly stable until 1983 and the extension of parole to short sentence prisoners (HMSO 1977). However, it must also be noted that the Jenkins initiative

[1] A pre-agreed question asked by an MP at the behest of the government.

represented the 'first significant attempt by a Minister to influence or control the overall policy of the Board' (Maguire 1992 p.183). While such measures were warmly welcomed contemporaneously, the Jenkins initiative had the unintended effect of normalizing Home Office interference in the work of the Parole Board. This prompted fresh calls for a more judicial body and established a 'policy-setting precedent' that was relied upon by Leon Brittan a number of years later with an altogether more negative reception (Maguire 1992 p.183). But in the short term at least, the extension of the parole system delivered the gains Roy Jenkins was seeking and helped to ward of the worst excesses of prison overcrowding. This had been achieved by flexing the existing legal framework, but such an approach offered increasingly marginal gains at a time when the prison population was expected to rise at a significant rate over the coming years. Throughout these deliberations the elephant in the room remained short sentence prisoners. The parole system as articulated in the Criminal Justice Act 1967 was explicitly designed to deal with medium- to long-term offenders and eligibility had been limited to those serving sentences of eighteen months or longer for the reasons set out in Chapter 4. In practice, this meant that the vast majority of prisoners fell outside of the scope of the parole system. The average sentence length in 1977 was 12.1 months with 77 per cent of the adult male population serving sentences of up to and including eighteen months (Home Office 1978). The extension of a system of early release to this category of offender had the potential to remove thousands of prisoners from the system at a stroke (and annually thereafter) while at the same time correct a perceived injustice that short-term prisoners had been excluded from the benefits of early release—what became known within the Home Office as the 'equity' argument (FOI: January 2013).

Policy Innovation: The Partly Suspended Sentence

Squaring the circle of early release for short sentence prisoners proved fraught with difficulty. On 31 March 1976, Lord Harris, Minister of State, and Dr Edith Summerskill, Parliamentary under Secretary, met with senior officials to discuss *Parole and Probation Matters* (TNA: HO 330/335). Dr Summerskill advised attendees that the Human Rights Sub-Committee of the Parliamentary Labour Party were minded to introduce a system of 50 per cent remission, a proposal that was ultimately rejected by Lord Harris who felt such a scheme would be unacceptable to judicial and public opinion in England and Wales (TNA: HO 330/335). In November 1976, the new Home Secretary Merlyn Rees came close to approving a scheme of 50 per cent remission and it was reported in the media that the Home Office had given serious thought to a prison amnesty as part of the Queen's Silver Jubilee celebrations scheduled for 1977 (*Daily Mail* 16 November 1976; TNA: HO 495/18). Policy discussion continued unabated but in the short term at least, the key developments in early release policy and practice did not emerge from within the Home Office but were driven from the more unlikely surrounds of the Lord Chancellors Department and the Royal Courts of Justice. While the Home Office was busy exploring new models of executive release there is evidence to suggest that the senior judiciary were driving a quiet revolution in sentencing practice and a new jurisprudence premised upon short sentences. As the rehabilitative ideal began to unravel many criminal justice practitioners staged a partial retreat from the reformative potential of prison to a less demanding faith in individual deterrence, the 'clang of the prison gates', and the modest window of opportunity to work constructively with prisoners during the first few weeks of their sentence. On 15 October 1976, the Lord Chancellor Lord Elwyn-Jones delivered an impassioned speech at the Annual General Meeting of the Magistrates' Association calling upon the magistracy to make greater use of shorter sentences (TNA: HO 495/4). The Lord Chancellor argued that the vast expense of incarceration, coupled with the bleak conditions within many local prisons prevented any meaningful reformative activity with prisoners. In the absence of any generalized rehabilitative effect it was the Lord Chancellor's belief that the first few weeks of a custodial sentence were most likely to influence an individual's propensity to re-offend and a short sentence was therefore more than sufficient to satisfy the deterrent and reformative effects of the criminal law.

> Imprisonment is a costly way of dealing with offenders. It now costs well over £3,000 to keep one man in prison for twelve months. At present we are clearly in a situation where we cannot as a nation find more money and more staff for more prisoners, or even for better prisons. In present circumstances our only hope of improvements in the prisons is by getting the population down so there is less over-crowding and less pressure on staff. A more sparing use of imprisonment, through shorter sentences, could be one way of achieving this. (TNA: HO 495/4)

In many ways this was a significant modification of the 'recognisable peak' argument that had proved so influential in the parole deliberations of the 'Longford Committee' (of which Lord Elwyn-Jones was a member) and the *Adult Offender* White Paper discussed in Chapter 3. In both instances the centrality of prison within the penal apparatus of the state remained but whereas many policymakers in the 1960s believed this effect was increased by sustained exposure to prison (up to a recognizable peak) their successors were now arguing for the opposite. The benefits from custody were most apparent in the first few weeks of a prison sentence and reduced thereafter as offenders became institutionalized and exposed to the detrimental effects of prolonged incarceration. This mindset quickly began to influence sentencing practice. As Mr Justice May (as he then was) would subsequently reflect in his address to the 8th Annual Overnight Conference of the Parole Board at Cumberland Lodge on 22 September 1977, 'the courts are increasingly taking the view that the maximum impact that prison has in that type of offender who has no record of violence occurs within the first six months of the sentence ... As a consequence of this view sentences that a year ago would have been in the 12 to 18 month range are now in the range of from six to twelve months' (FOI: BV3/52). In this context, it required only a small leap of imagination for policymakers to see a short 'taste' of prison as a credible alternative to immediate custody and the increasingly discredited fully suspended sentence (Bottoms 1979, 1981; Thomas 1982). Writing in *The Magistrate*, Professor Antony Allott (1976) offered one of the first cogent proposals for a framework of what became known as partial suspension. Reflecting on Lord Elwyn-Jones' call for shorter prison sentences Allott advanced a 'radical scheme for the partial implementation of the Lord Chancellor's suggestion' based upon the introduction of a new partly suspended sentence for first-time offenders and first-time prisoners. Under the terms of this new sentencing power an offender would immediately serve fourteen days in prison, at which point they would be released, subject to good behaviour, with the understanding that if they were sentenced for a further imprisonable offence within a twelve-month period they would serve the full balance of the original sentence as well as any additional penalties imposed by the court on the second occasion (Allott 1976 p.27). The idea of partial suspension was also considered by the Advisory Council on the Penal System (ACPS) in their 1978 Report *Sentences of Imprisonment*

(ACPS 1978 pp.118–123). The ACPS indicated that a form of partly suspended sentence had been considered as early as 1976 but the Council had not recommended legislation due to considerable uncertainty over how the power would be used by the courts and the likely impact upon the prison population (ACPS 1978 p.119). The ACPS was critical of individual deterrence as a justification for short sentences and expressed serious reservations about the possibility of the courts 'up-tariffing' individual sentences by using the power of partial suspension as an alternative to non-custodial options. However, the Council did conclude that if used in the right circumstances, particularly with first-time offenders, the penological foundations of the partly suspended sentence were sound and might provide a useful addition to the sentencing tool-kit of the courts.

> To sum up, we view the partially suspended sentence as a legitimate means of exploiting one of the few reliable pieces of criminological knowledge—that many offenders sent to prison for the first time do not subsequently reoffend. We see it not as a means of administering a 'short, sharp shock', nor as a substitute for a wholly suspended sentence, but as especially applicable to serious first offenders or first-time prisoners who are bound to have to serve some time in prison, but who may well be effectively deterred by eventually serving only a small part of even the minimum sentence appropriate to the offence. This, in our view, must be its principal role. (ACPS 1978 p.123)

Unfortunately, the proceedings of the Advisory Board were overtaken by political events and the nuance of this analysis was lost in the debates that followed. On 28 June 1977, Patrick Mayhew MP (a practising barrister and backbencher) moved an amendment to the Criminal Law Bill 1977/78, with the aim of empowering the Courts to partly suspend a short prison sentence (Hansard: Standing Committee E, 28 June 1977 c655). Mayhew's rationale for the new sentencing power was revealing. Gone was the post-war faith in indeterminate sentences and a 'recognisable peak' in prisoners' rehabilitation, replaced by a stripped back belief in deterrence and the value of prison as a 'short, sharp shock':

> ... it is the first few weeks that really bite and that really have a deterrent effect. If the memory of those first weeks is not dulled by acclimatising to life in prison—one does acclimatise to it fairly quickly—it will probably live forever and the prison sentence will have achieved for the offender its maximum deterrent effect, which is what we are hoping for. (Hansard: Standing Committee E, 28 June 1977 c656)

The Home Office indicated in Commons Committee that it was sympathetic in principle to this argument and Minister of State Brynmor John MP promised to bring forward more detailed proposals for the introduction of a partly suspended sentence on Report (Hansard: Standing Committee E, 28 June 1977 cc657–658). Efforts were made in both Houses to empower the courts to impose a supervision order on offenders serving sentences of partial suspension, but this was resisted by the government on the grounds that supervision was expensive and would place too great a burden on the already stretched resources of the probation service. The government's proposals were eventually accepted without division and added to the statute book on 29 July 1977. Section 47 of the Criminal Law Act 1977 stated that where a court passes, 'a sentence of imprisonment for a term of not less than six months and not more than two years it may order that, after he has served part of the sentence in prison, the remainder of it shall be held in suspense'. In this sense, partial suspension can be seen as the judicial counterpart to executive release and was closer in spirit to the fully suspended sentence than immediate custody with eligibility for parole (Bottoms 1979). The parole system operated on a discretionary basis and resulted in the subsequent modification of the sentence of the court by administrative action. In contrast, the partly suspended sentence frontloaded the release decision and empowered the sentence judge, in certain circumstances laid down by Parliament, to reduce the custodial element of a sentence and specify a prisoner's release date. These differences may seem abstruse but as we will see the timing and ownership of release decisions can have significant implications for the rule of law, the realization of strategic objectives, and the lived experiences of prisoners and their families (Hood 1974a; 1974b). In this context the partly suspended sentence was symbolic of the clash of interests that came to define the policy-making cycle as the Home Office explored options to deliver a viable system of early release for short sentence prisoners.

New Government, New Direction

One of the most intriguing twists in the brief history of the partly suspended sentence is just how quickly the idea was abandoned by the government. Senior officials were divided on the activation of the new power and without a broad base of support within the Home Office the partly suspended sentence quickly floundered. Several years later Lord Harris of Greenwich revealed that a breakdown of communication within the senior ranks of the department led the government to erroneously place the partly suspended sentence on the statute book in 1977. Upon realizing this error, a decision had been taken at the highest level to row back and block any activation of the power.

I have to tell the House that it is very rare for there to be failures of communication within the Home Office but, on this occasion, there was such a failure, for which Ministers must accept responsibility. I certainly accept my measure of responsibility; but, once we were apprised of what we had got ourselves into, we decided to extricate ourselves from it with the maximum speed, because, although I do not like and I do not think it appropriate to give details of official advice which was received nor to attempt to use the advice which was tendered to one particular Administration in a debate such as this, I must make it absolutely clear that the view we took was not taken in the teeth of determined opposition from our officials. (Hansard HL Deb 07 June 1982 vol 431 c104)

This indecision reflected Home Office concern that the courts were likely to misuse the partly suspended sentence as an alternative to non-custodial sanctions with the result that activation of s47 may well increase the prison population rather than reduce it. As the Home Office would later note, the partly suspended sentence:

has not been activated because of fears that the new sentence would be used to give a 'taste of imprisonment' in cases where at present the courts would impose a fully suspended sentence or non-custodial sentence ... there can be no certainty that implementing section 47 would achieve any reduction in numbers in custody and would not confer any advantage in the treatment of individual offenders. (Home Office 1981d p.14)

The prospects for partial suspension were dealt a further blow when the Conservative Party won a landslide victory in the 1979 General Election. Having held the shadow Home Affairs portfolio for a number of years William Whitelaw was appointed Home Secretary and from the earliest days of his tenure the Home Office moved to implement a two-pronged strategy in relation to penal policy (FOI: HO 495/21; January 2013). On the one hand, the Home Office began to examine options to reform the release arrangements of short sentence prisoners, a theme we take up in Chapter 6 (TNA: HO 495/4; HO495/18; HO 291/25). On the other, the Home Office sought to build a constructive dialogue with the judiciary in order to promote greater use of non-custodial sentences (see FOI: HO 495/21). Sentencing practice falls largely outside the scope of this book but it is impossible to understand the events that follow without an adequate account of the constitutional position of the judiciary and changing sentencing practice. The constitutional separation of powers between the executive and judiciary emerges as a key driver in the developmental trajectory of penal policy and officials, no doubt well versed in the work of A.V. Dicey, deferred to the courts across a wide range of sentencing matters (Faulkner 2006: 2006 p.30). This made it very difficult to predict with any degree of confidence how new policy initiatives, such as the partly suspended sentence, would be received by the courts. If the power was applied in the limited circumstances proposed by the Advisory Council, the partly suspended sentences could have precipitated a shift from long-term determinate sentences towards shorter custodial sentences with significant implications for the size of the prison population. However, if used incorrectly, partial suspension would have the opposite effect, encouraging the courts to 'up-tariff' by giving non-serious offenders a taste of prison when historically they would have been dealt with in the community (Advisory Council on the Penal System 1978; Home Office 1981b). The Home Office were all too aware of this predicament and considerable efforts were made to build bridges with the judiciary and raise awareness of the pressures building within the prison estate (FOI: HO 495/21). For example, Bob Morris, a former Assistant under Secretary of State in the Home Office, recalls attempts in the very early 1980s to broach these issues with the judiciary.

> I remember the Permanent Under-Secretary with Mr Whitelaw's permission conducting some initiatives which took the form of discrete dinners at gentlemen's clubs. The judiciary was then manifestly apprehensive about such approaches. It thought that the Home Office had only one agenda, which was to reduce the size of the prison population. That suspicion never disappeared entirely. (CCBH 2010 p.18)

This mistrust may have been well founded but improved lines of communication with the judiciary was seen as a central pillar of Home Office strategy. The following extract from a memorandum sent by the Permanent Secretary Sir Brian Cubbon to the Home Secretary on the topic of early release for short-term prison sentences offers a unique insight into the delicate tightrope the Home Office was walking in seeking to curb the prison population while also retaining the confidence of the judiciary (FOI: HO 495/21). As Sir Brian was acutely aware the government's best laid plans would stand and fall according to the co-operation of the judiciary.

I think we need to link this whole exercise (including the question of implementing section 47) with the approach to the Lord Chancellor and then to the Judges about sentencing practice and the prison population. We cannot go it alone. The courts can nullify the intended effect of any of the legislative schemes which have been canvassed, or conversely make them unnecessary if the main object is to reduce the prison population. We need to see if we can establish a dialogue with the judiciary in order to form a view of how best to move forward on the joint problem of sentencing practice and sentencing powers. Putting it very crudely, we need to establish which of three scenarios is the most likely:

(a) the courts, with encouragement following our initiative with the Lord Chancellor, go a long way towards solving the overcrowding problem by a sustained change in sentencing practice;
(b) the courts and the executive pull together in the same direction, either by a combination in changes in sentencing practice and new schemes for early release on the lines of Flag A [bullet point (a) above], or at least the courts do not nullify the effect of such a scheme;
(c) the executive and the legislature unilaterally make changes which are then offset by sentencing practice. (FOI: HO 495/21)

Initially there were reasons for cautious optimism that Cubbon's scenario 'c' could be avoided. A concerted effort was made by all parties to promote the use of non-custodial sentences. In the months following his appointment as Lord Chief Justice in April 1980, Lord Lane issued a series of practice directions in the cases of *R v. Bibi*[2] and *R v. Ian Albert Upton*[3] stating that, 'the time has come to appreciate that non-violent petty offenders should not be allowed to take up what has become valuable space in prison' (*Upton* p.133). Later, in *Aramah*[4] Lord Lane issued the

[2] (1980) 1 W.L.R. 1193.
[3] (1980) 2 Cr. App. R. (S.) 132.
[4] (1985) 4 Cr. App. R. (S) 407.

first in a series of guideline judgments intended to set down, 'general parameters for dealing with several variations of a certain type of offence, considering the main aggravating and mitigating factors and suggesting an appropriate starting point or range of sentences' (Ashworth 2010 p.36). These judgements helped to temper the use of immediate custody, at least in the short term, and contributed to a fairly stable prison population in the first half of the 1980s. Average sentence lengths for those aged seventeen and over fell from 13.2 months in 1975 to 10.3 months in 1982, while the Magistrates' Courts, often portrayed as particularly susceptible to punitive impulses responded by gradually reducing the number of males aged twenty-one and over that were sentenced to immediate custody throughout the 1980s.[5] Green shoots perhaps, but they were not deep-rooted. As Koffman has noted, guidance from the Court of Appeal was piecemeal, did not focus sharply enough on the most common offences, and without continued review of lower court decisions both sentence lengths and use of immediate custody began to rebound after 1984 (2006 p.283). Recognizing these deficiencies, the Home Office began exploring options for extending a system of early release to short sentence prisoners (TNA: HO 495/4; HO495/18; HO 291/25). Greater use of non-custodial sentences remained the aspiration for many penal reformers but given past experiences there was little sense in relying upon this outcome (Faulkner 2014 pp.99–108; TNA: HO 495/18). The government needed a contingency option and this came in the form of early release for short-term prisoners.

[5] Although this must be balanced against the increasing numbers sentenced to immediate custody by the Crown Court, typically for longer periods.

6

The Politics of Inertia

The Criminal Justice Act 1982

In this chapter we continue to explore the ever more complex policy debates that surrounded the efforts to extend a system of early release to short sentence prisoners. The chapter begins with an overview of the main candidates for reform and the strengths and weaknesses of these policy options. It explores the Home Office (1981b) *Review of Parole in England and Wales* and considers why these recommendations were so quickly abandoned in the face of political and judicial pressure. It then goes on to examine the passage of the Criminal Justice Act 1982, a significant piece of legislation which resulted in wide-ranging reform of parole in England and Wales. The chapter concludes with a number of reflections upon the policy inertia of the early 1980s and what that reveals about the changing aims and techniques of criminal justice at this time.

On the Horns of a Dilemma: The Question of Short-Term Prisoners

In October 1977, the House of Commons Expenditure Committee (one of several select committees established to scrutinize the activities of Her Majesty's Departments of State) announced a wide-ranging review of the penal system, with an explicit mandate to explore options for the 'reduction of pressure on the prison system'. In their Final Report, published in July 1978, the Committee recommended that, 'an independent inquiry should be instituted into the whole parole system though we have no views as to the form it should take other than that it should not be limited to an internal review by officials' (House of Commons 1978 p.XXXIII). The Home Office was unwilling

Getting Out: Early Release in England and Wales, 1960–1995. First Edition. Thomas C. Guiney. Published 2018 by Oxford University Press.

to accept this recommendation but a modest, internal review of the parole system was established with a broad remit to consider the organization of Parole Board hearings, the provision of reject reasons and recall arrangements (Home Office 1981b). The review gathered pace in May 1979 with Whitelaw's appointment as Home Secretary and at this point officials began to actively explore options for extending parole to those serving short prison sentences. Prisoners serving less than eighteen months made up the lion share of the prison population and despite the fact their offences had been deemed less serious by the courts they were liable to serve a longer proportion of their sentence in prison than long-term inmates. The extension of a system of early release to this category of offender had the potential to remove thousands of prisoners from the system while at the same time correct a perceived injustice that short-term prisoners had been excluded from the benefits of early release (Freedom of Information/ FOI: January 2013). For this reason the policy problem of short sentence prisons excited a great deal of creative thinking and four major schools of thought began to emerge within the Home Office, each with their unique constellation of strengths and weaknesses, supporters and detractors.

Remission

The first option under consideration by the Home Office was to amend the Prison Rules and increase remission from one-third to one-half of a sentence for all inmates. An increase in remission time was attractive for a number of reasons: it could be implemented swiftly by statutory instrument, it made no additional demands upon the prison or probation service, and did not rely upon the unwieldy machinery of the parole system. Records indicate that the influential Prison and Borstal Governors' Branch of the Society of Civil and Public Servants, a forerunner to the Prison Governors Association, had consistently advocated for an expanded system of remission to assist with the maintenance of order within prisons (1977, 1978; FOI: HO 495/21) and this view also found favour in the influential May Review which recommended that, 'executive intervention through remission schemes and parole should be kept under consideration' (Home Office 1979: 27). Since reform of remission arrangements was relatively straightforward and commanded the support of a powerful alliance of interest groups, it is easy to see why it remained on the political agenda throughout the period in question. That it had not been implemented can be attributed to two major shortcomings. First, Whitelaw strongly objected to the fact that remission could not be altered in such a way that would allow prison authorities to exclude certain categories of offender (HO 495/23). Remission applied equally to all inmates regardless of the gravity of their offence and this was fundamentally at odds with the Thatcher government's commitment to bear down heavily on violent offenders. As one official in the Crime Policy Planning Unit noted:

> If the prison system broke down it would be government's responsibility to take whatever measures were considered appropriate to deal with the emergency. However, at present the Home Secretary is extremely reluctant to contemplate the only kind of measures which would be possible (e.g. an increase in remission) because they would have to be indiscriminate, they could have unwelcome side effects on the administration of criminal justice as a whole, and they could only be a temporary palliative. (TNA: HO 495/23)

Second, and perhaps more decisively, the judiciary fiercely opposed further increases to remission on the grounds that automatic release represented an unacceptable level of interference with the sentence of the court. As the following note from Anthony Brennan, dated 1 May 1979, illustrates there was a clear and present danger that the courts would actively undermine the intended effects of remission by increasing the average sentence tariff:

> I had an interesting telephone call from the Lord Chief Justice arising from the exchange in the House yesterday on S of S's 'May' statement.
>
> He said that he had been concerned (going on the Press reports) about the apparent preoccupation with the idea of increased remission. He thought that there was a considerable danger of the judges and magistrates simply reacting by increasing sentences: this, he said, had happened in Canada. He wondered if the Home Office had given thought to an alternative approach. This would be to provide that every prisoner should automatically be paroled after a third of his sentence unless the judge had ordered, in his particular case, that he should serve the full term less normal remission. Of course, there would be much work to do on the detail of such an approach but he felt sure that it would be more acceptable to the Judges. I elicited that the LCJ was talking of a change that might replace the existing parole scheme—not just one for prisoners to whom that scheme does not apply. (FOI: HO 495/21)

Release on licence: The Northern Ireland model

The second option available to the Home Office was to adopt a system of release on licence analogous to the framework used in Northern Ireland. As a result of the long-standing political and sectarian tensions in Northern Ireland, coupled with the administrative difficulties of dealing with 'political prisoners', the system of parole introduced by the Criminal Justice Act 1967 was never extended to Northern Ireland (FOI: HO 495/21). Instead, the authorities pioneered a novel system of automatic release on licence. Under the scheme, introduced by the Treatment of Offenders (Northern Ireland) Order 1976, all prisoners, excluding lifers and those serving determinate sentences of under one month, became eligible for release after they had served 50 per cent of their sentence (House of Commons 1978 p.326; FOI: HO 495/21). Like the operation of remission in England and Wales, release was automatic and subject to forfeiture for bad behaviour, but where the Northern Ireland scheme differed was in relation to a prisoners' continuing liability for recall. Prisoners serving a sentence of more than twelve months were liable to recall for bad behaviour and could be ordered by the courts to serve the remainder of their sentence in custody as well as any additional penalties accrued for crimes committed while on release (House of Commons 1978 p.326; FOI: HO 495/21). There were good reasons to extend the Northern Ireland model to England and Wales. The scheme offered many of the advantages of remission but with the additional benefit that it provided a degree of control over offenders for the remainder of their sentence, along with a clear mechanism for further sanction should they offend while on release (FOI: HO 495/21). Furthermore, the Northern Ireland model did not require an elaborate administrative architecture and offered a clear, appreciable impact on the prison population that could not be guaranteed by discretionary systems. For this reason, the model attracted considerable support within the higher echelons of the Home Office, including Permanent Secretary Sir Brian Cubbon who had first-hand experience of the system from his time as Permanent Secretary in the Northern Ireland Office between 1976 and 1979. In the minutes of one meeting chaired by the Home Secretary it was recorded that:

> Sir Brian Cubbon said that many of the changes which had been urged would in fact increase rather than reduce the complexity of the parole

> scheme. In his view parole was probably not the right solution for the short sentence prisoner. On the other hand, the partial suspension of sentences, on the lines of Section 47 of the Criminal Law Act 1977, could have unforeseeable implications on sentencing practice. One possibility might be to examine further the adoption of the system in Northern Ireland of conditional remission, which enabled a prisoner to be released on conditions, after serving half his sentence. It might be feasible to combine both mandatory and discretionary elements in such a procedure, and in this way avoid the problems which had arisen following the introduction of suspended sentences. (FOI: HO 495/21)

Unfortunately, it was difficult to predict with any degree of confidence how the judiciary would respond to a scheme of automatic release and, unlike remission, it was likely that the adoption of the Northern Ireland model would require primary legislation. For these reasons, the Northern Ireland model of release on licence had proved difficult to transport across the Irish Sea.

Parole

With remission held in suspense as a reform of last resort, the third option under consideration by the Home Office, and alluded to by the Lord Chief Justice Lord Lane, was the possibility of reducing the minimum eligibility threshold for parole. Parole applied to only a small minority of the prison population and officials estimated that a system for short sentence prisoners might, if implemented correctly, reduce the prison population by more than 7,000 (Home Office 1981b). Unlike the crude tool of remission, parole was discretionary and the Home Office Research Unit had demonstrated that parolees were (marginally) less likely to offend in the first two years following release (Nuttall et al. 1977). The difficulty was devising a system that would operate effectively at scale, given the inevitable increase in caseload for the Home Office, the Parole Board, and probation. The portents were not encouraging. In a briefing to Home Office officials charged with developing a system of parole for short sentence prisoners it was noted that, 'as part of the background flavour, you should know that S of S regards the elaborate bureaucracy of the parole scheme as burdensome although he appreciates its utility (especially with the life prisoners) ...' (FOI: HO 495/21). This policy window generated a wide-ranging policy literature.

The Parole Board was by now a more assured policy actor with the resources, expertise, and access to influence Home Office thinking and set the terms of debate. In 1979, a Parole Board study group was established under the chairmanship of Sue Baring (then Chairman of Hampshire Probation and Aftercare Committee). At an early point in their proceedings a decision was taken to reject the case for automatic parole of short-term offenders on the grounds that such a system was likely to overload the Probation Service with a large number of prisoners who were unlikely to cooperate with their supervision arrangements. Instead, the study group endorsed a two-tier system of discretionary release whereby the Parole Board would retain responsibility for long-term prisoners with the case reviews of inmates serving less than four years devolved to prison-based Local Review Committees (LRCs) under the powers contained in the Criminal Justice Act 1972.

Summary of the New Proposed Two-Tier System

31(a) The LRC to deal with all cases where the sentence is 4 years or less plus those cases where the maximum expected available period of parole is not more than 3 months.

(b) The Parole Board to deal with all cases where the sentence is greater than 4 years except for those cases where the maximum expected available period of parole is not more than 3 months, plus the Home Office referrals. (FOI: BV3/30/2)

It is difficult to verify the study group's concerns about placing undue stress on the Probation Service with any degree of confidence. While this was an important consideration it is also likely that in championing a two-tier discretionary system the study group was safeguarding the gatekeeping role of the Parole Board and LRCs within that system. At the level of administrative expediency, the scheme had much to commend it, the Home Secretary already possessed the powers to bring about these changes and over time the LRCs had taken on a greater proportion of Home Office decision-making. But at a more strategic level the Parole Board was very much a lone voice amongst those seeking fundamental reform of the parole system (Hood 1974a; 1974b; Mackay 1980; Morris 1980). Penal reformers had made much of the running in criticizing the current operation of the parole system and within the sector there was almost universal support for a system of automatic release. In 1979, the filmmaker Rex

Bloomstein broadcast a two-part documentary '*Parole*' for the BBC *Inside Story* series (1979). With never-before-seen footage of Parole Board hearings, the film drew attention to the inner workings of a secretive and bureaucratic system that placed untold mental strain on prisoners and their families as they awaited the outcome of their parole applications. In a powerful critique, the film went on to question the viability of determining complex release decisions on the basis of paper files only, the justification for not providing reject reasons to unsuccessful applicants, and the desirability of a system that in many ways represented a form of re-sentencing without the legal protections expected in a court of law. Disappointed by the Home Office's 'half-hearted response' to calls for reform of the parole system, the Howard League established their own review in March 1980 (1981 p.vii). Chaired by Lord McGregor of Durris the working group published a highly influential report *Freedom on Licence* in 1981 calling for the creation of a system of automatic release on licence for prisoners serving less than three years:

> The scheme which we favour would operate as follows: All prisoners sentenced to periods of less than three years would automatically be eligible for release on licence after serving one third of their sentences. Prisoners sentenced to periods between three and seven years would also be eligible for automatic release but, in these cases, the court would be able, if it so wished and subject to appeal, to stipulate a minimum period which would have to be served before parole could be granted. In such a situation, the prisoner's case would be reviewed at the time stipulated by the court, and release would be at the discretion of the Parole Board. Prisoners sentenced to periods in excess of, say, seven years, would be subject to parole review at one-third of the sentence, as now. (1981 p.86)

Whether predicated upon discretionary or automatic release, the extension of parole to short-term prisoners attracted considerable support from those working within the criminal justice system. While there were clear concerns over the logistical and financial implications of extending parole to such a large class of prisoners this appeared to be a secondary consideration when contrasted with the wider benefits of reducing the prison population and extending the benefits of release on licence under the supervision of a probation officer. The question was whether similar advantages could be achieved without further modification of prison sentences by executive action.

The partly suspended sentence

The fourth and final contender for the early release of short-term prisoners was the partly suspended sentence. As we have seen, the Home Office had declined to activate s47 of the Criminal Law Act 1977 due to ongoing concerns about how the measure would be utilized by the courts. However, records reveal that officials were not ready to give up on the principle behind partial suspension entirely (FOI: HO 495/21; TNA: HO 495/18). From a technocratic perspective, the failing of s47 was the discretion it bestowed upon the courts and the inherent ambiguity of how the new power would be exercised by sentencing judges. To mitigate this uncertainty Home Office officials began to develop more ambitious plans for the partial suspension of all short sentences of imprisonment. This became known as the 'Bampton Proposal' after its author Stuart Bampton, a principal within H2 Division (Parole and Probation). In essence, the 'Bampton Proposal' sought to augment the partly suspended sentence provisions contained in the Criminal Law Act 1977 with the addition of a legislative presumption in favour of partial suspension and compulsory supervision in the community during the suspended period of the sentence (TNA: HO 495/18; HO 495/21). Mr Bampton outlined his proposal in the following terms in an influential discussion paper circulated widely within the Home Office on the 1 June 1979:

> The proposal is that the courts be given responsibility for allowing short sentence prisoners to serve part of their sentence in the community as happens with longer sentence prisoners who receive parole. If the provision allowing for partially suspended sentences were to be amended such that all sentences between, say, 3 and 15 months were required to be suspended for the middle third; and if during this suspended third the prisoner were to be on parole licence with the normal liability to recall, an almost immediate and dramatic effect would occur—providing sentence lengths were not increased. It should be possible to prevent this at least in part if the courts were given power to refuse parole for the middle third of sentence in exceptional cases with a proviso that reasons would need to be given.
>
> The proposal has much in common with Dr Hood's ideas for automatic parole but there are significant differences particularly in presentation. Thus automatic parole to prejudice the time people spend in prisons, or to ease the pressure on the prisons, would not be regarded kindly by public opinion. If, however, it is presented as a move to remove the anomaly that parole eligibility does not apply to all, it may attract much less criticism. The main difference, however, is that

whereas automatic parole will be seen as the Executive undermining court sentences, partially suspended sentences will remain within the responsibility of the courts—even though their discretion will be greatly circumscribed and either method will derive from the Executive and Parliament. (TNA: HO 495/18)

The second paragraph is particularly revealing. As we saw in Chapter 5, one of the great attractions of the partly suspended sentence was that it could be presented as an addition to the sentencing toolkit of the courts rather than a questionable act of executive control. By using an Act of Parliament to create a statutory presumption in favour of partial suspension, with a period of supervision on release, the practical import of the 'Bampton Proposal' in administrative terms was all but identical to that of executive release. For this reason, the 'Bampton Proposal' attracted a considerable degree of attention within the Home Office. While criticized by some within the Research Unit and Prison Department as an ornate technocratic fix, many others saw it as an ingenious solution to the myriad problems thrown up by the extension of early release to short sentences offenders (FOI: January 2013; TNA: HO 495/18). Perhaps of most significance the 'Bampton Proposal' quickly emerged as the option of choice within the Crime Policy Planning Unit who were coordinating the review of parole and regularly championed its benefits in their discussions with Ministers and senior officials (TNA: HO 495/18).

The Home Office Review of Parole in England and Wales

The Home Office agonized over the extension of early release to short sentence prisoners. At different times, each of these reform options could be considered in the ascendancy, before fatal weaknesses were identified and officials were forced to return to the policy drawing board. In part, this reflected the difficulty of grafting a new policy framework onto existing practice. At the outset of the review William Bohan, an Assistant Under Secretary of State in the Criminal Policy Department, set out a number of criteria that any reform package must satisfy before it could be considered a viable option for public presentation:

A. To minimise anomalies between different sentences so that some offenders are not released disproportionately sooner than others in proximate sentencing bands.

B. To negotiate satisfactorily the effects (direct or indirect) which its adoption would have on the main parole scheme.
C. To allow for likely compensating behaviour by sentencers,—e.g. to restore the original effect of their sentencing powers.
D. To be capable of—carrying the Scots since it would be difficult to operate two substantially different systems in Great Britain. (FOI: HO 495/21)

These measures of success proved extremely onerous. The Home Office undertook countless options appraisals to test their assumptions and quantify the likely impact upon the prison population (see Figure 6.1). In this sense, the policy-making process was of a very different character to the debates that accompanied the introduction of parole in the 1960s and the ease with which such considerations were located within a broader narrative associated with the rehabilitative ideal and the personalization of punishment. This made an already difficult policy issue even harder to resolve. Without a clear sense of direction, the department was seeking to address various, often mutually conflicting objectives through one package of reform.

A full three years after the Parliamentary Expenditure Committee had first recommended an independent review of the parole system, the Home Office published its *Review of Parole in England and Wales* in May 1981 (Home Office 1981b). A rather unambitious and conservative document, the *Review of Parole* offered a gentle critique of the parole system and acknowledged some long-standing issues of due process but ultimately shied away from radical departures (Howard League 1981; Parliamentary All-Party Penal Affairs Group 1981). Undoubtedly the biggest discussion point was the proposal to extend a system of release to short sentence prisoners. The Review acknowledged the conceptual and logistical difficulties of such a scheme but on balance came to the view that 'the attractions of extending the central idea of parole —release under supervision—to a greater proportion of the prison population are substantial' (Home Office 1981b p.16). In reaching this conclusion the Home Office working group sketched out a rather nebulous proposal to establish a distinct system of release on licence for short sentence prisoners:

One approach would be to recognise the impracticability of assessing short-term prisoners while in custody, and to make the element of supervision instead an integral part of the sentence as passed by the court.

EARLY RELEASE FOR SHORT SENTENCE PRISONERS

	Scheme	Advantages	Disadvantages	Effect on prison population
A	Half remission for those serving sentences of two years imprisonment or less	Simple. Introduction by amendment to Prison Rules	Resource constraints obvious motive. Possibility of a compensatory increase in sentence lengths	Steady state reduction of about 2,700
B	As at A but excluding those with four or more previous convictions	More likely to maintain confidence in system than A	Would need legislation. Would exclude many prisoners who were not necessarily serious criminals	Steady state reduction of about 500
C	As at A but excluding those convicted of offences of violence	As at B but at less cost in terms of reducing effect on prison population	Would need legislation. Would call into question current basis of sentencing "tariff" based on length of sentence as indicator of seriousness	Steady state reduction of about 2,300
D	Flexible remission	Could be manipulated to have a guaranteed effect on the prison population	Would introduce unacceptable degree of caprice and uncertainty into the system. Would be furthest removed in its effect from what the court decided in each individual case. Would need legislation	Would vary according to reduction desired by the executive
E	Partially suspended sentence of imprisonment	Can be introduced by bringing into effect section 47 of the Criminal Law Act 1977. Gives additional powers to the courts, not the executive	Serious risk of increasing proportionate use of imprisonment and prison population. Will put more pressure on local prisons already most seriously over-crowded prison establishments	Impossible to predict. Ranges from a reduction in daily average population of about 3,800 to an increase of about 8,000
F	Automatic parole after ⅓ sentence for all serving sentences of between 6 months and 3 years	Relatively easy to administer. Some saving on existing parole arrangements. Extends idea of parole to shorter sentences without damaging existing arrangements for those serving longer sentences	Courts likely to react by increasing sentence lengths. Would need legislation. Would need additional resources for probation service	Could be a reduction of about 6,500 but only if sentencing practice remains unchanged

Figure 6.1 Home Office options appraisal of early release for short-term prisoners

Source: FOI: HO 495/21 © The National Archives, 1980

In very broad outline, this might mean that the middle third of a short sentence would be held in suspense and the offender would be placed on release under the supervision of a probation officer for that period. Remission of the final third of the sentence could continue to operate as at present, with any loss lengthening the time spent in custody rather than shortening the period of suspension. The arrangements for supervision might be broadly similar to those for suspended sentence supervision orders. Offenders would be obliged to observe certain conditions, for example to maintain contact with the supervising officer, and if an offender were reconvicted while under supervision the court could reactivate the unexpired part of the period of suspension. (Home Office 1981b p.14)

The public presentation of this proposal was unusual. The writing style is unusually hesitant for a Home Office publication and despite detailed commentary, at no stage does the Review confirm this proposal as official government policy. Moreover, very little effort appears to have been made to communicate this complex recommendation to the public. In much of the media the reform package was reported as a system of automatic parole (*The Times*, 14 May 1981), or a hybrid of remission and parole (*The Guardian*, 11 June 1981a). In reality, it was best described as an articulation of the 'Bampton Proposal' for the introduction of a presumption in favour of the partial suspension of all short custodial sentences (FOI: HO 495/21). The evidence for this comes a little later in the Report when the authors note that, 'the new approach outlined above offers a rethinking of section 47, using a similar framework to extend the concept of parole to those at present ineligible' (Home Office 1981b p.14). An intellectual heritage recognized contemporaneously by Keith Bottomley (*The Times*, 21 August 1981) and latterly by James Dignan's in his excellent short history of the partly suspended sentence (1984). In essence, the Home Office was proposing a new statutory framework for short sentence prisoners underpinned by a presumption in favour of the partial suspension of all short sentences of immediate custody between six months and three years. Under these arrangements the middle third of a sentence would be held in suspense and the prisoner would be released under the supervision of a probation officer with clear instruction that if they were reconvicted during this time the court could reactivate the suspended portion of the sentence. Remission would then continue to apply to the final third of the sentence, subject to good behaviour. Critically, the *Review of Parole* was far stronger than previous policy statements in calibrating the burden of proof required to defeat this presumption. The *Review* recognized that there were circumstances in which the presumption in favour of suspension should be defeasible, for example, where a prisoner has continued to offend while under supervision or the offender posed 'some special threat to the community'. But, 'in the context of the chronic and severe pressure on the prison system' the Home Office indicated that strong adherence to the presumption of partial suspension was desirable given the governments' strategic commitment to reduce the prison population (Home Office 1981b p.15).

This publication was a defining moment in the history of early release for short sentence prisoners in England and Wales. Until this point the genesis of Home Office thinking from Anthony Brennan's note summarizing his discussions with the Lord Chief Justice had been that the courts would retain wide sentencing discretion (FOI: HO 495/21). The symbolic importance of a strong presumption in favour of partial suspension, albeit one that could be defeated in certain pre-defined circumstances, was considerable and despite the qualified nature of the Home Office proposal, the departure from this delicate constitutional settlement proved inflammatory. For the executive, it was a guarantee that the scheme would have the desired effect upon implementation. For the judiciary, it crossed the Rubicon into executive interference with the constitutional function of the courts. Why was the Home Office prepared to take such a risk? Reductions in the prison population loomed large over this discussion but it was not the only consideration. The Home Office was, at least in part, motivated by a desire to ensure that short sentence prisoners were treated in a fair and equitable manner by the courts who may otherwise apply sentences of immediate custody, fully suspended sentences and partial suspension in an inconsistent manner across England and Wales (FOI: HO 495/21). This was after all, a time before the creation of the Sentencing Council when very limited sentencing guidance was issued by the Court of Appeal. Allied to the above, one can also detect a clear desire to ensure that the majority of short sentence prisoners received some degree of supervision when on release—a feature of the parole scheme that had been widely celebrated (FOI: HO 495/21). Altogether less clear are the intentions of the Lord Chief Justice and the assurances, if any, he offered to the Home Office. There is some evidence to suggest that the Lord Chief Justice was rather more sympathetic to these measures than his fellow Lord Justices of Appeal, and the Home Office may have been confident that Lord Lane could bring the senior judiciary with him in support of these measures given that they were ostensibly an addition to the sentencing toolkit of the courts (FOI: HO 495/21). Whatever the unique constellation of reasons for this decision, there is no doubt that it represented a significant gamble on the part of the Home Office.

'Whitelaw Mark 1 and Whitelaw Mark 2'

The Home Office proposals began to unravel almost immediately. The senior judiciary were the first to turn against the government's plans for release on licence for short sentence prisoners (Maguire 1992 p.185). The nub of the issue was the level of discretion afforded to the courts at the sentencing stage. For many in the judiciary, a presumption in favour of the partial suspension of all short sentences of imprisonment represented an unacceptable fetter on the sentence discretion of the courts. Following a period of consultation the senior judiciary made it clear they could not support the proposals articulated in the Home Office *Review of Parole in England and Wales* (Dignan 1984). On 9 October 1981 the Lord Chief Justice wrote formally to the Home Secretary setting out the judiciary's opposition to the proposals (FOI: May 2013). A copy of that letter was released to this study under the Freedom of Information Act 2000 and given its historical significance a portion of this correspondence is set out at Figure 6.2. In that letter, Lord Lane informed the Home Secretary that he had consulted with the Lord Justices of Appeal with responsibility for criminal matters who were now unanimous in their belief that the removal of 'any element of discretion' from the sentencing decision represented an unjustifiable 'usurpation of the function of the judge' that could not be supported (FOI: May 2013).

In its place, the Lord Chief Justice encouraged the Home Secretary to re-visit the case for a discretionary system of parole and consider reducing the minimum threshold for parole eligibility to six months (FOI: May 2013). Days after receiving this rebuff from the Lord Chief Justice, Whitelaw suffered a further setback at the Conservative Party conference. The summer of 1981 had seen riots in cities across England, and Whitelaw was under significant pressure to toughen up the government's law and order credentials at precisely the same time as the Home Office began to promote the use of non-custodial sentences and expedite the early release of thousands of short-term offenders

(1)

Royal Courts of Justice,
London, WC2A 2LL

9th October 1981.

[redacted]

cc [redacted]

My dear Home Secretary.

With further reference to our discussion the other day and my letter to you on the subject, I have now had the opportunity of a long discussion with the Lords Justices who sit on criminal matters in the Court of Appeal.

The preponderance of opinion was rather similar to the Roehampton opinion namely that your split system of comprising one third of a sentence in custody was not a good idea. The Lords Justices thought that judges would probably do their best to honour their obligations without deliberately upping sentences but the view was that once any element of discretion is removed from the system and once the reduction becomes imposed without anyone ever having considered the merit of the case, it is very difficult either for a judge or for a member of the public to see how justice can be said to have been done in any particular case. It becomes obviously a direct usurpation of the function of the Judge. This plainly is going to cause you difficulty with the electorate just as it may cause you difficulty with the judges.

I should add that my idea of an amnesty was equally unpopular.

The system which eventually the Lords Justices were agreed would be the best was one which has been canvassed previously, if my recollection is correct, in a number of reports and articles, namely that the threshold for parole/ should be reduced to six months. This would require an amendment to Section 60, sub-section 1 of the Criminal Justice Act 1967 and to the Local Review Committee Regulation.

Quite apart from the obvious expediency of reducing the prison population in this way, there is another more palatable reason for doing it and that is the present un-fairness of the threshold of 18 months, which is emphasised when two people sentenced at the same time to different sentences may be released on the same day. If the threshold is reduced from 18 months to 6 months, it would make obviously a significant reduction in the prison population. As I understand it, without having the statistics in front of me, something like 45% of the sentenced prison population have 18 months or less to serve.

Figure 6.2 Letter from the Lord Chief Justice to Home Secretary, 9 October 1981

Source: FOI: May 2013, 'Letter from the Lord Chief Justice to the Home Secretary', 9 October 1981
(Contains public sector information licensed under the Open Government Licence v3.0.)

from prison. From the outset of the debate the atmosphere was hostile. Edwina Currie famously brandished a pair of handcuffs at Whitelaw and following an impassioned debate the law and order motion was defeated by a 'substantial majority' for the first time in decades (Conservative Party 1981). The political fallout from the conference was toxic and Whitelaw was left on borrowed time as Home Secretary. The Guardian would later report that 'an incensed Willie Whitelaw informed the Prime Minister that if she ever publicly supported critics of his policy again he would resign' (*The Guardian*, 9 October 1985). However, in the short term a reshuffle was politically unpalatable, Whitelaw was the Deputy Prime Minister and his personal support for Margaret Thatcher was vital given his strategic importance as a bridge to the 'one nation' elements of the Conservative Party who were still deeply sceptical of Thatcher's premiership (Farrell and Hay 2010).

With the Home Office fighting to contain the situation on two fronts the Government were forced into a politically embarrassing climb down. On 27 November 1981 Patrick Mayhew MP, now Minister of State, informed the House of Commons that the government had decided not to proceed with the proposals set out in the *Review of Parole in England and Wales*. Instead the government would move to activate the far more modest powers contained in s47 of the Criminal Law Act 1977, a policy shift the indefatigable Lord Longford dubbed 'Whitelaw Mark 1 and Whitelaw Mark 2' (Hansard: 24 November 1981 column 716). Mayhew rejected opposition claims that the proposals had been torpedoed by the judiciary, claiming instead that following high level discussions with a range of stakeholders the government had concluded that a strong presumption in favour of partial suspension was 'likely to counteract the very welcome downward trend in sentence lengths' (*The Guardian*, 27 November 1981). Left with few options the Home Office activated the partly suspended sentence provisions of the Criminal Law Act 1977 on 29 March 1982 with virtually no agreement on the likely effect on the prison population. After more than two years of intense policy discussion the Home Office had expended a great deal of political capital with little to show for its efforts. Henceforth, the Home Secretary would have to manage an altogether more volatile relationship with Conservative backbenchers who were emboldened by the 1981 Conservative Party Conference. Perhaps more significantly, some media outlets reported that Lord Lane had become so disillusioned with political initiatives to reform the penal system that he limited contact with the Home Office to all but the most unavoidable 'official business' rendering a policy of soft influence all but impossible (Windlesham 1993 p.184).

The Criminal Justice Act 1982

As had occurred so many times before, the Home Office sought to wipe the slate clean with primary legislation. A new Criminal Justice Bill was presented to Parliament on 20 January 1982. Commending the Bill to the House, Whitelaw indicated that the government was fulfilling a manifesto commitment, 'to provide the courts with more flexible and effective powers for dealing with the diversity of offenders who come before him' (Hansard: HC Deb 20 January 1982 vol 16 c294). He went on to defend the constitutional independence of the courts to determine the appropriate quantum of punishment in individual cases but made clear that 'the stresses that can occur within the prison system' required a more robust response from the Home Office (Hansard: HC Deb 20 January 1982 vol 16 c294). Under sustained questioning from Labour MP and Chair of the Parliamentary All Party Penal Affairs Group (PAPPAG) Robert Kilroy-Silk, Whitelaw accepted a degree of *mea culpa* for the period of political inertia outlined above but insisted it was right that the Home Office had responded to the views of the judiciary and other criminal justice stakeholders:

> Mr. Kilroy-Silk: Could the right hon. Gentleman tell the House what evidence he has that the introduction of a partially suspended sentence will reduce the prison population that is different from the evidence available to the then Minister of State when he spoke to the House in December 1979 and which was available to him when he wrote the review of parole in May last year, on both of which occasions it was said that the introduction of such a scheme would lead to an increase in the prison population?
>
> Mr. Whitelaw: I did what I believe is right in a democratic system; I consulted widely all those concerned. The result of the consultations led me to believe that in the current climate of shorter sentences this would be the case. This is what those who impose the sentences, both judges and magistrates, believe. I have every reason to trust their judgment and I have done so. If it is to be said that I should not trust their judgment that would be a great mistake. I believe they will show that this power will work to the best advantage. (Hansard: HC Deb 20 January 1982 vol 16 c299)

The Criminal Justice Act 1982 was a major piece of legislation. Largely remembered for the heated debates that accompanied the free votes on capital punishment, the Act introduced three very significant reforms to the early release architecture of England and Wales. Section 30(3) reduced the qualifying period for a partially suspended sentence from six months to three months and, in an attempt to guard against sentencing up-tariffing, Section 30(4) of the Criminal Justice Bill made clear that the courts should not impose a partly suspended sentence where the offender had no prior history of imprisonment or a fully suspended sentence would be appropriate. Section 32 granted the Home Secretary emergency powers to release non-violent offenders up to six months before their remission date should the situation within the prison estate become critical. Finally, Section 33 empowered the Home Secretary to alter the minimum eligibility period for parole as set out in the Criminal Justice Act 1967. Interestingly, this final provision did not feature in the original copy of the Bill. The reform that was to have the single largest impact upon the prison population in the 1980s was only incorporated into the Bill at Report Stage (Commons) following considerable pressure from PAPPAG, supported by a number of penal reform groups working outside of Parliament (HC Deb 12 May 1982 vol 23 cc777–780). Thereafter, the provisions on early release enjoyed a relatively smooth passage through Parliament as more controversial clauses of the Bill relating to life sentences and capital punishment bore the brunt of parliamentary scrutiny. The Criminal Justice Act 1982 received Royal Assent in October 1982 and the provisions relating to partial suspension came into effect on 31 January 1983 with the activation of the 'Eligibility for Release on Licence Order 1983'. For all the posturing, both inside and outside of Parliament, the partly suspended sentence provisions contained in the Criminal Justice Act 1982 had a modest impact upon sentencing behaviour. After an initial jump, the use of partial suspension plateaued at just over 12 per cent of all sentences between 1982 and 1985. Thereafter the use of partly suspended sentences fell into terminal decline and by 1990 only 1,400 such sentences were handed down in England and Wales (see Figure 6.3 below). By any measure this was an extraordinarily poor return on five years of intensive policy development and the significant political capital invested by William Whitelaw and his junior ministerial team. The simple fact was that by 1984 the partly suspended sentence had been comprehensively overtaken by events.

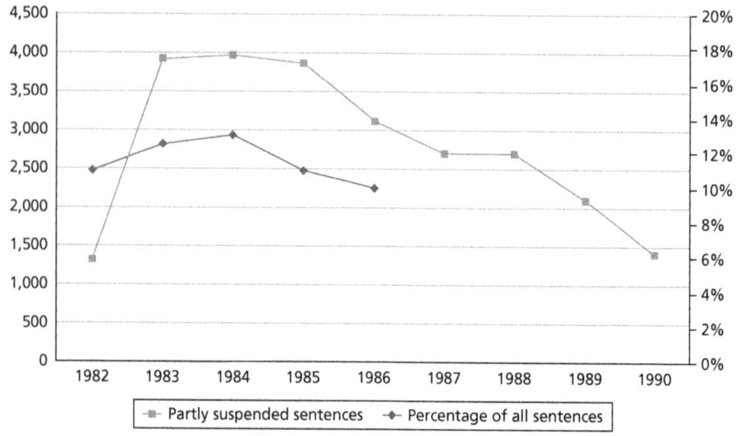

Figure 6.3 The use of partly suspended sentences, 1982–1990

Source: Various, Home Office Criminal Justice Statistics England and Wales, 1982–1990

In July 1983 Leon Brittan was promoted to Home Secretary and immediately signalled a change of policy direction from his predecessor (Conservative Party 1983 pp.1–22). Brittan had enjoyed a rapid ascent within the Conservative Party and as the youngest Home Secretary since Sir Winston Churchill was far more reliant upon the patronage of the Prime Minister than his predecessor. Moreover, as the senior Minister of State in the Home Office, Brittan had been privy to the policy discussions that would ultimately prove so damaging to Whitelaw at the infamous 1981 Party Conference. Keen to avoid a similar fate, Brittan used his inaugural speech to the 1983 Party Conference to signal his embrace of a 'tougher' approach to law and order. The centrepiece of his speech was a package of reforms intended to extend the benefits of parole to short sentence prisoners and require serious offenders to serve a far longer proportion of their sentence in prison (Conservative Party 1983 pp.1–22). In a written statement to Parliament on 30 November 1983, and set out in full in an appendix to the *Report of the Parole Board for 1984* (HMSO 1985 p.22), the Home Secretary provided further detail on the new parole arrangements that would begin with immediate effect. Relying upon the precedent established by Roy Jenkins in 1974, the Home Secretary made clear that prisoners serving five years or more for offences of violence or drug trafficking were to be denied parole until their final review by the Parole Board, and would only then be released on parole for the final few months of their sentence if it was clear they no longer posed a risk to the public (HMSO 1985 p.22). Changes were also made to the parole arrangements of those serving life sentences. At this time, the release of life sentence prisoners was solely a matter for the Home Secretary, subject to a favourable recommendation by the Parole Board and consultation with the Lord Chief Justice and Trial Judge where he or she was available for comment. Henceforth, the Home Secretary confirmed that in exercising his discretion, prisoners serving life sentences for murder of a police officer, prison officer, sexual or sadistic murders of children, terrorist murders, and murder by firearm would not be considered for parole until they had served a tariff of at least twenty years or longer in many cases (HMSO 1985 p.23). The cumulative effect of this announcement was that offenders found guilty of the most serious crimes could expect to serve a far longer proportion of their sentence in prison. To accommodate these changes the Home Secretary announced that the minimum eligibility threshold for parole would be reduced.

> It is also right that those who pose no such risk either do not go there in the first place or are released when they have suffered the first short, sharp shock of custody. It is for this reason that first, I intend to reduce from one year to six months the minimum qualifying period of custody before a prisoner can be considered eligible for parole. This will reduce our prison population substantially. Those released will be the least serious criminals. Their removal will ensure that there is room for the men of violence who must be imprisoned, often for substantial periods, if the public is to be properly protected. (Conservative Party 1983 p.21)

Foreshadowing the emergence of a more contested discourse on law and order, the restrictions Leon Brittan placed upon the operation of parole for serious offenders provoked fierce debate. For some the announcement represented a long overdue victory for common sense and truth in sentencing (*The Times*, 3 December 1983). Others expressed concern that the announcement was politically motivated, lacked empirical rigour and may in fact put the public at greater risk in the long run (see McCabe 1985). One member of the Parole Board, Dr Candy, a Consultant Psychiatrist at St John's Hospital in Aylesbury resigned from the Board in protest (as cited in Shute 2003 p.403) and legal proceedings were brought against the Home Office by a number of prisoners, eventually reaching the House of Lords in the landmark case of *Re Findlay*.[1] With the benefit of hindsight, the negative reception to the restrictive policy may have distracted public attention from the administrative implications of extending parole to short sentence prisoners, a policy that arguably had an equally corrosive impact upon the operation of the penal system in the medium to long term (Home Office 1989). For all the talk of half remission, automatic parole, and compulsory partial suspension it was a modified version of the existing discretionary parole system which finally succeeded in removing large numbers of short-term prisoners from the prison estate. The first releases under the new arrangements took place on 1 July 1984. Under the revised guidance issued to the Parole Board, LRCs, and prison authorities, the Home Office made clear that prisoners should only be considered for review if their sentence allowed for one month of compulsory supervision on licence before remission time took effect. In practice, this had the effect of reducing the minimum qualifying sentence for parole to 10½ months and the Home Office anticipated that the number of prisoners granted parole would increase to over 13,000 a year (HMSO p.18). Given the significant pressure this would place upon the parole system a truncated selection process was introduced for short sentence 'Section 33 cases'. Parole decisions should continue to balance the benefits to the individual against the risk to public safety, but given the short time frames associated with s33 cases this calculus would operate with a 'presumption in favour of parole' with selection procedures directed towards identifying inmates who may be particularly bad parole risks (HMSO 1984 p.19). As such, probation officers were not expected to prepare detailed release plans and cases would not be referred to the Parole Board except in the most exceptional of circumstances. Instead cases would be reviewed by prison-based LRCs who were authorized to grant parole in a far broader range of cases under the devolved powers set out in Section 35 of the Criminal Justice Act 1972 (HMSO 1984 p.19). Following a positive release decision, parole would operate in much the same way as it did for longer sentence prisoners; parolees would be released on licence under the supervision of the Probation Service

[1] Re Findlay [1985] AC 318.

with liability for recall if they breached the terms of their licence conditions.

As a technocratic exercise it is difficult not to applaud the Home Office for a solution which exhibited more than a passing resemblance to the proposals of the Parole Board study group Chaired by Sue Baring. The parole system was a well-established feature of the criminal justice landscape and it was the retention of a discretionary element of parole that ensured early release for short-term prisoners was palatable to the judiciary, at least in the short term (Maguire 1992 p.185). This was not automatic release but, in a system that placed a strong presumption in favour of release upon LRCs (who it should be remembered were part of the Prison Department machine), it was as close as it was possible to get to such a system while retaining the underlying philosophy of parole as a discretionary privilege. As a result, the number of prisoners released on parole swelled from 5,366 in 1984 to 14,769 in 1987, an increase of 175 per cent in just three years (see Figure 1.1). It is difficult to judge whether this simply accelerated the revolving door of minor offenders back into the justice system but what is clear is that the changes announced by Leon Brittan fundamentally altered the landscape of early release in England and Wales, and placed huge strain upon a criminal justice system that was already under considerable pressure. This proved to be unsustainable in the long term and the fallout from these reforms is considered in more detail in Chapter 7.

Conclusion: Administrative Realpolitik

If the establishment of a modern system of parole in England and Wales was initially grounded in principle, the picture was very different less than a decade later. Our analysis has shown that the extension of parole to short sentence prisoners was driven almost exclusively by pragmatic considerations and administrative realpolitik. Moreover, from a contemporary vantage point, the extant archival records possess a rather detached quality concerned with increasingly narrow technocratic points of difference rather than substantive questions of principle. One particularly frank official noted contemporaneously that the discussions lacked a clear guiding philosophy, '[s]o far, the discussion is like a ship without a rudder since we seem to be in perpetual motion around the same arguments but without moving them to a conclusion.

This is probably because the consideration of parole for short-term prisoners has become intertwined with the recurrent need to consider contingency planning should the prison population reach "bust"' (FOI: HO 495/21). Similar views were expressed by the Crime Policy Planning Unit who were responsible for co-ordination of the internal review of parole, '[s]uch considerations draw attention, of course, to the fact there is no strictly penological rationale for the scheme: the reason why it appealed to the Home Office (viz fewer people in prison) would be irrelevant to the courts once they had decided imprisonment was appropriate at all' (TNA: HO 495/18). In part this can be traced back to the economic turbulence of the early 1970s, and the significant reductions in the Home Office following the 1973 Public Expenditure Survey negotiations with HM Treasury which hindered the ability of the Home Office to recruit the probation officers needed to manage a larger community sentence caseload or expand the size of the prison estate to cope with a growing prison population. However, it also suggests a crisis of confidence in both the aims and techniques of penal policy as the rehabilitative ideal increasingly failed to provide a reliable guide to administrative action or a compelling narrative for the justification of such policy decisions. This general picture suggests that policymakers were struggling to apply a long-standing penal orthodoxy that was increasingly at odds with operational realities, professional experience, and the emerging evidence base. This saw many criminal justice decision-makers fall back to less demanding positions such as the deterrent effect of prison and the 'clang of the prison gates', a view that was particularly prominent within the judiciary who had always been more cautious in their support for the rehabilitative ideal (Interview F: 29 September 2014).

PART IV

Breakdown and Renewal, 1987–1995

7

Truth in Sentencing

The Carlisle Committee Review of Parole in England and Wales

In Part IV we explore the evolution of early release policy and practice between 1987 and 1992—a transitional period sometimes described as an 'Indian Summer' for liberal criminal justice policy (Windlesham 1993 p.28). Chapter 7 begins with a brief overview of the challenges facing the criminal justice system on the eve of the 1987 General Election. It goes on to consider the piecemeal modification of remission arrangements in July 1987, a measure to relieve pressure on the prison system that ultimately came at a high cost for the Home Office. It provides a detailed overview of the proceedings of the Carlisle Committee and the compromises that laid the ground for their final report *The Parole System in England and Wales* (Home Office 1989). The chapter concludes by reflecting upon the initial reaction to the Carlisle Report and the considerable uncertainty within the Home Office about how best to respond to these challenging proposals.

A Restricted Operating Space

On 11 March 1987, the Home Secretary Douglas Hurd and his Minister of State Lord Caithness met with the Director General of the Prison Service Chris Train at Queen Anne's Gate, the Whitehall headquarters for many Home Office staff after 1977. The meeting was convened to discuss the deteriorating conditions within the prison estate (*The Guardian*, 12 March 1987a). Records of the meeting are incomplete but there are indications that Hurd closed the meeting by instructing his most senior officials to begin contingency planning for the release

Getting Out: Early Release in England and Wales, 1960–1995. First Edition. Thomas C. Guiney. © Thomas C. Guiney 2018. Published 2018 by Oxford University Press.

of 6,000 prisoners under the emergency powers provided for in the Criminal Justice Act 1981 (*The Guardian*, 12 March 1987a; Zander 1988 p.292). If so, this marked a significant departure from the long-standing Home Office orthodoxy when it came to management of the prison estate (Zander 1989 p.297). As Hurd had noted in a keynote speech delivered to the Prison Governors Conference shortly after his appointment as Home Secretary, the department was committed to an 'open door' policy of accommodating those sentenced to custody by the courts:

> There is a school of thought which would place the emphasis entirely on containing the level of demand. This is unrealistic. The prison system must respond to the demands placed on it by the courts. It is true that Parliament has provided, for use in an emergency, a power of executive release applying to prisoners who are in the last six months of their sentence. But my predecessors have made clear that its use would be confined to extreme emergencies, losses of accommodation caused by fire, riot or the like. I stand by that position. (The Churchill Archives Centre: Churchill/KNNK 2/3/1/42)

Why were Ministers beginning to countenance a departure from the 'open door policy'? Hitherto, the penal system had been defined by a discourse of crisis and many symbolic lines in the sand had been drawn as the penal tide continued to rise. In 1975, Roy Jenkins had declared that if the prison population should reach 42,000 'conditions in the system would reach the intolerable' (*The Guardian*, 24 July 1975) and yet, in the years that followed, the system had, by-and-large, coped with a rising prison population thanks to sporadic prison building and the use of controversial tactical management strategies such as 'overcrowding drafts' (Faulkner 2014 p.41). What made the situation in 1987 qualitatively different from previous historical periods considered in this book was the coalescence of a deteriorating operational context and an obstructive political inheritance that limited the options available to the Home Office. There was simply nowhere left to go. As we will see in Chapter 9, the events described here would ultimately create the space for policymakers to pursue a more strategic approach to the administration of the criminal justice system, but in March 1987 Home Office decision makers faced a 'perfect storm' with few viable channels to circumnavigate through the operational turbulence they were experiencing.

A rising prison population

The tangled problems of our prisons took up ever more of my time at the Home Office. Several times we seemed on the edge of catastrophe. (Hurd 2003 p.344)

By early 1987, the Home Office had to contend with a prison population that had reached a post-war high of 51,000 (see Figure 1.5). While the headline figure was itself symbolically damaging for the Home Office, it was the logistical implications of accommodating so many prisoners within an inadequate prison estate that really began to tell (Windlesham 1993 p.140). Despite the Government's commitment to a comprehensive prison-building programme, the average prison population had grown 7,500 higher than the Certified Normal Accommodation (CNA) of the prison estate (Figure 1.5) and, contrary to Leon Brittan's pledge to end cell sharing by 1990, the number of prisoners sleeping either two or three to a cell had actually increased to an unprecedented 18,983 (Figure 3.2). When taken as a whole, an ageing prison estate, staff shortages, and the continued necessity of 'slopping-out' meant that many prisoners were confined to crowded, unsanitary cells with little opportunity for constructive activity. In his Annual Report for 1986, HM Chief Inspector of Prisons Judge Stephen Tumim noted that, 'the physical conditions in which many prisoners had to live continued, therefore, in many cases, to border on the intolerable ... Overcrowding, coupled with the lack of in-cell sanitation and the sharing of limited and inadequate facilities on the landings, represented much human misery' (HM Inspector of Prisons 1987 p.8). As conditions deteriorated prison indiscipline, a useful barometer of operational health, increased markedly. In the summer of 1986, many penal establishments throughout England and Wales experienced significant disruptions. HMP Northeye was partly destroyed, HMP Bristol was severely damaged, and at Erlestoke Youth Custody Centre, thirty-four young offenders escaped after destroying their living quarters. According to Home Office estimates, the damage to the prison estate would eventually cost the taxpayer more than £14.5m at 2017 prices (Home Office 1987 p.1). Growing unrest within the prison estate weighed heavily on the Home Office. During the course of one interview a former Home Office official described the 1986 'summer of discontent' and the events at HMP Northeye, in particular, as the 'worst moment' of Hurd's tenure at the Home Office (Interview B: 13 January 2014). Prison administrators feared widespread prison disturbances more than any other issue and this was not a remote threat. Local intelligence was indicating that further rioting was a real possibility should there be an extended period of hot weather in the summer of 1987 (*The Guardian*, 13 July 1987b).

The application of organized pressure

While the situation was dire, it was not inevitable that prison unrest would translate into policy change. Few votes were lost by enforcing tough penal regimes. Prisoners were largely alienated from the political process and unable to apply more than fleeting democratic influence. A strong humanitarian impulse did guide many politicians and their officials, but this exerted a rather nebulous influence over the trajectory of penal policy (Loader 2006). Far more telling was the sustained pressure applied by organizations such as the newly established Prison Governors Association (PGA), the Association of Chief Police Officers (ACPO), and the National Audit Office (NAO) who were tasked with embedding new public management techniques across Whitehall (Faulkner 2006 pp.29–30). In April 1986, the Prison Officers Association (POA) voted 13,106 to 3,100 in favour of industrial action in protest against substandard pay and conditions. This resulted in the eventual negotiation of the 'Fresh Start Agreement' and, as the Director General of the Prison Service, Chris Train would later note in a report to the Permanent Secretary this placed considerable strain on the Home Office: 'Fresh Start dominates the way ahead but we are beginning to be able to see, beyond the detail of implementation to the benefits on the horizon' (David Faulkner Personal Papers). Pressure also came from less obvious corners of the criminal justice system. The Police Service, as represented at junior and senior ranks by the Police Federation and Association of Chief Police Officers (ACPO), had long used their influence to criticize executive release and make the case for 'fair' sentences that kept criminals off the streets for an extended period of time (e.g. *The Guardian*, 17 November 1988a). This position began to soften as year on year increases in the remand population awaiting trial reached 11,162 in 1987 and began to spill over into police cells. In early 1987 the Metropolitan Police Commissioner, Sir Kenneth Newman wrote to Douglas Hurd warning the Home

Office that holding prisoners in police cells was diverting significant police resources from front line activity and represented an unacceptable drain on police capability (*The Guardian*, 13 July 1987b). The relative independence of crime rates and the prison population has been well documented (Cavadino and Dignan 2006a p.447) but here, for a fleeting moment in time, the use of police cells created a feedback loop within the criminal justice system that was most unwelcome to the senior ranks of the police service whose influence within political circles was unrivalled. As one Home Office official put it to this author:

> You know the police mattered hugely. If you lose the police you lose everything, and the police are absolutely crucial. You know you had the IRA campaign going on, you've just had the miners' strike, under public disorder you've got terrorism you've got the crime rate going up, I mean you know in terms of big politics, winning elections or losing elections the police are streets ahead of it ... the police really matter. (Interview B: 13 January 2014)

The cumulative and converging nature of this organizational pressure should not be under-estimated. Jointly and severally, these various interest groups enjoyed direct (and regular) access to the senior echelons of the Home Office and just as significantly this was backed up by the political and institutional firepower to disrupt the everyday business of the criminal justice system. While their agendas were very different, the constant reinforcement of a discourse of operational fatigue was slowly internalized by Home Office decision makers and weighed heavily in the Department's options appraisals.

A difficult inheritance

By 1987, it was all but impossible for the Home Office to exert any soft influence over sentencing practice or the use of non-custodial measures. A solution would have to be found within the Home Office's sphere of influence and historically this had meant turning to executive release and the creation of additional prison capacity. Unfortunately, for Hurd and his advisors this particular path had been well travelled by the Home Office. By the late 1980s early release had emerged as a key battleground between the executive, judiciary, and the various interest groups with a stake in the criminal justice system. The problem could be traced back to

July 1983 and Leon Brittan's maiden speech to the Conservative Party Conference as Home Secretary. As we noted earlier, Leon Brittan's move to introduce a bifurcated system of parole for serious and minor offenders served to destabilize the already delicate regulatory balance of early release policy and practice. In private, the Parole Board expressed serious misgivings with the operation of the 'restrictive policy' (FOI: BV3-38). More publicly, the Home Office was drawn into protracted judicial review proceedings as prisoners directly affected by the changes challenged the Home Secretary's power to revise the policy directions issued to the Parole Board without adequate consultation, a question that reached the House of Lords in the case of *Re Findlay*.[1] While the Law Lords eventually found in favour of the Home Secretary the damage had already been done. Prisoner morale, particularly amongst the long sentence population, was damaged and judicial discontent was mounting (*The Guardian*, 6 February 1984; *The Times*, 21 February 1984). Home Office guidance to Local Review Committees (LRCs) advising them that there should be a presumption in favour of parole for short sentence prisoners in s.33 cases provoked a storm of criticism from the judiciary and previously unseen records released to this study under the Freedom of Information Act reveal that:

> In the autumn of 1985 the Lord Chief Justice drew to the attention of the Home Secretary the mounting concern among members of the judiciary, and in particular among circuit judges (as evidenced at the Judicial Seminar at Roehampton in September), about the effect of the reduction in the minimum qualifying for parole (MQP) from 12 to 6 months under section 33 of the Criminal Justice Act 1982. It was against that background that the Home Secretary decided in December 1985 that a Working Group should be established, under the chairmanship of Mr S G Norris, Director of Operational Policy, Home Office Prison Department, with the following terms of reference:
>
> 'To explore further the concerns that have been expressed by the judiciary about the operation of section 33 of the Criminal Justice Act 1982; and, against that background and taking into account the independent role of the Parole Board and Local Review Committees, to look for ways in which that aspect of the parole scheme might be improved.' (FOI: HO 291/2081)

[1] Re Findlay [1985] AC 318.

Sir Maurice Drake, a High Court Judge and former Vice Chairman of the Parole Board represented the judiciary on the Working Group. At a meeting on Thursday 24 April 1986, Sir Maurice set out the concerns of the judiciary (FOI: HO 291/2081). He questioned whether it was possible to adequately assess the risk of short-term prisoners and took aim at the Home Office guidance that there should be a 'presumption in favour' of parole for eligible s33 prisoners (FOI: HO 291/2081). This approach, ingenious as it was in transplanting the concept of a presumption in favour of release from the 'Bampton Proposal' to the deliberations of the Home Office administered LRCs, was extremely unpopular amongst the judiciary who saw it as an unacceptable erosion of the sentencing function of the courts. This was executive influence 'by the back door' and Sir Maurice expressed his fear that many judges were now actively working to undermine the parole system (FOI: HO 291/2081). In the minutes to one meeting it was noted that, 'he [Mr Justice Drake] said that at a recent meeting which he had with the Lord Chief Justice, the LCJ had told him that there were now very clear indications that judges were increasing sentences to take account of the parole situation' (FOI: HO 291/2081). This difficult inheritance had profound implications for Hurd. As Shute has noted, parole had historically operated as a 'safety valve' when pressure on the prison population became particularly grave (2003 p.836). The problem for the Home Office in 1987 was that the parole system had reached its load-bearing capacity; its administrative coherence was unravelling, and the judiciary had already lost confidence in the system, particularly the new s.33 procedures (FOI: HO 291/ 2081). On the other hand, the bifurcation of parole, particularly the restrictive policy for serious offenders announced by Leon Brittan, had resonated with the tabloid media and the right wing of the Conservative Party and any moves to 'liberalise' early release arrangements were likely to draw negative criticism. Where Roy Jenkins, William Whitelaw, and Leon Brittan could turn to parole to mitigate the worst effects of the prison population this avenue was closed off to Douglas Hurd.

The Introduction of 50 Per Cent Remission

The Home Office never did exercise the emergency powers of executive release contained in the Criminal Justice Act 1982. The plans were leaked to Aileen Ballantyne, a correspondent at *The Guardian*, who ran a front-page exclusive on the 12 March 1987 entitled 'Crowding may free 6,000 prisoners' (*The Guardian*, 12 March 1987a). The story was politically damaging for the Conservative Party as it prepared for a summer general election and it was reported that the Prime Minister intervened personally to veto the plans and shore up the government's hard-earned law and order credentials (Zander 1989 p.292). The Conservative Party won a decisive victory at the General Election on 11 June 1987 and Hurd convened a series of meetings in June and July 1987 to scope out an alternative approach (Hurd 2003 p.347). Where past Home Secretaries had turned to parole it was remission that now emerged as the most promising lever at the disposal of the Home Office. While the operation of parole could only be altered by primary legislation, remission was entirely in the gift of the Home Secretary and could be quickly expedited by a change to the Prison Rules. Equally, remission required no formal assessment of inmates and placed no additional resource pressures on either the prison or the probation service. In administrative terms, the measure was resource neutral and likely to result in significant reductions to the prison population. The attraction was easy to understand but like Whitelaw before him, Hurd was well aware of the indiscriminate nature of remission and the deficiencies of a system that was both automatic and offered no continuing liability for recall once released. As he would later recall in his memoirs:

> By July 1987 the total of prisoners in England and Wales was 51,029, of whom 68 were in police cells. There was no particular rhyme or reason for this summer surge; it bore no relation to the figures of recorded crime, which were rising less fast than they had been. On 2 July I held a long and crucial policy meeting at the Home Office. 'Devise outline plan, including some 50% remission. Could be politically lethal.' (Hurd 2003 p.347)

Keen to capitalize on a dominant electoral victory, Douglas Hurd addressed the House of Commons on 16 July 1987 and announced a 'five-point plan' intended to signal immediate and decisive action to address the deteriorating conditions within the penal system (*The Times*, 17 July 1987). First, an army camp in Rollestone, Wiltshire would be converted into a temporary prison providing space for an additional 360 inmates. Second, in discussion with HM Treasury, there would be a substantial expansion and acceleration of the prison-building programme. Third, with immediate effect Hurd was establishing a new Prison Building Board within the Home Office to streamline the prison building programme and 'exploit to the full private sector techniques in bringing new prisons on stream' (*The Times*, 17 July 1987). Fourth, the Government would honour the Conservative Party manifesto commitment to 'institute a thorough review of the workings of the parole system' (Conservative Party 1987 p.57). Finally, pending the outcome of the parole review, the period of remission which could be earned by those serving sentences of up to twelve months was increased from a third to one half (*The Times*, 17 July 1987). This final measure provoked considerable unrest amongst Conservative backbenchers and resulted in a tense meeting of the Parliamentary Party as Douglas Hurd and his senior Minister of State John Patten sought to build support for the new proposals (Interview B: 13 January 2014). In a circular to Conservative MPs dated 20 July 1987, Hurd expanded further on these measures. While conceding that his plans might cause backbenchers some 'short-term discomfiture' in the medium-to-long term (The Churchill Archives Centre: Churchill/ILLD 2/14/10) it was hoped that Hurd's five-point plan would ensure that the prison system was not a thorn in the side of the government throughout the next electoral cycle. The rationale for introducing remission is particularly interesting and worth quoting at length.

> This will achieve two ends. First while the Review is being conducted it will reduce the anomalies caused by the interaction of remission and parole—especially in relation to the lower minimum qualifying period for parole introduced by Leon Brittan. These anomalies have been subject to growing criticism from the judiciary. Second, it will provide the prison system with some relief from the present levels of overcrowding and enable the important new 'Fresh Start' working practices to be implemented with very significant gains for prison regimes and value for money. The change in remission will affect only less serious offenders. The great majority of these are guilty of offences against property and less than a fifth are guilty of any use of violence. Indeed, the 'violent offenders' in this category will overwhelmingly be of the pub brawl or Saturday night fight type. The prison population will be reduced by some 3,500 and the maximum reduction in effective sentence length for any one offender will be two months, in most cases it will be much less. (The Churchill Archives Centre: Churchill/ILLD 2/14/10)

The changes to remission took effect on 16 July 1987[2] and provoked heated debate. Roy Hattersley, Labour spokesperson on home affairs, welcomed the announcement but castigated the government for a short-term approach to prison administration. The tabloid press was particularly critical (see Figure 7.1) and in an unusual step for a former Home Secretary and serving member of the Cabinet, Leon Brittan publicly criticized his successor on the grounds that

EXPRESS

OPINION

No justice in Hurd's Law

THE Home Secretary gave plausible reasons for authorising the early release of some 3,500 prisoners to ease jail overcrowding. However, they are not good enough.

Mr Hurd's predecessor, Leon Brittan, had the perfect response; to release convicted criminals simply because there is no room to house them is wrong in principle and contrary to the law.

No one denies our prisons are overcrowded. They were meant to hold 41,000; they now hold 10,000 more.

And, in theory, it seems no big deal to be letting men already entitled to four months remission to be given two months more.

But where does this leave the crucial notions of retribution and deterrence? Badly battered!

Criminals must pay

Those who will benefit from the Home Secretary's move were thought by the courts to have deserved the sentence they received. They surely deserve it no less now simply because the conditions in which they are kept are not ideal.

Is Mr Hurd incapable of imagining the impact his action will have on a public deeply worried about rising crime and soft sentencing?

On top of these worries we now have to contend with the spectacle of a *Tory* Home Secretary who calls for stiffer sentences one minute and shortens them the next.

The Government has a £690 million programme to build 17 prisons, yet it could be more effective if it incorporated a significant degree of privatisation.

Privatisation is a key to solving the problem of overcrowding. But the best way to solve it is to win the war against crime.

That means increasing the deterrent effect of punishment. Not, as Mr Hurd has now done, diminishing it.

Pal Maggie shows true understanding

WASHINGTON TV interviewers hoped to enlist the Prime Minister in their sly denigration of President Reagan, beset by Irangate.

Any criticism would have suited them perfectly but Mrs Thatcher was

EDWARD PEARCE ON WHY THE EASY OPTION ON PRISONS IS A DANGEROUS ESCAPE ROUTE

The fatal flaw in Hurd's plan for freedom

HOME SECRETARY Douglas Hurd is a civilised, fair minded and humane person who may one day turn out to be Prime Minister. But he may have got something wrong.

Mr Hurd is in the process of setting up an open prison camp, encouraging American style private sector involvement in prison building and releasing prematurely 3,500 offenders.

About the first two proposals there can be no argument. We actually need open prisons, lightweight prisons, whatever you like to call them, very badly. They are the only means of decanting quickly the numbers which are turning the prison system into a castellated nightmare.

American practice in letting private builders fully in on the act where prison construction is concerned is no more than common sense.

But the releases are dangerous. Not necessarily in themselves but because they involve the Government moving into the courts' area of responsibility and saying: "We can't cope, you let them out."

I have no quarrel with leniency and offer no comfort to the revenge and violence school of penology. But surely leniency (and severity) must come from the judge. A criminal court judge ploughs through hundreds of cases. He may sometimes get it wrong, but better than anybody else, he knows where generosity and second chance might work and where they won't.

Tragedy

The tragedy of our system is that judges are barred, by an historic failure to provide prison accommodation, from applying their wisdom of sentencing on merit. They are stuck with a purely administrative problem. Overall, we are stuffing 53,000 prisoners into prisons intended to take around 42,000.

A judge, often foolishly abused for softness, makes an individual decision knowing the prison service is begging him not to load the ship any nearer to the gunwales. He has to think numbers when he should be thinking cases.

There is an argument, popular in Opposition circles, that many offenders are petty offenders who shouldn't be in jail anyway. They are misfits, petty sexual miscreants, vagrants and other inadequates. That isn't exactly wrong, but it is desperately over-simplified. A sexual exhibitionist, for example, is not trivial in the eyes of the mothers of young girls.

If he (and the recidivist petty thief) do not belong in Parkhurst, they don't belong on the local housing estate either.

Another point never considered by progressive penologists is how much of the brunt of small crime is carried by working-class people who live where they cannot escape from it.

Clare Short, for Labour, spoke with philosophic disdain of "trivial" offences. I wonder how they define "trivial" in the harder bits of Coventry, where she is a local MP.

But if people are not to be set free when they need a form of confinement, we will need to expand the prison service and to sophisticate it. There is a spectrum which runs from murder to vagrancy. A satisfactory prison service would be calibrated to meet the distinctions instead of merely trying to put a ring fence around the most obviously violent and dangerous prisoners. A good prison service would be augmented by semi-voluntary vagrant hostels to hold the people who should be neither in prison nor casually at large.

Above all, the prison service we need would be big enough to give trial judges space to play with so that they can think seriously about sentencing.

With crime rising, the prison space deficit is made wider. And prisons are built in England under Civil Service procedures with the due deliberate haste of a seedling growing into a mature tree.

Mr Hurd announced that an Army camp at Rollestone, Wiltshire, would become a temporary prison for 360 inmates. I would like to see him multiply this capacity at least thirty fold by snatching up Government land wherever he can.

If we had small, tin-can, knock-together camps of Portakabins to accommodate the 12,000 least dangerous, least violent criminals [illegible] would be low security establishments, the Victorian stone hulks like Strangeways and Pentonville would have some light and air. The people inside would be able to breathe and the great prison riot to equal the 1981 riots will be avoided.

Douglas Hurd did what he did because the Home Office [illegible] fear of a big bang none of us wants to hear. To set up camps quickly and also to build the new stock of prison accommodation will cost money, lots and lots of it.

But why do we have prisons? Not for altruistic reasons. We have them to keep vicious, violent, dishonest and hopeless inadequates out of our hair.

Flashpoint . . . squalor and overcrowding in a typical prison

Hurd: Misguided

Figure 7.1 Media response to Hurd's introduction of 50 per cent remission

Source: *The Daily Express* 18 July 1987 © Daily Express/N&S Syndication, 1987

[2] Prison (Amendment) Rules S.I 1987 No 1256.

it is wrong in principle and quite contrary to the rule of law, and everything that we stand for, for convicted criminals to be released prematurely on whatever procedural means, not on the basis of individual consideration of their cases nor because of the application of some new or more liberal penalty, but simply because there is no room to house them. (*The Times*, 17 July 1987)

Despite this reception, the reform of remission arrangements had an immediate effect on the prison population; 3,500 prisoners were released early from prison in August 1987 and the prison population fell by an unprecedented 6 per cent in little over two months. This was the equivalent to administration of seven medium sized jails, and for a short time at least, was sufficient to draw the sting from the prison estate during the much feared warm summer months of 1987. In this very narrow sense, the changes to remission can be considered a success but in the long term it came at a heavy cost for the Home Office. As one former Home Office official would put it to this author:

... the damage we did to the credibility of sentencing by increasing remission to 50 per cent was seen in the arguments about 'truth in sentencing' that followed. I think we realized the anger, but finding a way of dealing with the population crisis in 1987 seemed to be the overriding priority, and of course all the sentencing reforms of the 1980s and the 1991 Act were tainted by the impression that they were do with reducing prison overcrowding and not to improving sentencing itself. (Interview G: 2 December 2014)

More than any other measure, the extension of remission came to be viewed as the high-water mark of executive interference in sentencing matters and created a powerful momentum towards greater truth in sentencing. As we will see, this set the tone for the deliberations of the Carlisle Committee and damaged the credibility of the Home Office as it embarked on an ambitious programme of criminal justice reform following the 1987 General Election.

The Carlisle Committee Review of Parole in England and Wales

In June 1987 the Home Office began preparatory work for a review of parole in response to a likely Conservative Party Manifesto commitment to 'institute a thorough review of the parole system'

(1987 p.57). Guidance notes issued with the Conservative Party manifesto, the so called 'war book', made clear that the review was commissioned to address; 'concern among the judiciary about the effect of parole on prisoners with short sentences; dissatisfaction in some quarters about the disparity between the time served in prison and the sentence handed down by the court ... and the effect of any changes on the prison population' (Oxford, Bodleian Library, Conservative Party Archive: CRD 4/30/7/26). Home Office officials briefed Lord Lane and the Deputy Lord Chief Justice Tasker Watkins prior to the General Election. By 19 June 1987, Mark Carlisle (as he then was), a former Secretary of State for Education and Science and junior minister in the Home Office, had been identified as the preferred chair of the committee (FOI: HO 291/2138). The Home Office also wrote to the Lord Chancellor's Department on 24 June 1987 seeking views on the membership of the committee. Judicial representation on the Review Committee provoked considerable unease within the Home Office with one senior official expressing concern about the judiciary's likely attitude towards the Review and early release for short sentence prisoners.

> In some ways I am not sure that it would be an advantage for the High Court Judge on the review to have had Board experience. On the whole they do not see the same range of cases as other members; and recent High Court Judges (Drake, McCullough, Popplewell) would approach the review with pretty closed minds about the merits of parole for short sentenced prisoners. Judicial opposition to section 33 is obviously a major issue for the review; but I am not convinced that membership should contain a leading antagonist (which Drake J, for instance, certainly is). (FOI: HO 291/2138)

It is unlikely that the Lord Chancellor's Department shared this view and compromise was needed to agree the terms of reference and membership for the review. The Home Secretary and David Faulkner met with Mark Carlisle on 21 July 1987 to finalize the terms of reference, membership, and an indicative timeline for the review (FOI: HO 291/2138). 10 Downing Street was consulted, and advice was put to the Home Secretary on the suggested arrangements for the committee (FOI: HO 291/2138). The final membership and terms of reference of the Carlisle Committee is set out in full at Appendix 3.

The Carlisle Committee convened for the first time in September 1987 and would go on to meet on twenty-two occasions before submitting its final report to the Home Office in October 1988 (Home Office 1989 p.1). Fact-finding visits were made to a number of prisons and probation services as well as overseas trips to Canada and both federal and state correctional facilities in the United States of America. Written and verbal submissions were received from a variety of audiences including NACRO, the Howard League of Penal Reform, and JUSTICE (Home Office 1989 p.1). On the face of it, the very act of establishing an independent review to examine the operation of the parole was surprising. Independent commissions were generally seen as a rather un-Thatcherite way to govern and evoked memories of a 'gentler age' of policy-making where Royal Commissions and Advisory Councils were common (Windlesham 1993 p.45). While it is true that the Thatcher government favoured decisive leadership and streamlined decision-making it was not averse to the use of independent reviews where they were politically expedient. For a short while, the Carlisle Committee was able to remove the complex issue of parole from the political agenda and allow for a detailed, independent review of the issues that the various stakeholders within the criminal justice system, particularly the judiciary, could support. Good news for the Home Office but as one *Guardian* newspaper editorial noted contemporaneously, the legacy of previous decisions, coupled with the density of interest groups and agendas that intersected on the question of early release, made the Committee's task extremely complex.

> That is not to say that there may not be a route out of the current mess that will avoid offending the conflicting interests of the judiciary, the Conservative Party, the popular press, the European Commission on Human Rights, the prison officers and—not least—the prisoners themselves. Merely to say that you would not, by choice, start from here. But that's the task that Mr Carlisle has been given. A tougher one in the law and order field it would be hard to imagine. (*The Guardian*, 22 July 1987c)

Through systematic archival research, it is now possible to peer behind the veil of the Carlisle Committee's deliberations in greater detail than has previously been possible. In his memoirs, Sir Oliver Popplewell observed that Lord Carlisle 'chaired the committee with 'consummate skills, bringing together disparate views from experts in their field, who expressed their views forcibly and with conviction'. Proceedings of the committee were described as professional and good-humoured and Popplewell recalls that, 'I cannot remember being on a committee which expressed such sensible or formidable arguments with such little rancour and with a flexibility which enabled members to change their minds after heavy argument on many subjects' (Popplewell 2003 p.250). Debate was inevitable given the composition of the committee and the very strongly held views of its members. As one member of the committee interviewed for this book would observe, there was a clear split between those members of the group who wanted to see a stronger emphasis upon punishment and the more liberally minded representatives of the Review Committee who adopted a progressive position concerned with the rehabilitative potential of parole to prepare offenders for life on release:

> I mean the key thing about the group was that it was split almost down the middle between softies and toughies. I mean that was the key dynamic in the long run, and this was pretty clear ... the toughies were ... Popplewell, Russell West, but Peter Wright and to some extent Mark Carlisle were sort of toughies. (Interview B: 13 January 2014)

This schism became a defining feature of the working group's proceedings and the final content of the Carlisle Report. The basis for a compromise position appears to have rested on the 'softies' conceding that prisoners serve half of their sentence in prison in return for support for stronger procedural safeguards and a concerted effort to reduce both the use of immediate custody and sentence lengths. One also gets a sense of the growing influence of a 'just deserts' penal philosophy that located the normative power of punishment in retribution and accentuated the importance of sentencing decisions to quantify the harm caused by the offence and calibrate the most appropriate quantum of punishment. This focus on proportionality and the sentencing decision came through strongly in the following discussion of the Carlisle Committee:

> I mean the deal really was that quite early on they formed—the Liberals formed a sort of faction to block too early a move to being tougher, but ... because Roger Hood had theoretical difficulties about early release and problems with the process stuff, and was well plugged into this American thinking about sentencing, he at the end of the day was prepared to countenance a shorter period of early release, and therefore more ... the great phrase 'more truth in sentencing', so long as you bore down on sentences to compensate for the fact that you're changing

> the currency, and secondly so long as you got a decent sort of due process enhancement into how it worked, and that was where the deal lay really. So the toughies got their way ... instead of getting out at a third you didn't get out until half-way. The Liberals got out that it would be a better process and you wouldn't just sort of ... it wouldn't be 50% of the sentence it was just you'd take all that into account. You know, they were happy that way because the judges weren't against due process, judges tend to run in favour of due process. So that was sort of where the deal lay. (Interview B: 13 January 2014)

While the Carlisle Committee did not agree with calls for the total abolition of parole, it did identify a number of significant weaknesses with the existing framework of early release (incorporating parole, remission, and partly suspended sentences). First, the Committee noted that the extension of parole to short-term offenders had undermined the integrity of the parole system in England and Wales. While laudable the practical implications were extremely damaging since, 'it is wrong in principle and, in any event, unworkable in practice, to try to operate a selective parole system for short sentence prisoners' (Home Office 1989 p.48). Second, the Committee concluded that recent reforms had eroded important differences in sentence lengths, 'the judges are right to object to the way in which the present system undermines proportionality by eroding, and in some cases removing entirely, the distinction between the amounts of time which offenders spend in custody under sentences of differing lengths' (Home Office 1989 p.48). Third, the Report made clear that Leon Brittan's 'restrictive policy' of curbing parole for many categories of serious crime was, 'flawed in principle and harmful in practice' (Home Office 1989 p.49). Fourth, the Committee drew attention to the role 50 per cent remission and short-term parole had played in creating, 'an unacceptable disparity between what sentences say and what they mean' (Home Office 1989 p.49).

When taken as a whole the Carlisle Committee were of the view that root and branch reform was needed to simplify the operation of early release in England and Wales, and restore meaning to the sentence of the court. The best available evidence indicated that it was impossible to operate a discretionary system of early release for short-term prisoners and in the view of the Committee the 'simplest and most defensible' way to operate a system of early release that blended elements of automatic and discretionary selection was on the basis of sentence length (Home Office 1989 p.65). As summarized in Figure 7.2, the Committee recommended that adult offenders serving sentences of up to twelve months should be released automatically at the halfway point of their sentence and remain on licence for the duration of their sentence. Prisoners serving sentences of up to, and including four years, would also be released automatically at the halfway point of their sentence but remain under the active supervision of a probation officer for the third quarter of their sentence, at which point they would serve the remainder of their sentence on licence with risk of recall for bad behaviour. In a significant departure from the existing system, the Carlisle Committee proposed that a discretionary parole system should be reserved for prisoners serving determinate sentences over four years and all indeterminate sentences (Home Office 1989 paras.269–280). As above, those serving longer determinate sentences were eligible for release under supervision for the third quarter of their sentence at which point they would serve the remainder of their sentence under licence with liability for recall. However, the Carlisle Committee recommended changes

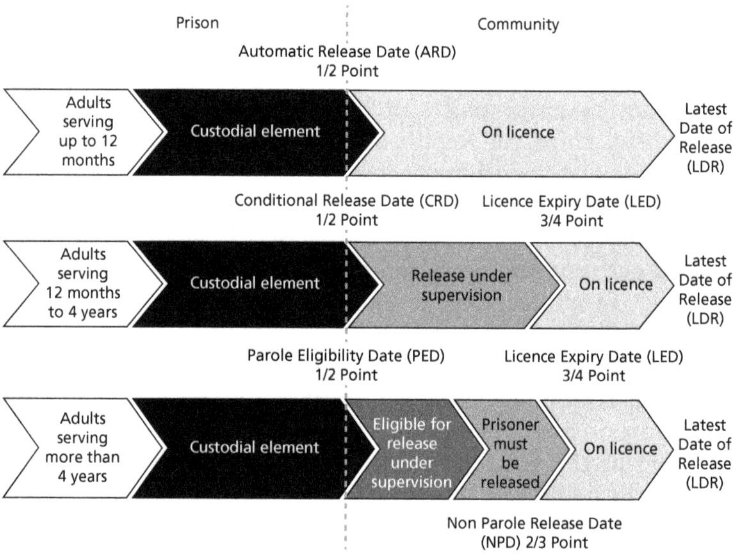

Figure 7.2 Summary of Carlisle Committee recommendations

Source: Home Office 1989

to the management of prisoners denied parole. Reflecting strong penological support for aftercare supervision, and mindful of the previous anomalous position of high-risk offenders denied parole only to be released unconditionally at a later date with no supervisory support, the Carlisle Committee recommended that prisoners who did not received a positive release decision from the Parole Board should nonetheless be released at the two-thirds point of their sentence (the non-parole release date) and placed under supervision until the three-quarters point of their sentence to embed a risk-based approach to the re-integration of serious offenders back into the community (Home Office 1989 paras.293–299). In most instances misconduct whilst in prison would result in the addition of extra days in custody and a delay to the key decision-making points (Home Office 1989 para.275).

The revised operational structure proposed by the Carlisle Committee had a number of administrative implications for the operation of early release in England and Wales. It necessitated the abolition of partly suspended sentences, already falling into disuse, because they were simply incompatible with a release framework based upon sentence length (Home Office 1989 paras.93–500). Given the significantly reduced workload of the Parole Board it also left no role for the prison-based LRCs that had provided the initial sift of eligible prisoners and proved so valuable when the Home Office abandoned the idea of compulsory partial suspension in favour of a system of discretionary parole for short sentence prisoners (Home Office 1989 para.317). Finally, it necessitated the abolition of remission, at least in the sense it had traditionally operated, since all prisoners would remain 'at risk' of recall until the end of their sentence (Home Office 1989 para.299). To oversee these changes the Carlisle Committee recommended a radical overhaul of the governance of the parole system. Rejecting the tripartite structure of the Home Office, Local Review Committees, and Parole Board, the Committee recommended that the Home Office should cease to be responsible for individual parole decisions with the Parole Board assuming executive powers in relation to prisoners serving determinate sentences. While the Home Secretary would retain ultimate responsibility to Parliament, particularly in relation to 'lifers', the Board would become a more autonomous body with an enhanced secretariat and Chairmanship function (Home Office 1989 pp.64–73).

Managing the Fallout

Undoubtedly, the biggest point of controversy in the Carlisle Report was the requirement that offenders serve one half of their sentence in prison and remain at risk of recall for the remainder of their sentence. The Carlisle Committee had been welcomed by many penal reformers as a once-in-a-generation opportunity to ease pressure on the prison estate, but for many that chance had been squandered. Far from bringing about a reduction in the prison population there was a very real risk that the changes recommended by the Carlisle Committee would actually increase prison numbers if it was not accompanied by an equivalent reduction in the use of immediate custody by the courts (FOI: May 2013; *The Guardian*, 26 November 1988b). This presented a number of problems for Home Office strategists. Limiting the scope of the review had been deemed necessary to prevent Carlisle morphing into a comprehensive review of the penal system, but in practice this meant the Committee could not predict the impact of its recommendations with any degree of confidence. Put simply, its success would stand and fall on the extent to which the courts could subsequently be persuaded to make better use of non-custodial measures. As such, the initial response to the Carlisle Committee report was lukewarm. Despite the enhanced procedural safeguards secured by the 'softies' (Interview B: 13 January 2014), Vivien Stern, Director of NACRO lamented the Committee's failure to push for radical reform: 'thousands of short-term prisoners who are now safely released on parole after one-third of their sentence will remain longer in prison' (*The Guardian*, 26 November 1988b). Barry Sheerman MP, then Labour home affairs spokesman, called upon the Home Secretary to go further by allowing automatic parole for those serving up to four years after one-third of the sentence (*The Guardian*, 26 November 1988b). A significant majority, including Harry Fletcher, Assistant General Secretary of the National Association of Probation Officers, called for the total abolition of the parole system in favour of a revised sentencing framework premised upon shorter determinate sentences (*The Guardian*, 26 November 1988b). At least initially, the Committee's recommendations in relation to sentencing were also given short shrift by the judiciary. As Sir Oliver Popplewell would later remark in his memoirs:

> We were not asked to express any view about sentencing. It was not within our terms of reference. The views that were expressed were done

> without any observations being sought from the Lord Chief Justice or other judges or without any evidence other than anecdotal evidence being put before the committee. Sensibly, the judges took no notice of this part of the report. (Popplewell 2003 p.254)

Within the Home Office the portents for the Carlisle Report also appeared gloomy. In January 1989, *The Independent* reported that key figures were minded to shelve the committee's recommendations, '... according to Home Office sources, although ministers are still discussing the plan, they have found many of the reforms politically unacceptable' (*The Independent*, 24 January 1989a). This concern appears to have rested upon a dual fear that sentencing reform would undermine the party's tough law and order credentials, and attract criticism from the senior ranks of the judiciary who continued to closely guard the court's sentencing discretion. In reality, the policy considerations were more complex. Following the publication of the Carlisle Committee Report an internal Home Office working group was established, initially under the direction of William Bohan, before handing over to Graham Angel who would reach the rank of Assistant Under Secretary in the Criminal Department (FOI: May 2013). The Working Group was guided by a number of assumptions that reveal a great deal about how the aims and techniques of punishment in England and Wales were evolving at this time:

> 1. In accordance with the spirit of the Carlisle Report, we have assumed that the objectives of change in the parole system should include the following:
>   a. bringing about greater parsimony in the use and length of custodial sentences for all but serious, violent crimes;
>   b. restoring greater proportionality between nominal sentence and time served in custody;
>   c. making conditional release at least relatively more effective in helping prisoners re-enter society and avoid recidivism;
>   d. making the parole process simpler and fairer, and seen to be such, by prisoners and the public. (FOI: May 2013)

The realization of these objectives was impeded by two significant administrative challenges. The first related to the dividing line between the automatic system of conditional release for short sentence prisoners and the discretionary system of parole for serious long-term prisoners. The Carlisle Committee had recommended a threshold of more than four years for the exercise of discretionary release, but this proved contentious. The government was committed to a tough, bifurcated penal policy and any reforms that were likely to result in the automatic release of violent or sexual offenders was seen to be politically risky given the real or perceived attitudes of the parliamentary party and wider electorate. On the other hand, custodial sentences of four years were common and any steps to shift prisoners from an automatic to a discretionary system of parole would have a clear and immediate impact upon the prison population. The second issue was whether the proposals would be acceptable to the judiciary and, in time, lead to a step change in sentencing practice. As the Carlisle Committee had noted, the requirement that offenders spend a longer period of their sentence in prison with continued liability for recall once released was likely to result in a significant increase in the prison population if it was not accompanied by an overall reduction in the use of immediate custody by the courts. No doubt fearing a repeat of the judicial veto that scuppered Whitelaw's plans for the introduction of compulsory partly suspended sentences, the Home Office fretted over the judicial response to the Carlisle Report. Records reveal that in May 1989, 'Mr Faulkner wrote to Lord Justice Tasker Watkins in May gently inviting comment but has received no reply' (FOI: May 2013). In parallel, the Home Office Statistical Unit was tasked with estimating how changes in sentencing lengths and the number of prisoners recalled to prison might affect the prison population in a range of different scenarios. The permutations set out at Figure 7.3 suggest that in the absence of significant offsetting reductions in sentence lengths by the courts the prison population was likely to rise by several thousand.

These deliberations were given added urgency by events outside of the Home Office. On 6 July 1989, David Evans a known sex offender was found guilty of the murder of Anna Humphries. The sentence followed a string of serious offences and bureaucratic failures in relation to his aftercare and risk management. In July 1978, Evans had been jailed for five years at Birmingham Crown Court for the attempted rape and the assault of two women. Evans was released by the Parole Board in July 1980 upon satisfying the panel that he was no longer a risk to the public but went on to rape another woman four months after his release on licence. Thereafter Evans was sentenced to ten years' imprisonment with the sentencing judge Mr Justice Drake, who would

ANNEX A

Estimated effects on prison population

1. Eligibility for early release and parole at 50% of sentence: effect of changes in the point at which early release becomes discretionary.

Sentence length	Percentage of offenders in restrictive parole policy	Prison population
3 years	57%	- 100
3+ years	57%	- 400
4 years (Working Party)	71%	- 500
4+ years (Carlisle)	72%	- 900
5 years	78%	-1000
5+ years	84%	-1400

2. Proportion returned to prison for breach of licence or re-offending before end of sentence.

10%	+ 900
20%	+ 1900
30%	+ 2800

3. Examples of net effect of 1 and 2.

(i) Parole eligibility at 4+ years (Carlisle)	10% recall	-
	20% recall	+1000
	30% recall	+1900
(ii) Parole eligibility at 4 years (Working Party)	10% recall	+ 400
	20% recall	+1400
	30% recall	+2300
(iii) Parole eligibility at 3+ years	10% recall	+ 500
	20% recall	+1500
	30% recall	+2400

4. Off-setting reductions in sentence lengths.

5% reduction in all sentence lengths	-2200
10% reduction in all sentence lengths	-4300
10% reduction in sentence lengths up to 4 years	-3500

Figure 7.3 Home Office impact assessment of the Carlisle Committee recommendations upon the prison population

Source: FOI: May 2013, 'Submission on Report of the Working Group on the Carlisle Review of Parole, 1989

later sit on the Home Office review of s33 cases, noting that, 'you are an extremely dangerous young man, particularly to young women. My duty is to protect the public from you' (quoted in *The Guardian*, 6 July 1989). An application for parole was rejected in

1985 but Evans was subsequently released on 13 May 1988 in accordance with remission procedures. Since remission of sentence amounted to unconditional release without supervision Evans was under no obligation to report to a probation officer. Six months later, he kidnapped and killed Anna Humphries. The murder of Anna Humphries exposed the deficiencies of the existing early release system and allowed the general public to peer behind the veil of early release policy and practice to an extent that had rarely occurred in post-war England and Wales. The fallout in the media was considerable. The story made front-page news and many commentators noted that the murder of Humphries could have been prevented if the Carlisle recommendations had been in effect (*The Independent*, 17 July 1989b; *The Times*, 6 July 1989a). Lord Carlisle also entered into the debate arguing that, 'if our proposals were implemented even those like David Evans, who did not get parole, would nevertheless be under a period of supervision once released. That would add to the safety and security of society' (*The Times*, 6 July 1989b). These events helped galvanize support for the Carlisle proposals. In an interim report to Ministers, the working group recommended the full implementation of the Carlisle recommendations, subject to a number of revisions to the scope of discretionary release and the Home Secretary's ability to veto the decisions of the Parole Board in the interests of public safety (FOI: May 2013). This was accepted and planning began for a modified version of the Carlisle framework to be included in a major Criminal Justice Bill planned for the 1991/92 parliamentary session. As we will see in Chapter 8, as the focus shifted away from the internal machinations of the Home Office towards the public presentation of these reforms, the proposals were re-packaged to fit within a wider criminal justice narrative.

8

A New System Takes Shape

The Criminal Justice Act 1991

In Chapter 8 we examine the legislative planning process that gradually refined the early release framework eventually given legal effect by Part Two of the Criminal Justice Act 1991. As we have seen, the publication of the Carlisle Report prompted a period of significant policy debate as the Home Office began to craft a reform package that was at once politically palatable to Ministers, commanded the support of the judiciary and remained true to the spirit of Carlisle. The chapter begins with a review of the post-election planning process that gathered pace following the 1987 General Election. It examines the Home Office strategic awayday held at Leeds Castle in September 1987 and goes on to consider the Green Paper, *Punishment, Custody and the Community* and an unprecedented conference at Ditchley Park which brought together senior decision-makers from across the criminal justice system. The chapter then examines the passage of the Criminal Justice Bill 1990/91 and reflects upon the dramatic backlash against the new parole system in the mid-1990s. The chapter concludes with a critical appraisal of the underlying tensions that defined the development of criminal justice during this transitional period.

The 1987 General Election: From Penal Pragmatism to a Strategic Approach

In parallel to the 'five-point plan' announced by Douglas Hurd in July 1987, Ministers, with support from their special advisers and senior civil servants, embarked upon a significant post-election planning process with a view to developing a long-term strategic vision for the criminal justice system. Matching the provision of places (geographically and by establishment type) to the flow of prisoners through the prison estate remained, in civil service parlance, the pre-eminent 'wicked issue' for Home Office planners. Sentencing trends had hardened since the mid-1980s with the result that courts in England and Wales were sentencing more people to immediate custody and for longer periods of time than anywhere else in Europe. A succession of Public Expenditure Surveys (PES) had resulted in real-time growth within the Home Office budget and a significant Prison Building Programme, but with increasingly sophisticated population forecasts indicating further growth in the prison population there was an appetite to take stock and re-appraise the government's objectives in relation to criminal justice. In the week following the 1987 General Election, senior Home Office officials met at the Ship Hotel Brighton under the Chairmanship of David Faulkner (Windlesham 1993 p.213). Accompanied by Hurd's top advisor Edward Bickham, the purpose of the meeting was to reflect on existing policy objectives and refine a number of flagship policy initiatives, including crime prevention, community policing, and efforts to tackle racial discrimination that would be taken forward in the next Parliament (Faulkner 2014). This was followed by a series of policy scoping exercises that culminated in a strategic planning day at Leeds Castle on 28 September 1987. The Leeds Castle meeting was a defining moment for the Home Office. As the Home Secretary noted in a discussion paper circulated to senior management in advance, the meeting was a unique opportunity to reach a collective understanding on the strategic priorities that would underpin the Departments work, 'over the lifetime of this Parliament, in relation to crime and the reduction of crime' (David Faulkner Personal Papers). Hurd encouraged open discussion with a view to developing a suite of practical proposals that could pass the following political tests:

> 1) Will they contribute to a reduction in crime, in criminality or in the fear of crime? 2) Will they help meet or satisfy the public demand for more effective action against crime, and do so in ways consistent with the Government's philosophy of emphasising the part to be played by the individual citizen's personal and social responsibility? 3) Will they encourage the more efficient and economic delivery of criminal justice services? (David Faulkner Personal Papers)

The Leeds Castle meeting, chaired by Douglas Hurd, covered the entire gamut of Home Office activity with substantive sessions on crime, policing, prisons, and criminal justice. In the morning keynote address, John Patten, with the full encouragement of Home Office officials, outlined the case for a tough 'law and order' narrative that had yielded considerable electoral success for the government. Rising crime demanded a robust response and Pattern urged the department to be less squeamish about taking 'credit for continuing increases of up to 25% in custodial sentences and sentence lengths for these offences over the period of the Parliament' (David Faulkner Personal Papers). This provided an important juxtaposition to the afternoon sessions on penal policy. Leading the session on prisons, Lord Caithness, and Chris Train, offered a bleak assessment of a prison system that in their judgment was rapidly approaching a 'doomsday scenario' (David Faulkner Personal Papers). As Lord Caithness noted in his opening presentation:

> All the projections about the growth of the population were gloomy. Since mid-1984 the male adult population of those sentenced to 18 months or more had risen steadily, from 13,000 to nearly 19,000. There was already the risk of a further overcrowding crisis in 1989. If sentences continued to increase a crisis was certain; a 25% upping of the tariff would mean an excess of 10,000 over [Certified Normal Accommodation] CNA then. It was hard to believe that there would be sufficient time or money to enable the Department to build its way out of the problem. A 9,000 increase by 1991 equated to 15 additional prisons beyond the 20 in the current programme and the further 10 that were being sought (but would not be achieved in full) in this year's Public Expenditure Survey. In very round figures the total capital cost of all of that was about £2 billion, of which the 15 prisons for the 9,000 increase (always assuming that it was possible to find the sites and build that additional number on that timescale) would cost about £750 million. They would also add about £100 million a year running costs. This all suggested that the building programme alone was not the answer. Something had to be done to stop the judicial ratcheting up of sentences. (David Faulkner Personal Papers)

The last sentence is perhaps the most revealing. Lord Caithness recognized that the Carlisle Committee 'gave the opportunity for a thorough overhaul of the arrangements for adjusting the outflow from the prison system which had grown incoherently and piecemeal in recent years', but this alone was insufficient (David Faulkner Personal Papers). The department had too often relied upon early release to avoid difficult decisions on penal reform and the Home Office must now reach a clearer position in respect of sentencing and punishment. The choice was a stark one. Despite significant investment in a prison-building programme, the number of offenders sentenced to immediate custody continued to outstrip the provision of new places and Ministers were invited to weigh the competing demands of political expediency and administrative utility. Officials offered no advice on the choice before them, 'regarding it as an essentially political decision' (Faulkner 2010 p.6). Summing up the discussion the Home Secretary made clear that, 'coping with the likely rise in the prison population was easily the single most difficult problem facing the Department. The present rate of building might be doubled but there was neither the time nor the resources to do much more. This meant that relief had to be found elsewhere' (David Faulkner Personal Papers). After much discussion, Ministers decided to, 'exert some downward pressure on the rise in the prison population' (Faulkner 2010 p.6). Since 'a repetition of emergency release (in any form) would be politically unacceptable' Ministers agreed to a concerted effort to promote the use of non-custodial sentences as part of a wider 'just deserts' penal philosophy (David Faulkner Personal Papers). Six overarching priorities emerged from the Leeds Castle discussions:

1. Prevent and reduce crime.
2. Establish a more coherent and principled basis for sentencing and parole.
3. Avoid the unnecessary use of imprisonment and stabilise the prison population.
4. Develop schemes of supervision in the community which would effectively reduce offending.
5. Give greater consideration to victims.
6. Make the system more efficient, effective and accountable. (Faulkner 2010 p.6)

The planning meeting at Leeds Castle has been lauded as a high watermark of progressive penal policy-making; both for the collaborative manner in which Ministers worked with their senior officials and the decision to partially row back from ever more punitive policies (Windlesham 1993 p.215). With the emergence of a clear and broadly accepted roadmap for reform of the criminal justice system, the Home Office embarked upon a concerted schedule of activity to secure approval for the new approach. Particular attention was paid to potentially critical audiences within the Conservative Parliamentary Party, the Judiciary, and the Probation Service.[1] This saw John Patten take personal responsibility for a 'hearts and minds' campaign in the House of Commons where he met with over 150 Conservative Backbench MPs over the course of the year to secure buy-in for the government's proposals (Windlesham 1993 p.215).

A Fragile Consensus: The Green Paper and Ditchley Park

Seeking endorsement for the strategic vision agreed at Leeds Castle, a new Green Paper *Punishment, Custody and the Community* was published (Home Office 1988a) seeking views on a range of policy issues including community sentences, the use of imprisonment, and electronic tagging. The centrepiece of the Green Paper consultation was an 'unprecedented and never repeated' conference at Ditchley Park in September 1989, which brought together senior criminal justice representatives in England and Wales (Windlesham 1993 p.242). A central objective of the Ditchley Park conference was to establish a sense of collective responsibility for the criminal justice system, built upon shared understanding, whilst also respecting the principles of judicial and operational independence. This necessitated a more constructive dialogue with the senior judiciary in relation to sentencing reform and the Carlisle Committee recommendations published in October 1988. In the summer of 1989 Lord Justice Tasker Watkins convened an exceptional conference of judges to discuss the Carlisle Committee proposals and despite Home Office nervousness the conference 'declared enthusiastic support for the key Carlisle recommendations' (FOI: May 2013). This was a significant milestone, but the Home Office would require more than supportive words if it was to secure Cabinet approval for new legislation. It was the Home Secretary's express hope that Ditchley Park would play a formative role in building that dialogue, and on 19 September 1989, the Home Secretary

[1] The suggested changes were particularly bittersweet for the Probation Service. Firstly, in terms of the additional numbers who would be subject to punishment in the community. Secondly because the service would have to adopt a far more punitive ethos if the re-branded non-custodial punishments were to be taken seriously by the judiciary and Conservative Party membership.

wrote to the Lord Chief Justice Lord Lane outlining a range of 'issues which need to be resolved on parole and sentencing' (David Faulkner Personal Papers). Chief amongst the outstanding areas of discussion was the need to reassure HM Treasury that any legislative proposals were robust, fully costed, and would not incur significant additional public expenditure.

> The Treasury will require convincing assessments if they are to agree to legislation. Many of the resource implications of Carlisle can and will be managed within the Home Office. But the effects on prison population are not within Home Office control .... The range of uncertainties in that (the Carlisle Committee) assessment is so great as to prejudice the acceptability of the whole package. If sentence lengths are not affected by Carlisle's recommendations, or if the proportion of prisoners returned to custody on reconviction to serve the remainder of their original sentence is significantly greater than the 20% he estimates, we could need up to four new prisons costing up to £300m at current prices with running costs of up to £50m a year, including an extra 1,500 or so staff. If Carlisle's assumptions are right, the effect on the prison population could be neutral or even produce a reduction. One cannot, however, expect those responsible for public expenditure to authorise policy changes without a clear view of the likely costs. (David Faulkner Personal Papers)

Positioning the Treasury as the key veto player in this process was an astute political manoeuvre and serves as an important reminder that the functional division of government within Whitehall can be a catalyst for action as well as an impediment. It provided a legitimate point of entry into extremely delicate discussions with the judiciary and allowed the Home Office to occupy an intermediary position (real or perceived) between the various policy actors with a stake in the criminal justice system. In turn, this privileged position enabled the Home Office to control the terms of the debate since the Home Office could on the one hand reassure the HM Treasury that it was doing everything within its power to secure a strong deal for the taxpayer whilst also positioning the department as on the side of the senior judiciary in seeking to implement the Carlisle Committee recommendations. In short, the Home Office and judiciary would have to find common ground on sentencing if they were to secure HM Treasury approval for new legislation. Given the huge sensitivities of broaching this issue with the judiciary, a confidential meeting was scheduled for the morning of the Ditchley Park Conference at the request of the Lord Chief Justice. In attendance was the Home Secretary Douglas Hurd, Minister of State John Patten, the Lord Chief Justice Lord Lane, and Deputy Lord Chief Justice Tasker Watkins. Understandably keen to avoid the mistakes of the past, the Home Office was careful to avoid any suggestion that it was presenting the judges with a fait accompli. As a briefing note to the Home Secretary made clear, the aim of the meeting was simply to open a dialogue with the Lord Chief Justice and repair a relationship that had broken down in recent years. Substantive discussion of Carlisle could wait for another time.

The Home Secretary is well aware of the delicacy of these discussions. The first objective is to establish a dialogue. The judges' opening position may be that resource implications of sentencing are not matters for them and sentencing policy is not really a matter for Ministers. The aim of the pre-Ditchley meeting is to agree that both parties have an interest in both topics and it is in the public interest for them to discuss how best to fulfil their concerns. The note, therefore, suggests starting by seeking the Lord Chief Justice's view on the key opinions expressed in the Carlisle report about the way the judges would use new powers and the effect of Carlisle's changes on sentencing policy. An early or direct bid for a deal on the resource implications of Carlisle could abort substantive discussion. Once the dialogue is going the implication can emerge that the Government's implementation of the Carlisle package is dependent upon the answers to questions about the resource implications. For this reason the draft does not deal with prison population issues in as detailed a manner as Prison Department might wish ... The discussions on Carlisle will be helped by the fact that the judiciary want his report implemented. The Government's proposals on sentencing policy are unlikely to have a comparable attraction for the Lord Chief Justice. (David Faulkner Personal Papers)

The preliminary meeting with the Lord Chief and Deputy Chief Justices was not minuted but attendees reported that it went 'as well as could have been expected, and better than might have been feared' (David Faulkner Personal Papers). There was qualified agreement that the Carlisle Committee recommendations 'would need to be accompanied by shorter sentences, especially in the range six months to two years' (David Faulkner Personal Papers). But, as predicted, the proposals for sentencing reform were not well received. In the summary note circulated after the meeting it was observed that, 'the judges were left rather bemused by the "just deserts" approach to sentencing: it will need further work and more explanation. (The expression "just deserts" was not used at the conference except in a reference to North America)' (David Faulkner Personal Papers).

Putting this pre-meeting to one side, the Ditchley Park conference is rightly seen as a significant stepping stone towards the development of a more strategic approach to the management of the criminal justice system. Held over two days from 22–23 September 1989 the Ditchley Park Conference considered a range of topics including 'the criminal justice scene', 'tackling crime', 'managing the system', and a summary session led by the Home Secretary on 'future patterns and structures'. The event was unprecedented in its scope and ambition with attendees including the Lord Chancellor, Lord Mackay of Clashfern; the Attorney-General, Sir Patrick Mayhew; the Metropolitan Police Commissioner, Sir Peter Imbert; John Hosking, Chair of the Magistrates Association; and Graham Smith, Chair of the Association of Chief Probation Officers. As was the case at Leeds Castle, the key contribution came from John Patten, who delivered the opening keynote speech and set out the two principles that underpinned the government's position in relation to sentencing:

> One is to establish firmly those principles of sufficiency and proportionality of response. The other is to reinforce the links between offenders and society and emphasise the importance of social responsibility. Our objective is better justice, with greater consistency and emphasis on the offender in society ... We have tried to interfere as little as possible with the independence and the discretion of sentencers. We are not proposing mandatory sentencing guidelines or a sentencing commission ... We prefer sentencers to be free to consider all relevant circumstances: but we do believe that their discretion should be properly limited so that it does not frustrate policy principles. (Faulkner 2010 p.5)

By and large, the Ditchley Park conference achieved the objectives set by the Home Office. It helped to secure broad approval for the objectives outlined in *Punishment, Custody and the Community* and began the slow process of healing the wounds of a working relationship that had been fractured in part by the events that led to Whitelaw's volte face on automatic parole for short-term offenders. As Sir Clive Whitmore, the Permanent Secretary, would note in his follow-up summary, 'Ditchley was a notable success both in terms of what was achieved on substance (and not only with the Lord Chief Justice and Lord Justice Watkins but with those from the other services too) and of the way the occasion was structured and run' (David Faulkner Personal Papers). Not for the first time the rationale for early release was evolving to reflect wider societal attitudes towards sentencing and punishment. As the locus for sentencing decisions shifted away from the forward-looking science of penology advocated by Baroness Wootton to a backward-looking emphasis upon the gravity of the offence a similar reconfiguration occurred within early release thinking. The emergence of a 'just deserts' penal philosophy left little space for indeterminacy or the 'recognizable peak' arguments that had exerted so much influence in the 1960s. Increasingly, the 'Home Office was under pressure to restore meaning to sentences and respect the 'punitive element' of the sentence handed down by the courts. Likewise, the early release framework advocated by Carlisle was positioned as a welcome addition to an increasingly actuarial approach to crime control premised upon public protection and effective risk management (Hood and Shute 1994; Shute 2003). Douglas Hurd left the Home Office shortly after the Ditchley Park conference and was replaced by David Waddington who was elevated to senior Cabinet rank from the role of Chief Whip. Despite Waddington's desire to revisit some of the more politically sensitive features of the Green Paper the policy framework developed during Hurd's time at the Home Office was too advanced for a fundamental re-think and the Government's White Paper, *Crime, Justice and Protecting the Public* was published in February 1990. Reflecting Hurd's desire to avoid a patchwork of initiatives authored by the various divisions within the Home Office, both the Green and White papers were drafted by Jean Goose, Head of the Criminal Department (CCBH 2010 p.6). This consistency of authorship imbued the White Paper with a rare clarity of thought built upon a strong 'just deserts' penal philosophy and the proportionality principle, 'the severity of the punishment matching the seriousness of the crime and a sharper distinction in the way the courts deal with violent and non-violent crimes' (Home Office 1990a p.i). In relation to early release, the White Paper welcomed the Carlisle recommendations and committed the government to implementing the lion share of the review committee's recommendations. Following the proposals set out at Ditchley Park, the White Paper concluded that a system of early release could be made to work alongside a 'just deserts' sentencing approach. However, *contra* to Carlisle, the government felt that in the interests of public protection the discretionary system of early release should apply to all offenders serving sentences of four years and over (1990a: 28–34). Moreover, the government was unable to accept the Carlisle Committee view on the governance arrangements for the new system or the case for augmenting the Parole Board with additional executive powers (Home Office 1990a p.31). Mirroring the situation in 1967, the Home Office erred on the side of caution and confirmed that the Home Secretary would retain the final say over the cases of all serious offenders.

From a contemporary vantage point, these stepping stones towards a more strategic vision for the criminal justice system are fascinating. It is striking that when confronted with the competing claims of an explicitly populist law and order posture or a concerted effort to exert some downward pressure on the prison population Ministers elected to pursue a more nuanced package of reforms and place greater emphasis upon the use of non-custodial sentences. Given similar evidence, it is not at all clear that Ministers today would alight upon a similar balance. Nor was this a simple presentational exercise. Significant political capital was invested by the whole ministerial team with John Patten at the forefront of a hearts and minds campaign to win over backbench Conservative Party MPs and translate this overarching strategic vision into tangible policy propositions. These events also demonstrate a rather more collegiate approach to management of the criminal justice system than was typical of the Home Office for much of the post war period. While it is easy to overplay the importance of the conferences at Leeds Castle and Ditchley Park they do appear to symbolize, albeit for a fleeting moment in time, a genuine attempt to break free from the shackles of penal pragmatism and build support for a more strategic approach to administration of the criminal justice system. There were undoubtedly grounds for cautious optimism, but the delicate handling of the judiciary reveals just how precarious the Home Office position remained after the 1987 General Election. Even policy windows have their limitations it seems. By resisting calls to introduce a sentencing council or extend the successful steps taken to limit the use of custody for young offenders in the Criminal Justice Act 1988 the Home Office paid a high price for judicial acquiescence to their policy proposals. Whether unwilling or unable, the failure of senior policymakers to challenge judicial autonomy in sentencing at the Ditchley Park conference ensured that the government's flagship criminal justice policy was once again hostage to fortune and dependent upon soft influence of the judiciary to achieve its policy aims. Pre-commitment emerges time and time again as an essential ingredient of long-term policy change and without it the Home Office were left dangerously exposed as the backlash against the policy framework set out at Leeds Castle, and agreed at Ditchley Park, began to gather pace in the mid-1990s.

The Criminal Justice Act 1991

The Criminal Justice Bill 1990/1991 received its Second Reading on 20 November 1990. Commending the Bill to the House David Waddington noted that it was an 'important reforming measure which sets out to increase society's confidence in the criminal justice and penal system and its effectiveness in dealing with offenders' (Hansard: HC Deb 20 November 1990 vol 181 c138). In relation to early release, set out in Part II of the Act, Waddington went on to argue that radical reform of the existing dual system of parole and remission was needed to restore meaning to the sentence of the court and build public confidence in the criminal justice system. In his words, 'release at the one third point of sentence, which can occur if a person gets maximum parole and maximum remission, lead to an unacceptable erosion of the value of the sentence passed by the court. That is bad for respect for the criminal justice system' (Hansard: HC Deb 20 November 1990 vol 181 c140). The Second Reading debate is significant for at least two reasons. First, it is arguable that events outside the Chamber had a more decisive impact upon the long-term trajectory of criminal justice policy in England and Wales than the debates raging within it. While the Second Reading debate unfolded the Conservative Party was engaged in a leadership ballot prompted by Geoffrey Howe's resignation from the Cabinet and Michael Heseltine's subsequent decision to challenge Thatcher for the leadership of the party. During the Second Reading debate word reached the House that Margaret Thatcher had lost the confidence of the Party and her position as Prime Minister had become untenable. The events that followed have been well documented (Watkins 1992). Margaret Thatcher resigned as party leader on 23 November and John Major was eventually confirmed as Prime

Minister on 28 November 1990 following a divisive leadership contest. In the ensuing Cabinet re-shuffle David Waddington was elevated to the House of Lords and Kenneth Baker, who had previously served as the Chancellor of the Duchy of Lancaster, was appointed Home Secretary. This fundamentally altered the balance of power at Cabinet level and as Farrall and Hay (2010) have noted, it was the Major Government that would accelerate the tough law-and-order policies that are so often identified with the Thatcher years. Second, in a move intended to signal a more assertive posture on law and order, the Labour Party took the unusual step of tabling a 'reasoned amendment' to prevent the Bill from achieving its Second Reading and frustrate the government's criminal justice reform package. Explaining Labour's position home affairs spokesperson Roy Hattersley emphasized the Labour Party's support for the Carlisle Committee recommendations but expressed his fear that the requirement that all prisoners serve half their sentence in jail may result in a net increase to the prison population if it were not accompanied by a tangible decrease in the use of custodial sentences. This, Hattersley suggested, could only be guaranteed by the creation of a sentencing council with the authority to direct sentencing behaviour. Since the Bill did not provide confidence on such matters as crime prevention, remand prisoners, or concrete steps to manage the 'unacceptably high prison population' in England and Wales it could not be supported by the opposition (Hansard: HC Deb 20 November 1990 vol 181 c151). In pushing for a 'reasoned amendment' the Labour frontbench would have been all too aware that they had no prospect of success given the relative strength of the political parties within the Commons and so it proved. The government held the division comfortably by 350 votes to 190 but this adversarial reception helped set the tone for a Bill that would be subject to considerable disagreement as it progressed through Parliament. Perhaps in anticipation of a turbulent reception, the Bill was tightly marshalled through Parliament. Two Ministers of State (John Patten and Angela Rumbold) were assigned to shore up the Home Office position in Standing Committee. The time allocated to the scrutiny of the Bill was carefully choreographed and Ministers benefited from the resources and know-how of an extensive 'bill team' of civil servants led by Robert Fulton, a career civil servant who would later serve as Principal Finance Officer and Director of Strategy and Performance. The Criminal

Justice Bill reached the Lords on 12 March 1991. Introducing the Bill, Earl Ferrers repeated the policy position John Patten had first articulated to the senior judiciary at the Ditchley Park conference in 1988:

> The main purposes of the Bill are to reform sentencing practice—the way in which a sentence is determined—and the way in which sentences are actually carried out. The sentence in an individual case is, of course, a matter for the magistrate or the judge concerned. It is not a matter for Parliament. It is, after all, only the sentencer who will know all the facts of the case. What we seek is consistency of approach in sentencing, not uniformity. We have, therefore, resisted the temptations of those who would like to see detailed and rigid sentencing rules imposed upon the courts, which would require particular offences to be sentenced within only a very narrow range of options. (Hansard: HL Deb 12 March 1991 vol 527 c73)

This was followed by a re-statement of the principles first articulated in the *Crime, Justice and Protecting the Public* White Paper (Home Office 1990a). The Bill took as its foundational principle the retributive intuition that punishment should be determined by the seriousness of the offence. Imprisonment, it was argued, frequently does more harm than good and the government was committed to making better use of punishment in the community (Hansard HL Deb 12 March 1991 vol 527 c74). Serious offenders could expect to receive long custodial sentences while 'petty offenders', particularly those who perpetrate property offences, would be dealt with through non-custodial measures. The root-and-branch reform of early release, recommended by the Carlisle Committee, was intended to give expression to this policy framework by restoring credibility to the sentence of the court and streamlining the work of the Parole Board. Aside from parole, the discussion of partly suspended sentences and remission reveals how far penal 'orthodoxy' had travelled since the 1960s. While some, like Lord Monson and sitting Law Lord, Lord Ackner, remained wedded to the notion of a 'short sharp shock' and a broad toolkit of sentencing disposals (Hansard: HL Deb 12 March 1991 vol 527 c124), many more were in agreement with the Carlisle Committee and considered the operation of partly suspended sentences as incompatible with the new early release system introduced by Part II of the Act. As we noted in Chapter 6, the decision to locate the power of release in the hands of judges rather than the executive was seen as symbolically powerful even if the administrative differences between a partly suspended sentence and the system of automatic parole for short sentence prisoners introduced by Leon Brittan were negligible. By 1991, that symbolism had all but drained away and partly suspended sentences were seen as an anomaly that represented only 5 per cent of court disposals in criminal cases. The notion of a 'short sharp shock' was anathema to the government's political commitment to long prison sentences for the most serious offenders and the central recommendation of the Carlisle Committee that all prisons should serve 50 per cent of their sentence in prison so as to restore meaning to the sentence of the court. There was simply no room for the partly suspended sentence in the post 1991 release architecture. What was true of partly suspended sentences was also true of remission. As Lord Hunt, the first Chair of the Parole Board noted the fusion of parole and remission had created a distinctly British system of early release that had unleashed a number of operational anomalies on the penal system that were eventually exposed by the brutal murder of Anna Humphries and subsequent conviction of David Evans (Hansard: HL Deb 12 March 1991 vol 527 c105). Lord Hunt went on to note that this hybrid approach had exerted a negative influence on the operation of early release and the continued existence of remission could no longer be justified:

> I am particularly glad that remission time is to go. It was always excessively long for the needs of prison discipline and it constituted too large a reduction of the intended sentence of the court. It is quite interesting to recall that its retention in 1967 was the reason why—the matter arose when we were discussing the criminal justice legislation in 1967—parole eligibility had to be fitted in during the middle third of a sentence and could be awarded after only one-third of a sentence had been served. It was quite unlike any other conditions obtaining in other countries which my colleagues and I on the then Parole Board visited in order to discuss early conditional release systems. That fact did not endear parole to a number of people, including the judges, in the early days, and it has been alleged that it may have led to some lengthening of prison sentences. (Hansard: HL Deb 12 March 1991 vol 527 c 105)

Despite such wide-ranging contributions, the early release provisions contained in Part II of the Bill were not subject to systematic scrutiny. With limited time and resources, legislators focused instead on the politically sensitive question of prisoners serving life sentences. In the Lords, the government came under significant pressure to respond to the judgment of the European Court of Human Rights (ECtHR) in *Thynne, Wilson and Gunnell v. United Kingdom*,[2] published just weeks before the introduction of the Bill. The petition was bought by a number of prisoners who claimed that the operation of parole for those serving discretionary life sentences infringed their Article 5 right to a fair trial. Granting the appeal, the ECtHR held that the UK was in breach of its obligations since, 'neither the Parole Board nor judicial review proceedings—no other remedy of a judicial character being available to the three applicants—satisfy the requirements of Article 5(4)' (European Convention on Human Rights [ECHR] para.80). The Court called upon the UK Government to introduce a suite of measures intended to move the review of discretionary life sentence prisoners onto a judicial footing with greater regard for due process, provision of legal representation, and a right to address the court. At this time the ECHR had no direct legal effect in British law, but the United Kingdom did have a general duty to comply with the Convention. The government initially resisted all attempts to act upon the judgment in *Thynne*, but this began to shift following a number of high profile defeats in the Lords on the question of mandatory life sentences. In 1989 the House of Lords Select Committee Murder and Life Imprisonment chaired by Lord Nathan had recommended that the mandatory life sentence be abolished in favour of a system of discretionary life sentences that empowered the courts to fix the tariff prisoners could expect to serve according to the particular circumstances of the case (House of Lords 1989). Faced with organized and effective opposition to the Bill in the Lords the Government was forced to bring forward a number of concessions that might otherwise have been avoided. Chief amongst them was a series of government amendments on Report (Lords) that established a more court-like process to consider the parole applications of prisoners serving discretionary life sentences. As Lord Waddington noted, the government had wanted further time to consider the ruling of the ECtHR but given the pressure exerted in the Lords it had decided to accelerate the timetable for reform.

While, as I indicated in Committee, we should have preferred to take more time to consider the full implications of the judgment of the

[2] (1991) 13 E.H.R.R. 666.

European Court of Human Rights, we have decided that it would be right to respond to the views expressed in your Lordships' House by introducing amendments to the Bill during its later stages to deal with that point ...

Clearly, the European Court of Human Rights judgment requires cases involving discretionary life sentence prisoners to be considered by a body having the status of a court. That body should have the power, once the initial term set by the trial judge has passed, to order the prisoner's release if it is safe to do so. Clearly, the body should operate in a judicial manner, giving the prisoner the opportunity to appear before it and to be legally represented. However, the Government wish to offer alternative proposals on some of the more detailed points. We believe, for instance, that it may be preferable for the tribunal function to be carried out by the Parole Board, operating under a special procedure in the cases concerned rather than that a completely new tribunal should be set up. The relevant panel of the Parole Board would, however, be constituted under the chairmanship of a judicial member of the board .... (Hansard: HL Deb 20 May 1991 vol 529 c60)

This unplanned, and largely unwanted reform, would have a defining impact upon the operation of parole in England and Wales. With the extension of automatic release to prisoners serving short custodial sentences the Parole Board was released to focus on the more resource intensive cases of prisoners serving long sentences for serious offences. As the number of prisoners serving discretionary life sentences for public protection increased the more court-like approach to parole decision-making set out in the Criminal Justice Act 1991 would become a central feature of the Parole Board's work (Padfield et al. 2012a p.955).

The Criminal Justice Act received Royal Assent on 25 July 1991 and radically altered the early-release landscape for determinate sentence prisoners, those serving discretionary life sentences and mandatory life sentences. Under the Chairmanship of Lord Belstead, a former HM Paymaster General, the Parole Board became a more judicial body with an enlarged secretariat to manage the administratively complex liaison between the Parole Board and the prison-based 'parole clerks' that replaced the Local Review Committees (Hood and Shute 2000 p.iv). During this transition the last vestiges of the Criminal Justice Act 1967 framework that had been extended, modified, and adapted to meet the changing needs of the penal system passed into the history books. Gone was the penal optimism associated with the 'recognizable peak' and the personalization of punishment that were so central to the justification of the Criminal Justice Act 1967. Gone was the 1970s confidence in the reformative potential of a 'short sharp shock' or the enhanced individual deterrent effect of the partly suspended sentence. The system of 50 per cent remission introduced by Hurd as a measure of last resort in 1987 was also abolished as were the prison-based LRCs that had carried so much of the administrative burden once the judiciary had made it clear they would not support a system of compulsory partial suspension. In its place, the Act introduced a stripped back, rather functional system of early release premised upon proportionality in sentencing, active risk assessment, and robust supervision when prisoners were released on licence. However, as we will now see, the Criminal Justice Act 1991 did not definitively settle the issue of early release for a generation as many had hoped.

The Backlash Begins

The transition to the legal arrangements set out in the Criminal Justice Act 1991 took place against a backdrop of considerable political and economic volatility. John Major won a tightly contested General Election in April 1992, and in September 1992 'Black Wednesday' forced the UK government to withdraw from the European Exchange Rate Mechanism (ERM) at significant cost to the taxpayer. In May 1993, the Chancellor Norman Lamont resigned from the government (having declined a demotion to Secretary of State for the Environment) and in the ensuing cabinet re-shuffle Michael Howard was appointed as Home Secretary. Largely remembered for the rhetoric of 'prison works', Howard's tenure at the Home Office has become synonymous with the development of a more populist law-and-order discourse in England and Wales. David Faulkner has described the populist backlash against the Criminal Justice Act 1991 as, 'probably the most sudden and the most radical which has ever taken place in this area of public policy' (quoted in Gibson et al. 1994 p.84) and the abolition of early release quickly emerged as a cause célèbre within this emergent populist punitiveness (for a detailed history of events see Windlesham 2001 pp.1–53). At the 1995 Conservative Party Conference Michael Howard signalled his intention to introduce a system of mandatory sentences and abolish the early release framework first recommended by the

Carlisle Committee. Once again, the theme of truth in sentencing featured strongly; 'it's time to get honesty back into sentencing. Time to back the courts. And time to send a powerful message to the criminal. No more automatic release. No more release regardless of behaviour. And no more half-time sentences for full time crimes' (cited in Windlesham 2001 p.3). The speech was heavily criticized by the Lord Chief Justice Lord Taylor (*The Times*, 13 October 1995) and penal reformers, such as the Penal Affairs Consortium (1996), for unacceptable executive interference in the sentencing function of the courts. But despite such concerns, the move was seen as electorally popular and the policy was worked up in further detail by Home Office officials. In early 1996 the Home Office published *Protecting the Public: The Government's Strategy on Crime in England and Wales* a 'controversial' White Paper (Shute 2003 p.429) that called for the total abolition of the early release framework contained in Part II of the Criminal Justice Act 1991.

> The Government believes that the sentence passed by the court should mean what it says. Accordingly, the Government proposes that the present early release arrangements should be abolished (although the Parole Board will continue to consider cases involving the release on licence of life sentence prisoners). Instead, prisoners will have to earn early release by co-operation and positive good behaviour. No part of this will be granted as of right—it will have to be earned. Behaviour will be continuously assessed throughout the sentence. (Home Office 1996 p.44)

With this policy statement the Home Secretary entered into a longstanding inter-generational dialogue about the administration of the penal system and the termination of prison sentences. A dialogue that goes back at least as far as Captain Alexander Maconochie's decision in the mid-nineteenth century to introduce a 'marks system' at the notorious Norfolk Island penal colony and encompasses the introduction of a modern system of parole in the Criminal Justice Act 1967, Whitelaw's volte-face on compulsory release on licence for short sentence prisoners, and Leon Brittan's restrictive policy of denying parole to violent offenders. The politics of early release have always vied with the claims of administrative experience, but it is clear that over time the relationship between these two normative drivers of public policy has become altogether more contested with implications for the humanity, fairness, and effectiveness of the criminal justice system (Garland 2001; Lacey 2008). It is striking that thirty years before the White Paper the May Committee Inquiry into the United Kingdom Prison Services had reflected on exactly the same question before arriving at a very different conclusion:

> From time to time it has been proposed that remission should be positively earned rather than awarded automatically subject to the proviso that it can be forfeited for bad behaviour. Such a system was used in Britain during the last century and formally abandoned only in 1940. Under this scheme, prison officers awarded 'marks' to inmates who had behaved well and, on the basis of the number of marks acquired, an inmate could accelerate his progress through the system and gain additional privileges. Unfortunately, officers very rapidly fell into the habit of awarding full marks to almost every inmate, preferring to rely on disciplinary procedures when dealing with recalcitrant inmates; the scheme was, therefore, effectively abandoned long before its formal abandonment in 1940. (TNA: HO 263/148)

Despite such historical portents, the White Paper was followed by the legislative proposals contained in the Crime (Sentences) Bill. The Bill received its Second Reading on 4 November 1996 and the subsequent passage of the legislation through Parliament reveals something of the emerging contours of the new law-and-order landscape in England and Wales. Opposition to the Bill in the Commons was muted. As Newburn has noted, New Labour were at pains to safeguard a tough law and order image and, 'during the passage of the Bill, the shadow home secretary, Jack Straw, had been careful not to appear to be especially hostile' (2007b p.439). In contrast, a concerted effort was made in the House of Lords by a cross-party alliance of former Home Office ministers, senior judges, and the Chairman of the Parole Board, Lord Belstead, to water down the proposals for mandatory sentences and restore a measure of sentencing discretion to the courts (Windlesham 2001 pp.1–53). Under growing pressure to conclude parliamentary business, the amendments made in the Lords were reluctantly accepted by the Home Secretary in return for acquiescence to the government's proposals for a scaled back system of early release which would require prisoners serving three years or more to earn the right to apply to the Parole Board for release on licence, once they had served five sixths of their sentence. Despite fierce opposition to the circumvention of usual procedures the offer was accepted, and the Bill was passed on 19 March 1997 just days before Prorogation and the conclusion of Parliamentary business (Windlesham 2001 pp.1–53). In the ensuing general election, the Labour Party was returned to power on a landslide victory, but any hope that the New Labour government would repudiate The Crime (Sentences) Act was short lived. The new Home Secretary Jack Straw committed the government to introduce the mandatory sentences powers incorporated in the Act but, in a significant departure from Conservative policy, Straw confirmed that the government would not activate the powers relating to early release. Instead, a system of 'honesty in sentencing' would be introduced that would require the sentencing judge to explain what the sentence would mean in practice (Windlesham 2001 pp.1–53). As a direct result of these wider political forces, the system of parole established by the Criminal Justice Act 1991 received an unlikely reprieve.

Conclusion: Penal Policy at a Crossroads

The events described in Part IV of this book illustrate a criminal justice system in the midst of significant flux. While there is little doubt that the pre-eminence of penal welfarism had come to an end, making sense of the more contested world of criminal justice that was beginning to replace it is an altogether more difficult task. In this book, we have traced the evolution of early release through a succession of reforms intended to modify the sentence of the court and extend the scale, scope, and reach of executive release. Initially this reforming project was primarily orientated towards the treatment of prisoners serving long sentences but over time this logic began to work through the system with significant implications for the management of prisoners serving short custodial sentences. These reforms were principally justified on instrumental grounds; initially as a way of giving administrative expression to indeterminate sentencing and the personalization of punishment (Cross 1962, 1966; Walker 1962) and latterly in pragmatic terms as a way of achieving significant reductions in the prison population (Home Office 1976). This dynamic began to change in the mid-1980s with Leon Brittan's decision to radically curtail parole eligibility for serious offenders. This marked the beginning of a swing away from instrumental justifications for early release in favour of a retributive view of punishment as intrinsically valuable in marking out the unique seriousness of the offence. When viewed in this way, early release starts to become problematic, both as a means of watering down the punitive element of the sentence imposed by the courts (the populist argument) and in undermining the complex assessment of harm and proportionality at the point of sentence (the 'just deserts' argument). As early as 1976 Von Hirsch had argued in *Doing Justice* that parole was incompatible with the basic tenets of a 'just deserts' sentencing philosophy:

> In the name of 'individualization', sentencing judges in most jurisdictions have been given wide leeway ... Parole boards have similar sweeping powers. When a prisoner becomes eligible for parole (usually after about one third off his sentence has expired), the parole board has discretion to order his release or continue to hold him until the expiration of sentence. Frequently, a parole board does not state any reasons for its decisions; no precedents are set; and no standards for release of continued incarceration are formulated. Moreover, the parole board makes the sentence indeterminate: the imprisoned offender will not know what portion of his sentence he will actually serve in prison until the parole board finally makes its decision about release. The most obvious drawback of allowing wide-open discretion in the name of 'individualization' is the disparity it permits. (von Hirsch 1976 p.29)

This oppositional tension between consequentialist and retributivist justifications for punishment defined the work of the Carlisle Committee and subsequent period of policy development that culminated in the Criminal Justice Act 1991. It can be seen in the division between the 'softies' and the 'toughies' on the Carlisle Committee (Interview B: 13 January 2014) and it can be seen in the final Report where the Committee noted that, 'we are satisfied that one of the main defects of the present system is that things too often do not mean what they say. We believe that there is a strong case for restoring some meaning to the full sentence imposed by the court' (Home Office 1989 p.61). It is also evident in the deliberations of the Home Office working group who wrestled with the political implications of the Carlisle Report and the dividing line between the automatic and discretionary elements of the new system (FOI: HO 291/ 2081). Truth in sentencing was the new demand and as a Criminal Law Review editorial noted contemporaneously, 'the Committee falls into the pattern of recent committee reports in Canada and Australia ... in trying to assimilate the "bark" and the "bite" of custodial sentences, thereby increasing "truth in sentencing"' (Editorial 1987 p.653). The Carlisle Committee is historically significant because it accepted the force of this critique and recommended the first significant rolling back of early release in England and Wales since the Criminal Justice Act 1967 first came into effect (Home Office 1989 p.64).

In this book we have considered three critical junctures in the evolution of early release policy and practice; from the confident penal optimism of the 1960s, through the uncertainties of the 1970s, to the complex process of breakdown and renewal that defined the development of early release in the late 1980s. These detailed historical case studies reveal a complex picture of both continuity and change (Faulkner 1991). In Part V we return to the questions set out at the outset of this book and reflect upon the key dynamics that have influenced the historical trajectory of early release policy and practice in England and Wales between 1960 and 1995.

PART V

Discussion

9

Organizational Factors in Early Release Policy and Practice

> Without denying the importance of both the social context of politics and the motives of individual actors ... institutional analysis posits a more independent role for political institutions. The state is not only affected by society but also affects it. Political democracy depends not only on economic and social conditions but also on the design of political institutions. (March and Olsen 1984 p.738)

At the outset of this book we posed two questions to guide our exploration of the evolving aims and techniques of early release as a public policy concern. First, in what ways did the policy and practice of early release develop in England and Wales between 1960 and 1995? Second, how might we account for these changes? In turn, it was noted that these concerns offered a promising point of departure for a wider discussion of the changing aims and techniques of criminal justice. In Part V, we return to these questions and reflect upon the institutional dynamics that helped shape the unique historical trajectory of early release in England and Wales between 1960 and 1995. This is not to downplay the importance of individual or structural factors. Our analysis builds upon and confirms many of the conclusions from earlier research on penal policy (Downes and Morgan 2002, 2007, 2012; Garland 2001; Loader 2006; Ryan 2003), but it does suggest that institutional dynamics have played an altogether more important role within the wider political economy of crime control than has hitherto been recognized. As we noted in Chapter 2, 'a way of seeing is a way of not seeing' (Poggi 1965 p.284) and in this book we have advanced the case for a quizzical and historically grounded institutionalism that examines public policy 'as life is lived' rather than taking a snapshot of those interactions at one point in

Getting Out: Early Release in England and Wales, 1960–1995. First Edition. Thomas C. Guiney. © Thomas C. Guiney 2018. Published 2018 by Oxford University Press.

time (Sanders 2006). In particular, our interest in the evolution of early release over a thirty-five-year horizon has proved particularly well suited to a 'theory of the middle range' which seeks to explain a limited aspect of political life, and occupy a position intermediate to general theories of social systems and empirical particulars. As Mahoney and Rueschemeyer have noted, this iterative approach to theory building has allowed us to explore this important area of public policy in greater detail than would otherwise have been possible:

> By employing a small number of cases, comparative historical researchers can comfortably move back and forth between theory and history in many iterations of analysis as they formulate new concepts, discover novel explanations and refine pre-existing theoretical expectations in light of detailed case evidence. (Mahoney and Rueschemeyer 2003 p.13)

When approached in this way our dialogue between the theoretical building blocks of historical intuitionalism and the archival record begins to illuminate the complex processes that have shaped the unique historical trajectory of early release policy and practice in England and Wales between 1960 and 1995. In Chapter 9 we investigate the 'spatial' dimensions of this mediating role, in order to signal a sharper focus upon how policy-makers operate within and interact across institutional settings. The chapter re-visits the 'stewardship function' of the Home Office and examines how functional tasks were assigned, interpreted, and resolved within the Department. It then looks outwards to better understand the fluid and uneven distribution of power between the various actors with a stake in the administration of early release. Particular attention is paid to the dynamic relationship between the judiciary and the executive which, more than any other, has exerted a significant influence over the development of early release in England and Wales. The chapter concludes with a call for greater focus on the production of a liberal democratic statecraft and the central role these techniques have played at critical junctures in the development of criminal justice policy and practice.

Inside the Home Office: From Plurality to Action

It is impossible to understand the events described in this book without a critical appraisal of the Home Office, and the mediating role of central government departments more generally, within the British political system (Smith et al. 1993). Within the media, and very often amongst politicians, there has been a tendency to portray Whitehall departments as monolithic institutions and this has often seen the Home Office equated with the personality of the Home Secretary or imbued with a corporate identity that thinks and speaks with common purpose (a discussion of this tendency can be found in Lowndes 2010 pp.67–71). In reality, the Home Office has proved to be a far more complex, heterogeneous entity and more research is needed to better understand how the Home Office has coped with plurality and translated a multiplicity of views, options, and agendas into a singular course of action (Faulkner 2014; RIPA 1982; Windlesham 1993). Ryan was surely right in his description of post-war criminal justice administration as the preserve of a 'small coterie of somewhat self-satisfied, well connected, [white?] middle class, mostly male, metropolitan reformers, academics and a few sympathetic judges, sharing authority with powerful civil servants and ministers in pursuit of their own private agendas' (2003 p.40). Similarly, Loader's discussion of 'liberal elitism', a complex worldview premised upon civilizing values, the use of expert knowledge and the careful management of public opinion offers a powerful insight into a governmentality that framed the proper conduct of government towards crime in post-war England and Wales. But within this broad cultural framework, systematic analysis of the Home Office as a policy actor remains rare (Gibson 2008). Speaking at the Royal Institute for Public Administration symposium to mark the Bicentenary Anniversary of the Home Office (RIPA 1982), James Callaghan, the only modern politician to have occupied all four Great Offices of State, offered a fascinating insight into the centralizing tendencies of the Home Office, the autonomous workings of each Department, a heavy legislative workload and a rather myopic outlook that prioritized short-term crisis management over long-term strategic planning (Callaghan 1982 pp.9–22). More recently, David Faulkner has offered a unique insiders perspective on the Home Office as an institution, its culture and configuration (Faulkner 2014). Faulkner describes a department grappling with the appropriate balance between citizen and state, an administrative culture rooted in case management rather than large public expenditure transfers and an unusually eclectic portfolio of policy interests (see also

Faulkner 1991). As Douglas Hurd would also reflect on his time at the Home Office:

> ... the Home Office in 1983 handled a more bizarre ragbag of unconnected matters than it does today. As the senior Minister of State I found myself at once coping with criminal justice, the police, the regulation of broadcasting, civil defence, gambling, racing and anything else which happened at the time to need a ministerial presence or signature. Each of these subjects had its own hierarchy within the Home Office, and its array of pressure groups outside. (Hurd 2003 p.288)

Each of the case studies described in this book draws attention to how organizational factors shaped the everyday experiences of Ministers and officials, and influenced their disposition towards the management of early release as a public policy concern. At a very practical level the initial geographical spread of the Probation and After-Care Division, the Criminal Department, Prison Department, the Home Office Research Unit and Parole Board secretariat across four separate buildings presented a very real challenge to the effective administration of the new parole system and required new forms of collaboration between the various agencies with a stake in the new parole system (TNA: PCOM 9/2261). More deeply embedded was the uneven distribution of power within the various divisions of the Home Office. Historical institutionalism requires the student of politics to go beyond the first face of power and the authority to make decisions to better understand the more demanding ways in which those with power influence the decision-making agenda and shape the preferences of others. In this regard, the Home Office has always been a rather asymmetric department and there is good evidence to suggest that the Police Department dominated in terms of power and prestige while the Probation and Aftercare Division, as it then was, was seen as the junior partner and able to command only fleeting influence over the wider policy agenda (Interview B: 14 January 2014). This asymmetry helped to close down certain policy options and make others more likely. For example, the steps taken to protect police investment in the 1973 Public Expenditure Survey contributed to the eventual disinvestment from the flagship prison-building programme and historic underinvestment in the Probation Service. These choices about resource allocation cast a long shadow over the administration of criminal justice throughout the decade, at a time when the Probation Service lacked the necessary personnel to cope with a significant increase in non-custodial disposals by the courts and the prison estate struggled to cope with significant further increases in the average prison population. In this context, it is little surprise that reform of early release emerged as such an important tool in the administration of the penal system when so few other levers of control were available.

More subtly, this analysis reveals that within the broad cultural outlook Loader has described as 'liberal elitism' there were subtle variations of light and shade (Loader 2006). Our analysis reveals significant differences in how the various Home Office divisions with a stake in the early release system viewed the world according to their functional responsibilities, policy objectives, and the real-time feedback they received from the unique constellation of professional relationships that built up around every team. As Peter Hall has noted, 'policymakers customarily work within a framework of ideas and standards that specifies not only the goals of policy and the kind of instruments that can be used to attain them, but also the very nature of the problems they are meant to be addressing' (1993 p.279). While subtle, these cognitive scripts help to frame the ongoing interpretation and contestation of public policy concerns that define the day-to-day business of government within any large Department of State. Consider, for example, the following extracts from a Home Office dossier setting out the development of the 'Bampton Proposal' of compulsory partial suspension discussed in Chapter 5 (TNA: HO 495/18). Following the initial presentation of the proposal to a select group of officials in July 1979, Stuart Bampton's paper was circulated for comment to the Assistant Secretaries of each division of the Home Office with an interest in the management of short sentence prisoners. Feedback was collated by the Crime Policy Planning Unit and a discussion paper was prepared for consideration by the Crime Policy Planning Committee in November 1979.

Sydney Norris, Assistant Secretary, P3 'Adjudications' Division of the Prison Department. Note to the Crime Policy Planning Unit, 16 July 1979,

> Returning to the general nature of Mr Bampton's proposal I do not believe that the provision for supervision and recall would in any way satisfy those who would see this as a step by Parliament to interfere with the present sentencing practice of the courts, not for any good reason of penal policy but simply on resource

> grounds ... We have said we would consider half remission as a means of dealing with crisis of population. Half remission is easy to understand, it is inexpensive and I do not think it carries a worse risk of sentences being lengthened than does Mr Bampton's proposal. (TNA: HO 495/18)

John Croft, Head of Home Office Research Unit. Note to the Crime Policy Planning Unit, 17 August 1979:

> I cannot say that I am particularly sympathetic to this scheme, however ingenious, for tinkering with a parole system which I should like to see abolished, provided there is substituted for it a commission independent of the Home Office (but accountable to Parliament) for the review of prisoners sentenced to long terms. As a criminologist, I have never understood the penological justification for the system (although I understand the sociological and political 'justification' only too well). Scientifically, such empirical evidence as there is about the benefits of supervision on parole has never struck me as particularly convincing. In short I think we are attempting to tackle an admittedly complex problem from the wrong end and that we do well to have regard to continental experience in this matter. (TNA: HO 495/18)

Margaret Clayton, Assistant Secretary C1 'Criminal Policy' Division. Note to the Crime Policy Planning Unit, 12 September 1979:

> If there were any possibility of allowing the courts full discretion as to parole on short sentences, I think it would be much better to implement section s47 of the 1977 Act with, if necessary, additional provision for supervision during the suspended part of the sentence. This would be less confusing, less controversial, and easier to defend yet, so far as I can see, the end result would be the same. (TNA: HO 495/18)

K. A. O'Neill, C4 'Probation' Division. Note to the Crime Policy Planning Unit, 28 November 1979:

> One aspect which the paper does not discuss at any length, however, is the possible implications for both the courts, police, and others of having these people back in the community. A high rate of recall is envisaged, which presumably implies some behaviour involving fresh offences. While this must be balanced against the obvious advantages of emptying the prisons of offenders, the following ought I think also to be taken into account;
>
> a) probably further pressure on the courts, if further offences are committed by those on parole,
> b) an extra load on the police, who would perhaps have to bring these offenders in again,
> c) additional hazards for the public if offenders are at large (and extra costs to the Health Service if there are crimes of violence!)
> d) alternative accommodation to house those released who are socially inadequate and have nowhere to go.

These contributions suggest that the organizational basis of the Home Office had a significant and largely overlooked impact upon the interpretation and contestation of early release policy and practice. While individuals no doubt differed in their personal attitudes towards such complex policy problems, and could to an extent shape the view of their division or department, it is also the case that comments such as these were made 'on the record' after significant discussion and reveal something of the distinct divisional cultures that built up within the Home Office. These divisional worldviews were largely resilient to the turnover of individual staff and it is surely no coincidence that officials responsible for prison adjudications favoured an extended system of remission given the low administrative burden presented by such a scheme, while the Probation and Aftercare Division worked tirelessly for a system that incorporated active supervision while on release. It also hints at one final possibility; that the decision to assign a task, project, or problem to a particular department or division was in many cases just as significant as the deliberations and recommendations that followed. In some instances, there was a conscious decision to exploit such differences and a savvy Permanent Secretary would no doubt allocate tasks to the teams most likely to elicit the desired response and support amongst external stakeholders. But more generally such decisions were shaped by a series of unwritten rules, assumptions and norms of appropriate conduct that informed how the allocation of tasks was to be undertaken amongst the various divisions of the Home Office. It is quite conceivable that over time this functional division of government tasks closed down some likely avenues of reform while favouring others. In part, this is why the Crime Policy Planning Unit was established in the 1970s; to coordinate the policy-making process across the Home Office and bring a more strategic approach to such deliberations. When taken as a whole this suggests that powerful norms of appropriate conduct, coupled with the precedents set by previous budget allocations and the informal pecking order amongst Home Office divisions, exerted a significant, albeit largely unnoticed, influence over criminal justice policy in England and Wales.

The Mediations of Political Power

The Home Office may have occupied a privileged position within the criminal justice system but to an important extent this power was negotiated between and mediated though other institutional actors. The US President Lyndon B Johnson once famously observed that, 'power is where power goes' (Caro 2012 p.159) and, as we have seen, the political centre of gravity within the criminal justice system was continually shifting in response to subtle variations in personal authority, parliamentary majorities, moments of crises, and broader socio-economic conditions. These mediations of political power left their mark on the evolution of early release in England and Wales between 1960 and 1995. In Chapter 6, we examined the political manoeuvres that led William Whitelaw to abandon his plans to introduce a system of partial suspension for all short prison sentences in England and Wales. In the absence of concerted electoral pressure from the Labour Party internal party politics took on added significance. The defeat of the law and order motion at the 1981 Conservative Party Conference seriously weakened Whitelaw's position and made it all but impossible to build momentum for his penal reform programme once it became apparent that the senior judiciary did not support his proposals. Indeed, these events are all the more interesting because they happened despite Whitelaw's qualities as a leader and administrator, not because of them. A glimpse of this is seen in the political diaries of Chris Mullin MP who noted in one entry, 'to the Oxford and Cambridge Club in Pall Mall to deliver yet another book talk … Among those present, Sir Brian Cubbon, a former permanent secretary at the Home Office. Who, I inquired, was the most impressive minister he had served? Without hesitation, he nominated Willie Whitelaw as both the most effective and the most affable' (Mullin 2010 para. Thursday, 18 March). Whitelaw was almost universally regarded as an excellent Secretary of State but even this most experienced of politicians could not foresee or control these forces entirely (see Figure 9.1).

These power dynamics can also be seen at each stage of the policy-making cycle. In developing new policy positions Ministers and their officials were often forced to navigate a dense network of interest groups perceived to have a stake in the criminal justice system and invested considerable departmental resources to help 'win the argument' with those who could frustrate their policy objectives. As Home Secretary Douglas Hurd noted in the 1987 edition of *The House Magazine*, a weekly journal of the Houses of Parliament:

> Of the diverse responsibilities which a Home Secretary has to bear, it is questions of law and order that inevitably weigh most heavily with

Figure 9.1 Caricature of Home Secretary William Whitelaw in *New Society*, June 1980

Source: Morris, T (1980) 'The case for abolishing parole' New Society 19 June 1980. The original image is reproduced with the permission of Michael Bennett © Michael Bennett, 1980

him. It is ironic perhaps that despite high expectations—and I don't for a moment complain about that—I have my hands on very few levers of control. In fact, just about the only bit of the system that I am totally responsible for is the running of our prisons. Needless to say, I don't have control over the numbers that come into them. (Hurd 1987 p.14)

Hurd's comments, made as they were at the height of the late 1980s prison boom, betray more than a hint of 'plausible deniability' and it is important not to overstate this point. The strategic review of criminal justice following the 1987 General Election demonstrated that where clear policy objectives had been identified the Home Office did have access to a great many levers of control such as legislation, patronage, policy directions, and resource allocation that were more than sufficient to transform the criminal justice landscape (Faulkner 2006; 2014). Rather the point being made here is that the development of early release policy and practice was continually impeded, refracted, and sometimes catalysed by the unequal and constantly shifting distribution of power within the criminal justice system. It can be seen in the Public Expenditure Survey (PES) negotiations between the Home Office and HM Treasury that established the resource envelope, both revenue and capital, available to the criminal justice system. It can be seen in the relationship between the Home Secretary and the Prime Minister and the reception of government policy within the wider political party, Parliament, and the various civil society organizations with an interest in penal reform. But, just as significantly, this process continued as the focus turned from policy to practice. The Home Office was reliant upon a complex chain of delivery agents to administer the parole system, whether represented jointly by the Society of Civil and Public Servants on behalf of the Prison Governors (latterly the Prison Governors Association), Prison Officers Association (POA), and National Association of Probation Officers (NAPO) or severally by senior Prison Governors and Chief Constables. As Faulkner noted in his address to the Breda Conference in October 1990, this added a further degree of complexity to the development of criminal justice as a public policy concern.

> So our system is complicated. It is not well designed for systematic planning, or indeed for efficient day to day operation at national or local level. Planning and co-ordination have to take place along three separate dimensions—within central government; between central government and the locally provided services and so far as possible the judiciary; and between the services themselves, again including the judiciary so far as possible. (Faulkner 1990 para.7)

To this we may add the growing influence of intermediary bodies such as the Parole Board. As noted in Chapter 4, the Home Office were initially keen to resist the creation of an independent parole board on the grounds that it might frustrate the Home

Secretary's efforts to reduce the prison population. A decade later senior officials expressed similar concerns that the Parole Board lacked the necessary dynamism to implement the 'Jenkins initiative', a key plank of the government's penal reform programme intended to extend the scale, scope, and reach of the parole system. As it became a more established feature of the penal landscape, the Parole Board emerged as a more confident policy actor prepared to use its resources, expertise, and access to influence Home Office thinking and public debate. The working group convened under the Chairmanship of Sue Baring had recommended an extension of the discretionary parole system and greater delegated powers for the prison-based LRCs and this was close in form to the scheme finally adopted by Leon Brittan in 1983. The key point being, that jointly and severally these relationships restricted the operating space of the Home Office, and helped shaped the unique trajectory of early release in England and Wales.

Law's Empire

More than any other, the relationship between the Home Office and the senior judiciary has, and will continue to, exert a defining influence on the evolution of early release policy and practice in England and Wales. While the wider family of criminal justice agencies outlined above enjoyed varying degrees of influence over the Home Office, the independence of the judiciary is hardwired into the British constitutional system and could both impede and catalyse policy change. Over time this creative tension played out in multiple spheres of influence including parliamentary debates, bilateral discussions between the Home Office and the senior judiciary, as well as in the application of sentencing guidance. To an important extent, the Criminal Justice Act 1967, which fused the new parole arrangements onto the existing system of remission, was itself a product of these forces. As we noted in Chapter 3, the Home Office sought to justify the new parole system on the rehabilitative grounds that long-term prisoners reached a 'recognizable peak' in their training at which point continued incarceration was no longer justified by any useful purpose (Home Office 1965 p.4; LSE Archive and Special Collections: Morris T/6). Whether this was a purely presentational device, or not (Shute 2003 p.385), the desire to extend the scope and reach of executive release had to be balanced at all times against the very real danger the senior judiciary would not support the proposals or, just as significantly, stand with the Home Office to pre-empt any threat of sentencing inflation that could undermine the strategic objectives of the fledgling parole scheme. Speaking to *The Observer* on 4 December 1966 Louis Blom-Cooper, then a member of the Home Secretary's Advisory Council on the Penal System reflected upon this dilemma and questioned whether the Home Office had struck the appropriate balance in this regard:

> The proposed release system also suffers from two major defects:
>
> It places far too much trust in the co-operation of the courts. If judges, expressing what they feel to be a public reaction to crime, simply step up the length of sentences, the whole project of early release will be jeopardised in one blow.
>
> Ever since the White Paper announced these proposals there have been signs that some judges—particularly at Quarter Sessions—have reacted in precisely this way. Thus the 'parole' system is at the mercy of judicial sentencing—not a happy augury.
>
> Secondly, the decision whether a prisoner has responded to treatment will be made by Home Office officials, based on prison governor's reports (and in turn, upon the say-so of prison officers). Nothing could be more calculated to upset the therapeutic relationship of prison officers and prisoner than for the former to have a conclusive say in the latter's liberty. (Churchill/HLSM 2/17/22)

This critique suggests that the Home Office were, at least in part, motivated to prioritize judicial approval for the new parole system over the realization of other strategic objectives. This calculation meant that a scheme based upon the automatic release of prisoners, such as an expanded system of remission, was considered an unacceptable extension of executive action and interference with the sentencing discretion of the courts. It ensured that the final parole framework was premised upon a complex process of discretionary release which, given the size of the prison population in England and Wales, required a two-stage decision-making process incorporating an initial sift by prison-based Local Review Committees (LRCs) followed by the final decision by the Parole Board. Finally, in echoes of the Victorian marks system, it meant that parole was positioned strongly as a privilege and not a right, despite the well-known difficulties prison authorities had historically experienced in administering a discretionary system of punishment and incentives. Each of these compromises would become a source of ongoing conflict and frustration for the Home Office, the judiciary and the various practitioners charged with the day-to-day delivery of the parole system. But in an important sense, they were necessary trade-offs within a liberal democratic system of government where more was at stake than just the administrative expediency of early release. As Loughlin (2003) has noted, the separation of powers, rule of law, and political pre-commitment are inherently bound up with the legitimacy and ongoing governability of the liberal democratic state. In this sense, compromises in the form and function of early release were generated through the creative tensions implicit in liberal democratic governmentality and the benefits the 'state', encompassing the executive, legislature, and judiciary, has accrued from this separation of powers. Over time the Home Office enjoyed both successes and failures in managing these delicate relationships and this had a significant impact upon the realization of policy objectives in the medium-to-long term. As we have seen the laboured attempts to extend a system of early release to short-sentence offenders provides a cautionary tale of the implications of failing to secure buy-in from the senior judiciary at key moments of reform. As the Home Office Crime Policy Planning Committee reported, rather matter-of-factly, after the Lord Chief Justice had written to the Home Secretary making clear that he could not support the proposals set out in the Home Office Review of Parole in England and Wales:

> ... the Planning Unit had been engaged in the preparation of a scheme for possible legislation on early release for short sentence prisoners. Such a scheme was developed in some detail and discussed by senior management in July [1981]; but the more closely the possible options were explored, the less desirable they became. The final assessment was that the scheme (and viable variants) would have no predictable impact on the prison population, that it might vitiate the effect of calls for shorter sentences, and that it could not in any event be implemented for 12 months because of the administrative complexities. The Home Secretary wrote to the Lord Chief Justice in September enclosing a summary of the Planning Unit's work, and the Lord Chief Justice's reply made it clear that he would not endorse legislation before his recent judgements on sentencing had had time to make an effect. It was therefore decided that plans for an early release scheme should be put on one side, at least for the time being. This decision has been reflected in subsequent Ministerial statements which have been to the effect that although some form of direct intervention cannot ultimately be ruled

out the Court of Appeal's initiative must be given a chance. (TNA: HO 495/23)

Putting aside philosophical questions about the relationship between liberalism and democracy (Dworkin 1986; Laws 1995), a debate given added impetus by the recent Supreme Court judgment on the process of Britain's exit from the European Union, it is clear that the Home Office repeatedly struggled to ascertain the intentions of the senior judiciary. This was perhaps understandable given that the judicial branch of the State also represented a diverse and heterogeneous constellation of institutions comprising the Magistrates Association, Lord Chief Justice, and the idiosyncratic position of the Lord Chancellor and the Lord Chancellor's Department that grew in size and complexity between 1960 and 1995. This made it exceptionally difficult to predict with any certainty how the senior judiciary would respond to new policy proposals such as the Carlisle Committee recommendations and just as importantly, how the courts would make use of new sentencing powers such as the partly suspended sentence. This contingency, or basic unknowability at the heart of criminal justice policy and planning, exerted a profound influence over the trajectory of early release between 1960 and 1995. Throughout the period in question the Home Office oscillated between strategies of soft and hard influence in seeking to manage demand on the prison system and the fallout from these engagements can be seen in the policy and practice of early release. Following the failure of the *Review of Parole in England and Wales in 1981*, a document perceived to cross the Rubicon in terms of executive interference with the constitutional function of the courts, the Home Office did seek to develop a more robust dialogue with the senior judiciary resulting in the Ditchley Park Conference and a series of bilateral meetings between David Faulkner and the Deputy Lord Chief Justice Tasker Watkins (David Faulkner Personal Papers). The legacy of these efforts is open to debate, but it does serve to focus our attention on the immediacy of the relationship with the Lord Chief Justice, historically, the second-highest ranking judge in England and Wales after the Lord Chancellor and, prior to the Constitutional Reform Act 2005, responsible for the administration of the Criminal Division of the Court of Appeal. Unlike Ministers of equivalent rank, the Lord Chief Justice did not enjoy the support of a large private office and this appears to have imbued working relationships with a level of immediacy that must be considered rare within modern government. This intimacy stands out from the formality and detachment of prose that are so typical of the archival record (FOI: May 2013, HO 495/21). Unlike correspondence between Ministers and other holders of high office which were carefully choreographed by civil servants through formal correspondence, exhaustive briefings, and carefully prepared meeting agendas, engagement with the Lord Chief Justice was largely unencumbered from bureaucratic procedure. In one such exchange Deputy Under-Secretary of State Anthony Brennan describes taking a call from the Lord Chief Justice to discuss a recent Parliamentary debate on the May Committee enquiry into the Prison Service. In a special edition of BBC '*Panorama*' aired on 22 February 1982 presenter Tom Mangold pressed Lord Justice Lawton on why the judiciary had raised concerns about the proposals set out in the *Home Office Review of Parole in England and Wales* (Home Office 1981b) and was offered the following account of his discussions with the Lord Chief Justice:

> The Lord Chief Justice asked all the Lord Justices who deal with criminal appeals to have a talk with him in his room and he then told us what the Home Secretary's suggestion was. We were told by the Lord Chief Justice that the Home Office were not in favour of giving any discretion to the trial judge. We felt that this was wrong both in practice and we thought too that the public would resent it because so many of these recidivist burglars will be in circulation again within a very short time of being sent to prison. (BBC '*Panorama*' 1982)

Shortly thereafter some media outlets reported that Lord Lane had become so disillusioned with political initiatives to reform the penal system that he limited contact with the Home Office to all but the most unavoidable 'official business' (*The Guardian*, 10 November 1990; see also Windlesham 1993 p.184). Engagement with the Lord Chief Justice was inter-personal rather than bureaucratic and ascertaining the views of the Lord Chief Justice or the collective position of the Lord Justices of Appeal with responsibility for criminal matters surely presented a unique challenge to Home Officials who relied upon the regular exchange of information to advise Ministers effectively. Like any traveller to foreign lands, the events described in this book suggest that the Home Office consistently struggled to navigate the very different institutional rules, practices, and structures of meaning they encountered within law's empire.

Conclusion: Criminal Justice as Statecraft

In this chapter, we have reflected on the organizational factors that shaped the unique historical trajectory of early release policy and practice in England and Wales between 1960 and 1995. We began by exploring the divisional organization of the Home Office and how policy-makers interacted to translate a multiplicity of views, options, and agendas into singular courses of action. We went on to locate the Home Office within a wider institutional ecosystem where power is negotiated across Whitehall and exercised through a range of criminal justice delivery partners (Faulkner 1990 para.7). More than any other, we noted that the dialectical relationship between the executive and the senior judiciary exerted a defining influence on the evolution of early release policy and practice in England and Wales. It bears repeating that the skill and finesse with which policymakers are able to navigate this dense institutional fabric and cultivate an effective liberal democratic statecraft has exerted a significant impact upon the trajectory of early release, and the development of criminal justice more generally. Criminologists have been particularly attentive to the ways in which political elites (Ryan 2003) and the contestation of political ideas (Downes and Morgan 2007) have influenced the development of criminal justice in England and Wales, but our analysis should offer a powerful reminder that the various ways in which power is harnessed and subsequently exercised in organizational settings can be just as significant as the aims pursued. As Jim Bulpitt noted in his pioneering study of the early Thatcher governments:

> What is statecraft? The crude answer is that it is the art of winning elections and achieving some necessary degree of governing competence in office. It is not synonymous with, though it may be related to, pragmatism or expediency. It is concerned primarily to resolve the electoral and governing problems facing a party at any particular time. As a result it is concerned as much with the 'how' as the 'what' of politics. (Bulpitt 1986)

This recalibration of policy analysis to focus on the 'how' as well as the 'what' of criminal justice raises some intriguing questions.

Why was Roy Jenkins able to exert more influence over criminal justice in his first term as Home Secretary than his second? Were the proposals for short sentence offenders set out in the Home Office *Review of Parole in England and Wales* (1981b) ill-judged or did the government simply fail to lay the necessary groundwork with within the Conservative Party and senior judiciary? Leon Brittan's 'restrictive policy' of denying parole to prisoners serving long sentences of imprisonment may have been politically advantageous in the short term but in the long term did it render the administration of the penal system unworkable? The post-1987 General Election planning process culminating in the planning days at Leeds Castle and Ditchley Park represented an attempt to embed a more collegiate approach to criminal justice policy and planning, but to what extent was this more successful than the command and control governmentality that had proved so influential within the Home Office following World War Two? More than almost any other area of public policy, criminal justice is inherently bound up with the exercise of power, the appropriate balance between citizen and state, and the legitimate role of punishment within a liberal democracy (Padfield 2007; Padfield et al. 2012a). Within such a complex landscape the ability to cultivate an effective liberal democratic statecraft can often be the difference between policy inertia and action.

10

Temporal Factors in Early Release Policy and Practice

In Chapter 10 we explore how temporal factors have influenced the development of early release in England and Wales. The chapter begins with a number of broad observations upon the everyday business of penal administration and offers a view of policy development that departs from the standard model of the policy-making cycle. It goes on to explore the central role of path dependency in shaping the trajectory of early release policy and practice in England and Wales between 1960 and 1995, before turning to the less well understood catalysing role of 'timing and sequence' at key moments of policy reform (Pierson 2004 pp.54–78). The chapter concludes with a critical appraisal of the complex picture of continuity and change that emerges from this book, and advances the case for greater use of comparative historical study given how little attention is given to historical lessons in much contemporary public policy debate (Rock 2005).

Policy-Making in Real-World Settings

> ... every single political phenomenon lives in history, and requires historically grounded analysis for its explanation. Political scientists ignore historical context at their peril. (Tilly 2006 p.433)

One of the central arguments advanced in this book is that the study of public policy in comparative historical perspective can help to reveal a richer account of how the liberal democratic state has sought to justify and, in turn, administer a system of criminal justice. Moreover, with reference to the new institutionalist critique of policy-making offered by March and Olsen (1984; 1989), we have sought to understand the policy-making process 'as it is,

Getting Out: Early Release in England and Wales, 1960–1995. First Edition. Thomas C. Guiney. Published 2018 by Oxford University Press.

rather than how it ought to be'. This has revealed a picture of public policy development that is somewhat at odds with conventional accounts of the policy-making cycle, including the HM Treasury *Green Book* (2011) which sets out detailed guidance to all government departments on how new initiatives should be developed before committing public funds to a policy, programme, or project. Such accounts often emphasize a pluralist framework where policymakers work sequentially through a series of decision-making steps and seek to balance the competing interests of economic constraints, political expediency, the findings from academic research, and the voices of special interest groups (Faulkner 2006; Walker and Giller 1976; Windlesham 1993). Our analysis of early release policy and practice in England and Wales between 1960 and 1995 indicates an altogether more contested, messy, and contingent view of policy-making defined by the following characteristics:

- **Early release in perspective:** In Chapter 1 of this book we set out the case for the study of early release in comparative historical perspective. There is however a danger that the selective use of archival records to trace the development of this particular public policy concern can overstate the prominence of early release within overall government decision-making. For the avoidance of doubt our review of the archival records, particularly the records pertaining to the Prime Minister, Cabinet, and the various sub-committees on Home Affairs, reveals that, apart from a short period of scrutiny in the 1960s, early release barely featured as a policy issue at the top-tier of government. This is not to dismiss the importance of early release as a public policy concern but to place such issues in their appropriate context. The relative standing of early release, like penal policy more generally perhaps, helps to explain why these issues are so sensitive to upstream policy choices and the shifting objectives of the Home Office, which was by and large free to manage these public policy concerns with little intervention from collective Cabinet decision-making structures.
- **The law of unintended consequences:** Allied to the above, our analysis has demonstrated just how often the trajectory of early release policy and practice was shaped, not by the conscious decisions of policymakers, but unanticipated changes within cognate areas of public policy or wider political manoeuvrings. These externalities can be seen throughout the events described

in this book. In Chapter 3 we noted that the modernizing project associated with the rehabilitative ideal led to the abolition of penal servitude with unanticipated implications for the release and aftercare arrangements of prisoners serving long determinate sentences. Harold Wilson's decision to reshuffle his Cabinet in advance of a possible 1966 General Election resulted in Roy Jenkins' appointment as Home Secretary, an appointment that started to challenge the hierarchical culture of the Home Office and unlocked a period of unprecedented creativity that saw the Criminal Justice Act 1967 re-imagined as a far more ambitious piece of legislation than would otherwise have been the case. In Chapter 5 we explored how the global economic insecurity of the early 1970s shaped the Treasury's attitude towards the Public Expenditure Survey (PES) negotiations with Whitehall Departments and made it more likely that the errors in the Home Office's prison population projections would be used as the basis for disinvestment from the flagship prison-building programme.

- **Contingency**: This book has revealed just how contingent many episodes in the historical development of early release policy and practice have been. There was nothing certain or pre-determined about the events described here and it is easy to see how things could have worked out very differently. Would the Criminal Justice Act 1967 have been such an ambitious piece of legislation if Roy Jenkins had taken the job as Secretary of State for Education or lost the confidence of the Prime Minister over his handling of the Shepherd's Bush murders and the escape of George Blake? How would the administration of criminal justice in the 1970s have differed if Robert Carr, then the Home Secretary, had convinced the Treasury to maintain its commitment to the prison-building programme? Would the populist backlash against the Criminal Justice Act 1991 been at all different if Margaret Thatcher had not lost the leadership of the party during the passage of the Bill? We will never know the answer to these questions, but they offer a useful caution against an overly deterministic interpretation of policy change and a reminder of why there has been such significant variability in political responses to crime across time and space despite broadly similar exposure to the socio-economic forces of late twentieth-century modernity.

- **Compromise:** Policymakers struggled to shape penal policy within circumstances that were not always of their own choosing. Decision-makers rarely had absolute discretion to make the choices they would have liked; many inherited unwanted political and fiscal commitments from their predecessors and successive Secretaries of State were forced to take policy choices in a succession of 'lesser of two evils'-type scenarios. Douglas Hurd's room for manoeuvre on early release was significantly limited by the choices of previous Home Secretaries. While popular within the Conservative Party, the bifurcation of parole introduced by Leon Britain served to undermine the administrative coherence of early release in England and Wales. The restriction of parole for serious offenders embroiled the Home Office in protracted judicial review proceedings and while the House of Lords ultimately found in favour of the Home Secretary in *Re Findlay*,[1] the extension of parole eligibility to short sentence prisoners in s33 cases was universally derided by the judiciary. This led to the establishment of an internal Home Office working group chaired by Sydney Norris that would prove to be an important precursor to the Carlisle Committee proceedings (FOI: HO 291/ 2081). This inheritance is critical to our understanding of why the Home Office elected to revise the Prison Rules and move to a system of half remission—a policy shift that more than any other served to undermine the integrity of the sentence system in England and Wales, and prompt calls for greater truth in sentencing. (Interview G: 2 December 2014)
- **Imperfect knowledge:** It is striking how often policymakers were forced to make decisions on the basis of imperfect knowledge and struggled to predict the likely consequences of their decisions with any degree of confidence (see also Jessop 1990; Hay 2002 pp.126–134). This was particularly true when it came to anticipating how policies would 'travel' as they were interpreted and implemented by a succession of delivery agents within the criminal justice system. Home Office officials worried about the creation of an independent Parole Board because they feared it would frustrate the Department's policy objectives in the medium to long term (TNA: HO 384/99). This

[1] Re Findlay [1985] AC 318.

anxiety remained well into the 1970s when, on advice from officials, Roy Jenkins took steps to pre-commit a conservative and risk averse Parole Board by announcing his plans to extend the scale and reach of the parole system in response to a dangerously high prison population. (TNA: HO 303/98)

Path Dependence

These insights strengthen the case for conceptualizing criminal justice 'as life is lived' rather than a snapshot of those interactions at one point in time (Sanders 2006 p.39). It has become somewhat axiomatic to claim history matters in the study of public policy (Tilly 2006), but the legacy of historic policy choices is writ large throughout this book. As noted in Chapter 2, relatively minor choices at one point in time can have major implications at a later point in a temporal sequence and this is especially likely when policy choices introduce 'positive feedback'—a process that facilitates further moves in the same direction and increases the costs of changing direction (Pierson 2001). As Margaret Levi has noted, positive feedback creates developmental trajectories that are hard to reverse once in motion (1997 p.28), with the implication that once institutional norms and rules of appropriate conduct have become established they become resilient to change and this 'stickiness' can close off some policy avenues while encouraging others. The events described in this book indicate that the landscape of early release policy and practice in England and Wales has been shaped, to a significant degree, by the forces of path dependency. One such example stands out above all others: the decision to graft the new system of parole onto the existing remission arrangements in the Criminal Justice Act 1967. This decision exerted a significant influence over the development of early release in England and Wales, a legacy which could still be felt well into the 1990s with the gradual transition to the Carlisle Committee framework enshrined in the Criminal Justice Act 1991. As we noted in Chapter 4, this compromise was by no means inevitable. If reductions in the prison population were the primary driver of penal reform, the obvious option would have been to extend remission to 50 per cent of a prison sentence, a move that was championed by prison governors who favoured remission as a tool of prison discipline. Remission was inexpensive to administer, did not require a complex decision-making framework, and could be amended easily by statutory instrument. Conversely, if this reform agenda was driven purely by the modernizing project associated with the rehabilitative ideal it would have been entirely understandable if the Home Office had taken the opportunity to abolish the outmoded system of remission altogether and replace it with a straightforward system of parole as was common in many other Western jurisdictions at this time (Turner 1966a, 1966b). The preference for incremental change reveals a great deal about the pragmatic instincts of the British political establishment at this time (Ryan 2003), but for present purposes the key point is that once the decision had been taken to adopt a hybrid rather than a pure system of either parole or remission this began to exert a path-dependent impact upon the trajectory of early release policy and practice in England and Wales. For eligible prisoners and their families it created a legitimate expectation that their cases would be considered for parole at the one-third point of their sentence and the prison service invested heavily in a new rank of Assistant Prison Governors who were responsible for the complex computation of early release dates and professionally invested in the task of overseeing the aftercare arrangements of inmates (Interview H: 20 January 2015). Moreover, a whole new administrative apparatus was created to deliver the new system; appointments to the Parole Board were highly prestigious, Local Review Committees were established in facilities across England and Wales, and a new parole unit was established within the Home Office. The system was supported by the Treasury as a way of reducing the financial costs associated with the penal system (TNA: T 227/2292) while the mainstream penal lobby comprised of organizations like the Howard League of Penal Reform (1981) and NACRO (Cavadino et al. 1977) were all broadly supportive of the new arrangements, particularly as a way of offering hope to those within the prison system and a vehicle for reducing the prison population. Initially, at least, the Criminal Justice Act 1967 commanded strong cross-party support which helped to shield the fledgling parole system from controversy when high profile cases such as Sydney Williams began to hit the headlines (*Daily Mirror* 12 August 1968). But in the long term the significant investment of time, money, and people in the new parole system provided a further level of insulation by heightening the costs of unwinding this complex infrastructure. Despite the self-evident limitations of this system the process of positive reinforcement incentivized the Home Office to work within this framework and heavily discount alternatives that would have required a radical departure from this settlement.

What did this mean in practice? By dividing the time available on release between the automatic system of remission and the discretionary system of parole, the Home Office had secured judicial and practitioner support for the new system but over time this arguably made 'root and branch' reform of early release policy and practice more difficult. The interaction between the two systems of release meant that the computation of early release dates was extremely complex and created anomalies like the example of a high-risk offender refused release on parole only to be released unconditionally under remission arrangements (Home Office 1989 p.4). It also meant that many of the reforms outlined in this book applied to only one portion of a prison sentence. Over time this encouraged prison authorities to focus on 'net widening' exercises like the 'Jenkins initiative' or the increasingly technocratic efforts to extend a system of parole to short sentence prisoners as described in Chapter 6. But more than this, it was the division of the automatic and discretionary elements of the system into two separate legal and administrative regimes that generated so many of the tensions outlined above. Somewhat counter-intuitively, the events described in this book suggest that remission is the key to understanding the idiosyncratic evolution of parole in England and Wales. Remission enjoyed high levels of support within the Prison Department who saw it as an invaluable disciplinary tool that offered a simple, cost-effective method to quickly expedite the release of a large number of inmates from the prison estate. But this came at a cost. Remission applied automatically to all prisoners regardless of the seriousness of their offence and contained no provision for aftercare, even when it was recognized that a prisoner was likely to be a threat to public safety without effective supervision and liability for recall. This trade-off appears to have resulted in a form of decision-making paralysis; the Home Office were unwilling to abolish remission altogether, but at the same time they repeatedly shied away from further reform and expansion until 1987 when all other options for reform had been exhausted. As a result, the focus of attention was continually shifted from remission, the elephant in the room, to the altogether more pliable parole system. As conditions in the prison system became more acute and only modest additional capital investment came on stream from HM Treasury, the Home Office turned with increasing regularity to the parole system to help control the prison population. As we have seen, this typically entailed efforts to water down the discretionary element of parole and introduce a degree of automation that would guarantee significant reductions in the prison population. This can be seen in the 'Bampton Proposal' for compulsory partially suspended sentences (FOI: HO 495/21; TNA: HO495/18), and later on with the Home Office issued guidance to LRCs stating that there should be a presumption in favour of release when dealing with s33 cases of short sentence prisoners. Viewed in isolation these proposals did not represent a fatal interference with the sentencing power of the courts, but since they operated in addition to a system of remission that already shortened all sentences by a third, even modest attempts to place parole on a more automatic footing were problematic and perceived as unjustifiable executive action by the judiciary. Over time this created something of a vicious circle that contributed to a deteriorating relationship between the Home Office and senior judiciary. It exacerbated the concerns of the judiciary who were increasingly sceptical of executive interference with the sentencing function of the courts and it limited the ability of the Home Office to exert some semblance of soft influence over sentencing practice and alert a somewhat distant and remote judicial class to the deteriorating conditions within the prison estate. The key point being that many of the difficulties and frustrations experienced by policymakers in the 1980s can be traced back to the legislative decisions made in the run up to the Criminal Justice Act 1967. A settlement that created strong path dependencies that only began to unravel as consequentialist justifications for punishment fell out of fashion and the 1987 General Election created a policy window where genuine root and branch reform became possible.

Continuity and Change

Path dependence can help us to explain the continuities in early release policy and practice for much of the period in question but what about the periods of upheaval and transformation we have described in this book? These dislocations can be difficult to articulate within an institutionalist framework (Streeck and Thelen 2005). On the whole, historical institutionalism has been far more effective in explaining 'institutional stability' than it has at making sense of seismic political change—a vulnerability that links back to the structuralist tendencies of the 'new intuitionalism' outlined in Part I of this book. Faced with this challenge many theorists have fallen back upon the idea of 'punctuated equilibrium', an explanatory model derived from the evolutionary theory of biologists Niles Eldredge and Steven Gould (1972) which holds that institutions remain in a state of equilibrium until they are faced with an external or exogenous shock, to account for policy change (see Thelen and Steinmo 1992). While frequently employed within the literature, Thelen et al. (1992) have criticized this conceptual model on the grounds that it sees institutional analysis too readily abandoned for base forms of structure and agency at precisely the point when history is at its most important and interesting:

> The problem with this model [punctuated equilibrium] is that institutions explain everything until they explain nothing. Institutions are an independent variable and explain political outcomes in periods of stability, but when they break down, they become the dependent variable, whose shape is determined by the political conflicts that such institutional breakdown unleashes. (Thelen and Steinmo 1992 p.15)

For Pierson (2004), a more profitable explanation of the apparent tension between the simultaneous stability and fluidity of historical events can be found in the integration of path dependence and 'timing and sequence'. While path dependence and positive reinforcement are often seen to have a stabilizing influence on public policy, timing and sequence can introduce contingency and variation, most notably when 'policy windows' are opened by the regular operation of the electoral cycle or exceptional events in domestic and foreign policy (Kingdon 2003). This leads Pierson to argue that where self-reinforcing processes are at work political life is likely to be marked by the following characteristics:

1. Multiple equilibria. Under a set of initial conditions conducive to positive feedback a range of outcomes is generally possible.
2. Contingency. Relatively small events, if occurring at the right moment, can have large and enduring consequences.
3. A critical role for timing and sequencing. In path-dependent processes, 'when' an event occurs may be crucial. Because early parts of

a sequence matter much more than later parts, an event that happens 'too late' may have no effect, although it might have been of great consequence if the timing had been different.

4. Inertia. Once such a process has been established, positive feedback will generally lead to a single equilibrium. This equilibrium will in turn be resistant to change. (Pierson 2003 p.43)

Using these tools, we can begin to construct a richer understanding of the key periods of reform and renewal described in this book. Take, for example, the efforts to secure a more strategic approach to management of the criminal justice system following the 1987 General Election. In the years following the Criminal Justice Act 1967 the compromise system of early release fusing remission and parole had proved extremely adaptable; it adjusted to the changing needs of the criminal justice system and accommodated an almost continued process of reform as the objectives of penal policy evolved (Tata 1990). But this elasticity had its limits and by 1987 the operation of early release in England and Wales had been stretched to breaking point. The options for further piecemeal reform were increasingly limited, and as the influence of retributivist justifications for punishment grew, so did popular discontent with the operation of parole which had always rested upon consequentialist logics. This policy problem helped to place early release on the policy agenda, but it is arguably the proximity of these events to the 1987 General Election, and the significant growth in the prison population, that ultimately proved decisive. The Conservatives were returned to power on 11 June 1987 with a healthy majority of 100 MPs and a strong mandate to implement their law and order commitments, including a review of parole in England and Wales. An extended period of hegemony had also strengthened the Conservative Party position in the House of Lords where they commanded 531 Peers to a Labour grouping of 117. Refreshed and re-energized by a strong Conservative performance in the General Election, Douglas Hurd returned to Queen Anne's Gate as a considerably more experienced Home Secretary with a strong command of his Departmental brief and the political appetite to undertake the wide-ranging strategic review of penal policy outlined above (Hurd 2003; Interview B: 14 January 2014). When taken as a whole, the mounting incoherence of early release and Hurd's growing self-confidence as Home Secretary, coupled with the policy window created by the 1987 General Election, all helped to create the political momentum for wide-ranging reform of early release. Nonetheless, there were any number of occasions when reform of early release could have fallen off the political agenda, most notably following the lukewarm reception to the Carlisle Report within government, the judiciary, and penal lobby (*The Independent* 1989a). It is critical that on this occasion, unlike the criticism that accompanied Whitelaw's proposals for short sentence prisoners, the interests of key power brokers within the criminal justice system aligned to reinforce the case for change rather than frustrate it. Hampered by the continuing practice of cell sharing the police were more aware than ever of pressures in other parts of the criminal justice system. The strategic review of criminal justice following the 1987 General Election had done much to build a collective vision for management of the criminal justice system amongst senior Home Office officials and Ministers (Faulkner 2006; Windlesham 1993). It was also hugely significant that the senior judiciary, so critical of the operation of s33 cases, came out in support of the Carlisle Committee proposals that went a long way to restoring meaning to the sentence of the courts (FOI: May 2013). Despite her punitive instincts, the Prime Minister gave Hurd significant discretion to manage the Home Office as he saw fit (Hurd 2003 p.341), while the tragic murder of Anna Humphries helped to galvanize public opinion and offered a powerful reminder of why the status quo was no longer tenable (*The Times*, 6 July 1989a). Put simply, this constellation of policy actors and interest groups had more to gain from reform of early release than they did with sticking with an increasingly dysfunctional status quo, a strategic calculation that helped tip the balance in favour of accepting the Carlisle Committee proposals and the measures given legal effect by the Criminal Justice Act 1991.

This is however only a partial explanation for the signal events and episodes of policy change described in this book. By its very nature the systematic study of 'official' records will tend to generate a picture of public policy as seen from the perspectives of the establishment, of senior officials, politicians, practitioners, and academics. When viewed from afar, the disruptive influence of the general public, of activists, of prisoners and their families can be lost. Far from a neutral and objective store of information the archive itself emerges as an active participant in the creation of 'official history' and all the disputes over power, legitimacy, and hegemony that come with it. Reflecting on this point in a fascinating 1994 lecture *Archive Fever: A Freudian Impression*, Derrida (1996) described the archive as a powerful symbol of state authority and a profound example of collective 'remembering' and 'forgetting' (1996 p.77). All historians must remain vigilant to the 'violence of the archive' and elaborating on this theme the historian Michelle King reminds us that the archival is never an objective site of memory and preservation but also a place of forgetting and destruction (1996 p.7).

> Put more plainly, every act of remembering and preserving is fixed to its shadow of loss and forgetting; ideas and experiences are written down in the first place so that they may be forgotten; documents are selected for inclusion into archives by acts of exclusion; the very preservation of documents in an archive exposes [them] to destruction. (King 2012 p.18)

This is somewhat unavoidable in a study of this nature, but it does not entirely preclude a consideration of social movements or what Barker has described as the dynamic and disruptive potential of 'civil engagement' (Barker 2009 pp.35–42). As Sanders has noted, historical institutionalism can be used to undertake 'top down' studies of ruling elites or 'bottom up' accounts of everyday people and social movements (2006 p.44). Take for example the growing influence of human rights across a wide range of public policy areas in England and Wales, including early release decision-making. In 1975 the academic Eryl Hall Williams published a highly influential article, *Natural Justice and Parole* where he argued that since parole proceedings were of an administrative rather than judicial nature, and intended by Parliament as a privilege rather than a right, there was no compelling argument for applying the strictest requirements of natural justice to parole decision-making. This argument, and variants of it, proved to be extremely influential in the formative years of the parole system, and were frequently cited by the Parole Board to resist calls for the introduction of reject reasons and a more court-like approach to parole decision-making (BBC *Inside Story* 1979). However, as the human rights movement grew in influence, and society became less deferential to those in positions of authority, it became increasingly difficult to justify such a paternalistic system (Nevitte 1996; Uslaner 2002). Calls for greater recognition of human rights and procedural justice were moving up the political agenda and the 1980s saw a steady stream of judicial review applications from prisoners and public interest lawyers seeking to challenge the long-standing administrative assumptions that underpinned the parole system. We have encountered a number of these cases already, but there were many others: In *Payne v. Lord Harris of Greenwich*[2] the Court of Appeal considered whether a prisoner had a right to see the reasons why the Parole Board had rejected his or her application for parole; in *Weeks v. United Kingdom*[3] the ECtHR examined the recall arrangements for parolees whose parole licences have been revoked and in the landmark case of *Thynne, Wilson, and Gunnell*[4] the ECtHR directed the UK Government to place parole hearings for prisoners serving discretionary life sentences on a more judicial footing with greater regard for due process, provision of legal representation, and a right to address the court. It should be noted that in many of these cases the courts found in favour of the Home Office but over time this growing body of case law gave credence to those calling for greater recognition of individual human rights and stronger safeguards against state infringement of individual liberties (Elliott 2007). This re-casting of the balance between administrative expediency and human rights took place at a time when the administration of early release was already coming under intense strain. As a direct result of repeated interventions by the Home Office the scale, scope, and reach of the early release system had been extended far beyond anything anticipated by policymakers in 1967. In 1968, a total of 4,347 applications for parole were considered in England and Wales, a figure that grew to 23,136 in 1988, a staggering rise of 432 per cent in just two decades (see Figure 1.1). No reliable data is available on either the number of personnel sitting on prison-based LRCs, the performance of the central Home Office Parole Unit, or the real term costs of administering the parole scheme in totality. However, we do know that the lay membership of the Parole Board for England and Wales, including the Chairman, grew from seventeen appointments in 1968 to a total of sixty-nine in 1988 (HMSO 1969; 1989). In parallel, the Annual Reports of

2 [1981] 1 WLR 754.
3 (1988) 10 E.H.R.R. 293.
4 (1991) 13 E.H.R.R. 666.

the Parole Board indicate that expenditure rose from £504,281 in 1978 to £954,652 by 1988 (at 2017 prices). When taken as a whole, the longstanding administrative assumptions that had made the delivery of a discretionary system of parole possible in 1967 were simply no longer feasible at the end of the twentieth century. As the Carlisle Committee noted, 'we are satisfied that it is wrong in principle and, in any event, unworkable in practice, to try to operate a selective parole system for short sentence prisoners ...' (Home Office 1989 p.48). As the criminal justice system grew in size and complexity it was simply impossible to assemble the necessary documentation to take robust release decisions for the vast majority of short sentence prisoners. Yes, the politics and presentational implications of reform loomed large over the policy-making process but at all times this had to be balanced against the likely impact of such proposals on the prison population and the resources needed to operationalize the new early release framework (FOI: HO 291/ 2081). In this sense, the evolution of parole has much in common with the historical trajectory of remission as it evolved from the discretionary 'marks system' of earned privileges that was common in Victorian prisons, to a settled administrative framework based upon a presumptive entitlement. In both instances, what began as a purely discretionary system, positioned as a 'privilege not a right' evolved into a largely automatic system as prison authorities struggled to deal with an increasing volume of cases in a fair, consistent, and equitable manner that did not antagonize a volatile prison population or offend changing social attitudes towards human rights and 'natural justice' (Liebling 2007; TNA: HO 263/148). This dynamic should also serve as an important reminder, if one were needed, that not all policy change emerges from within Westminster or Whitehall. As Padfield et al. (2012a) have noted the ECtHR has been a key driver of reform in England and Wales, prompting the Parole Board to improve its procedures, 'to make them more "court-like" and bring them more into line with the principles of natural justice and the European Convention on Human Rights' (Nichol 2007 pp.1–19). Likewise, much of the momentum for the Carlisle Committee reforms was driven by the courts, both domestic and European, civil society organizations, and the effective use of judicial review to re-balance the relationship between state and citizen (Padfield 2007; Padfield et al. 2012a). In this way the use of judicial review, local activism, and push-back from prisoners and their families can open provide some relief from the implicit 'violence of the archive' (Derrida 1996).

Conclusion: The Merits of Comparative Historical Study

By examining early release in broad historical perspective this book has revealed some of the stepping stones that led from the confident and optimistic world of the 'rehabilitative ideal' (Allen 1981) to the altogether more contested politics of law and order that emerged in the mid-1990s. During this time early release has demonstrated remarkable plasticity as a tool of public policy, supporting such varied aims as the personalization of punishment, incentivizing good behaviour and compliance with prison regimes, reducing pressure on the prison population, and a powerful symbol of changes in government policy. Just as significantly, early release has often provided the policy crucible where the inherent tensions and contradictions of liberal democratic criminal justice have clashed; indeterminacy and determinacy, consequentialism and retributivism, the judiciary and executive, political expediency, and the administrative implications of a more contested discourse of punishment (Garland 2001). Despite such upheavals, the events described in this book are just as intriguing for what they reveal about the significant continuities of post-war criminal justice policy and how frequently the same dilemmas, trade-offs, and mistakes re-emerge within penal policy (Faulkner 1991). How might we begin to reconcile this picture of continuity and change? In thinking about policy change it is helpful to return to Peter Hall's work on policy paradigms and the distinction between first and second order policy refinement and profound 'third order' changes to the aims, techniques, and overarching hierarchy of goals behind public policy (Hall 1993 p.279). When viewed in this way, the development of early release in England and Wales between 1960 and 1995 was largely defined by first and second order change. Namely, incremental adaptations to the aims and techniques of early release within a settled interpretative framework defined by a strong consequentialist ethos, a preference for technocratic fixes over substantive sentencing reform, and an orientation towards the business of government Loader has characterized as liberal elitism (Loader 2006). As

Hood and Shute noted in their description of the 'changing face of parole in England and Wales':

> The concept of parole—by which we mean the discretionary release of prisoners from custody under some form of supervision before the expiration of their sentence—has a long, honourable, yet turbulent history within the English penal system. Parole has assumed a number of different forms and had a variety of justifications. But fundamentally it has always rested on the assumption that the court, when imposing a sentence of imprisonment, especially a long sentence of imprisonment, is not in a position to judge the precise period for which it is necessary to keep an offender in custody for the protection of the public. Parole, therefore, has always been linked to some degree of indeterminacy of sentence based on consequentialist criteria. As such, it has existed in actual or potential conflict with classical, desert-based approaches to the allocation of punishment. (Hood and Shute 2002 p.835)

It is only in the mid-1980s that we begin to see the emergence of a substantive 'third order' realignment in the hierarchy of goals underpinning the criminal justice system. Wider shifts in the political economy may have begun in the 1970s with the breakdown of Keynesianism and an ascendant neoliberalism (Garland 2001; Young 2007) but these effects were not immediately felt in the criminal justice system. Rather, it took time for this transformation to work through cognate areas of public policy and materially influence the development of early release policy and practice. Two elements of this shift were particularly noteworthy. First, early release has always been defined by the oscillation between consequentialist and retributive justifications for punishment but as the 1980s progressed the terms of debate shifted decisively in favour of greater truth in sentencing. This shift towards a 'just deserts' conception of punishment saw the emergence of a retributive critique of parole that was seen as undermining the complex assessment of harm and proportionality at the point of sentence. As Andrew Ashworth noted contemporaneously:

> the spread of 'just deserts' has been associated with the decline of parole and moves towards 'real time' sentencing, developments which may be regarded as natural concomitants of an approach whereby the proportionate sentence is calculated at the outset, not to be subverted by decisions taken at later stages which alter the effective sentence length. (Ashworth 1989 p.351)

Second, as criminal justice became more politicized, parole was subject to a populist backlash from those who were critical of early release for watering down the punitive element of the sentence imposed by the courts. This line of attack had been anticipated in 1967, but by and large the parole system had been insulated from such pressures by a cross party consensus on the benefits of early release, the cautious outlook of the Parole Board and, it should also be recognized, a lack of transparency about the practical workings of the parole system in practice. This began to change in the 1980s. When viewed in comparative historical perspective, Leon Brittan's inaugural speech as Home Secretary at the 1983 Conservative Party Conference must be seen as a significant waypoint in the emergence of a recognizably 'populist punitive' critique of early release in England and Wales (Maguire 1992). Focusing on key conservative values like personal responsibility, the rule of law, and security, Brittan made great play on the 'great wave of anger against the wanton violence which disfigures our society' and drew upon this threat, either real or perceived, to justify his decision to restrict the use of parole for violent criminals:

> When it comes to the most serious and violent offenders, there is growing public criticism about the gap between the length of sentence passed and the length of the sentence actually served. I believe that in the cases where public concern is greatest, that gap can endanger public confidence in our criminal justice system. People want to know with some certainty what a sentence that has been passed actually means in practice .... I intend to respond to that feeling, and to ensure that those who commit serious crimes of violence do actually serve long terms of imprisonment. The system of remission for good behaviour is something staff need as an essential instrument of control but parole is a very different matter. What I intend—and the precise way of achieving it will be worked out with the Parole Board—is that no one sentenced to more than five years' imprisonment for an offence of violence to the person shall be released on parole except where release under supervision for just a few months before the end of the sentence is likely to reduce the long-term risk to the public, or in circumstances which are genuinely exceptional. Similarly, I regard drug traffickers sentenced to more than five years imprisonment as people who have cynically put at risk the lives of others and have often brought about their deaths. They must be treated with regard to parole in exactly the same way as serious violent offenders. They should not get it. (Conservative Party Conference 1983)

Systematic historical analysis can help to sharpen our perception of these subtle gradations of policy change. Moreover, it can equip us with the analytical tools to push back against the 'belief that we live in "new times" ... that demand new concepts, ideas, understandings' that is prevalent in so much policy development and analysis (Rock 2005 p.473). In an age of social media and the twenty-four-hour news cycle the pace of politics may have quickened but by-and-large the everyday business of government remains defined by institutional stability and incremental first and second order changes to the aims and techniques of criminal justice administration. This challenges us to think differently about contemporary policy problems. It has become almost ubiquitous to emphasize the distinctiveness of the contemporary world and the novelty of present day concerns. By failing to recognize our connection to past events, a bias Paul Rock has described as 'chronocentrism' (Rock 2005 p.473), we preclude the possibility of developing a more effective statecraft that is better attuned to the lessons of history and the opportunities to exercise power more effectively.

Postscript

In drawing this book to a close this postscript reflects upon the recent history of early release in England and Wales. A detailed account of these events is beyond the scope of this book and this postscript takes up the more modest task of tracing the headline reforms that have defined the policy and practice of early release in England and Wales since 1995. Given the space available, this involves painting with broad brush strokes and this postscript is loosely divided into three political interludes: the early years of New Labour, 1997 to 2003; the later stages of the New Labour project, 2004 to 2010; and the Coalition and Conservative governments that have followed since 2010. Unless otherwise stated the events described here are based upon existing secondary sources.

Context

When viewed in comparative historical perspective the 1990s can be seen as a watershed moment in the evolution of criminal justice in England and Wales. The decline of penal-welfarism (Garland 2001 p.34) created the space for new modes of crime control but the drivers of public policy described in this book did not fade from view entirely. Longstanding concerns, such as a rising prison population, greater recognition of human rights, financial pressures, and a desire to support the successful rehabilitation of offenders in the community continued to influence the development of early release policy and practice. Increasingly, however, these considerations were seen through the lens of the new public management, an emergent field of actuarial justice (Feeley and Simon 1992; 1994) and the politicization of crime as a fiercely contested electoral issue (Downes and Morgan 2002; 2007; 2012). While many of these forces can be seen as important, albeit foreseeable, long-term pressures on the criminal justice system, Bottoms has argued that the ascendancy of a 'populist punitiveness' characterized by 'politicians tapping into, and using for their own purposes, what they believe to be the public's generally punitive stance', was largely unpredicted and came to exert a defining influence over criminal justice towards the end of the twentieth century (Bottoms 1995 p.40). Stripped of the old certainties that defined the post-war consensus (Dutton 1997; Kavanagh and Morris 1994; Marsh et al. 1999), politicians of all stripes have sought to reconcile these countervailing forces within a 'strategy of bifurcation', that distinguishes between the moral blameworthiness and appropriate treatment of low-level acquisitive crime and dangerous offenders convicted of violent or sexual offences (Bottoms 1977). As Cavadino et al. (2013) have noted, this bifurcated approach to penal policy must be understood as both a pragmatic response to the necessary prioritization of limited resources and an active political strategy intended to project an image of toughness on questions of law and order:

> In this way 'a bifurcated policy allows government to get tough and soft simultaneously'. From the point of view of the resources crisis, bifurcation looks like a rational response: because there are so many more 'run of the mill' than 'serious offenders', a bifurcated policy should save many more resources than it costs. In terms of legitimacy with the general public such a strategy could also be effective since the public can be reassured that the really 'serious' offenders about whom they are most concerned will be kept locked up for long periods. Bifurcation can thus be seen as a pragmatic response to the combined crises of legitimacy and resources conditioned by law and order ideology. (Cavadino et al. 2013 p.27)

Over time, the logic of penal bifurcation has fundamentally reshaped sentencing practice in England and Wales, but its influence on early release is no less significant (Padfield 2012b p.104). Since Leon Brittan's speech to the 1984 Conservative Party Conference, the termination of prison sentences has emerged as a fiercely contested battleground in the 'law and order arms race' (Lacey et al. 2017 p.16) with significant consequences for the operation of parole. We will see that as the political, financial, and administrative pressures on the prison estate have grown more acute, policy-makers have pushed the bifurcation of early release to its limits in order to expedite the swift release of short sentence prisoners and restrict the pathways to release for serious offenders subject to discretionary release by the Parole Board.

1997–2003

Following the 1997 General Election, the New Labour government embarked upon an ambitious public service reform programme (Tonry 2003) but, at least initially, the policy and practice of early release was largely insulated from this reforming zeal. Following his appointment as Home Secretary, Jack Straw declined to activate the sweeping powers contained in Part II of the Crime (Sentences) Act 1997 and in the absence of wholesale reform, the early release framework established by the Criminal Justice Act 1991 was subject to incremental change. The Crime and Disorder Act 1998 revised the release arrangements of prisoners serving extended sentences for sexual or violent offences and took advantage of recent advances in electronic tagging to introduce a system Home Detention Curfew (HDC) designed to, 'manage more effectively the transition of offenders from custody back into the community' (Prison Service Order 6700). HDC initially applied to prisoners serving three months to four years who, in addition to existing parole arrangements, could apply for release on 'tag' for the final two months of the custodial portion of their sentence. As one of the few politically palatable ways to 'manage down' the prison population, the use of HDC was gradually extended under the Blair government. In May 2002, the Home Office introduced a presumption in favour of HDC for those serving sentences of three to twelve months, and in December 2002 the maximum period of time a prisoner could spend on HDC was extended to ninety days, eventually reaching 135 days in July 2003 (Padfield 2009 p.169). Steps were also taken to re-position release on temporary licence (ROTL) as a more commonplace and productive feature of prison life. Rule 9 of the Prison Rules (given legal effect by the Prison Act 1952) empowered the Home Secretary to release prisoners on compassionate grounds, but this had developed as an exceptional measure to be assessed by individual Prison Governors on a case-by-case basis. As the prison population grew, a higher volume of cases was considered by prison administrators and this prompted calls for greater equity in the treatment of inmates. Recall arrangements for those on temporary license had already been tightened by the Prisoners (Return to Custody) Act 1995 and substantial changes were introduced by the Home Office in 2001 with the publication of new guidance in Prison Service Order (PSO) 2300 and latterly PSO 6300. ROTL remained a discretionary entitlement to be decided on a case-by-case basis according to stringent risk assessment, but under the new prison rules ROTL was to be encouraged as a more common place feature of a prison sentence where it would enable prisoners 'to participate in necessary activities, outside of the prison establishment, that directly contribute to their resettlement into the community and their development of a purposeful, law-abiding life' (PSO 6300). As a result of these changes four categories of ROTL licence were made available to prison authorities, although more recent policy guidance has both curtailed and extended the use of these powers:

1. Special purpose licences: to visit dying relatives, attend funerals, for marriage or religious services, to receive medical treatment and to attend court, tribunal or inquiry proceedings.
2. Resettlement day release licences: to participate in reparative and community service projects, maintaining family ties, housing, employment, life and work skills training/education courses.
3. Resettlement overnight release licences: to maintain family ties and to make arrangements for accommodation, work/training on release, to spend time at their release address and as such is a key goal for prisoners reaching the end of their sentences.
4. Childcare resettlement licences: for those in open or semi-open conditions or categorised as suitable and who have sole caring responsibility for a child under 16. (Padfield 2009 pp.167–168)

Thereafter the pace of reform quickened. In February 2000, the Home Office announced a Quinquennial Review of the Parole Board with a remit to 'examine the parole and lifer systems, identify the key issues to be faced over the next five years and recommend appropriate changes to improve the efficiency and effectiveness of the relevant procedures' (HMPS 2001). In the ensuing discussion paper *The Comprehensive Review of Parole and Lifer Processes* over one hundred recommendations were made on matters of policy and practice (HMPS 2001). This was swiftly followed by the long-awaited 'Halliday Review' which had been established by the Home Secretary in May 2000 to consider the sentencing framework in England and Wales, with particular reference to the treatment of repeat offenders. The review was chaired by Deputy Under Secretary of State John Halliday and his final report, *Making Punishments Work: A*

Review of the Sentencing Framework for England & Wales was published in July 2001 (Home Office 2001). From the outset, Halliday was highly critical of the sentencing framework enshrined in the Criminal Justice Act 1991 for placing undue focus on the harm caused by the offence at the expense of the risk posed by the offender. More should be done, it was argued, to break the cycle of persistent offending and this required a redefining of the proportionality principle 'to take clearer and more predictable account of previous convictions. Simply requiring them to be "taken into account" is not enough' (Home Office 2001b p.iii). This ethos ran through the Halliday Report and necessitated a significant rethinking of early release policy and practice in England and Wales. Halliday recommended that for prisoners serving twelve months or less 'sentences should normally consist of a period in prison (maximum three months) and a period of compulsory supervision in the community, subject to conditions and requirements whose breach may lead to return to prison' (Home Office 2001b p.iv). For those serving fixed-term determinate sentences of twelve months or over, the focus should be on a more coherent sentencing pathway with offenders serving half their sentence in custody, followed by automatic release on licence in the community under the supervision of a probation officer. Given the increasing emphasis placed on dangerousness and risk management, a system of discretionary release should be reserved for high-risk offenders serving extended sentences (determinate and indeterminate). Halliday argued that in these more serious cases release decisions should be taken by the Parole Board on the basis of a robust risk assessment. Under the Halliday proposals, all prisoners would remain liable for recall until the termination of their sentence (Home Office 2001b p.iv).

The recommendations from the Halliday Review were largely accepted by the Home Office who set out their commitment to comprehensive sentencing reform in the White Paper *Justice for All* (Home Office 2002b). The resulting legislation, the Criminal Justice Act 2003, represented the most significant reform of the criminal justice system in England and Wales in over a decade. Under the new arrangements, the release date for prison sentences of less than twelve months was to be fixed by the courts. The Act created a new sentence of 'custody plus' consisting of an initial 'custodial period' of two to thirteen weeks, followed by a period of release on licence for a minimum of twenty-six weeks. However, this was never activated due to ongoing concerns about the likely impact of this new power upon the prison population (Ashworth 2010 p.295). For prisoners serving fixed-term determinate sentences over twelve months, the Act placed a new statutory duty on the Secretary of State to automatically release prisoners at the 'requisite custodial period' in their sentence, typically the halfway point. As Padfield has noted:

> Sections 244–246 of the 2003 Act abolished discretionary parole, as we knew it ... Under the new framework, the Home Secretary is under a duty to release any fixed-term prisoner (apart from those serving extended sentences) when he has served 'the requisite custodial period'. Offenders serving sentences of 12 months or more will be released automatically on licence at the halfway point of their sentence (with executive release up to 135 days earlier on home detention curfew ('HDC'), now possible for all determinate sentences. Upon release, the second part of their sentence will be subject to standard licence conditions and any combination of the additional prescribed conditions that the Secretary of State may determine by order. For new custodial sentences of 12 months or more, licence conditions may be imposed right up to the end of the sentence. (Padfield 2006 p.3)

In contrast, offenders sentenced to custody for serious offences were subject to a far more restrictive regime, underpinned by ongoing risk management. Chapter 5 of the Act introduced a suite of new powers to deal with 'dangerous offenders' in cases where a violent or sexual offence had been committed, as 'specified' under Schedule 15 of the Act, and 'the court is of the opinion that there is a significant risk to members of the public of serious harm occasioned by the commission by him of further specified offences'. Largely remembered for the ill-advised indeterminate sentence for public protection, or IPP (Annison 2015), the Act also made changes to the life sentence for public protection and created a lower tier sanction known as the extended sentence for public protection (EPP). The EPP was a determinate sentence available to the courts in cases of serious offending where the sentencing guidelines specified a maximum sentence of ten years' imprisonment. In such cases the courts could impose an extended period of supervision on licence, to be added to the custodial element of a sentence, where it was considered necessary for the purposes of protecting the public from serious harm. Release from the custodial element of an extended sentence was automatic at the half way point of the sentence and the offender remained on licence under the supervision of an offender manager up to a period of five years for a specified violent offence and up to eight years for specified sexual offences, as set out in Schedule 15 of the Act.

2004–2009

The Criminal Justice Act 2003 was the first major legislation of its kind in over a decade and the revised purposes of sentencing, set out in Section 142 of the Act, give some indication of just how far the aims and underlying assumptions of penal policy had travelled during that time.

(1) Any court dealing with an offender in respect of his offence must have regard to the following purposes of sentencing—
  (a) the punishment of offenders,
  (b) the reduction of crime (including its reduction by deterrence),
  (c) the reform and rehabilitation of offenders,
  (d) the protection of the public, and
  (e) the making of reparation by offenders to persons affected by their offences.

Punishment was now the primary purpose of sentencing and this had significant implications for the operation of early release. As originally conceived, the modern system of parole in England and Wales was justified on the basis of a 'recognisable peak' in an individual's rehabilitation where the interests of the community were better served by the careful reintegration of the offender back into the community rather than their continued incarceration (Shute 2003 p.385). With the emergence of a more contested discourse on law and order this calculus was almost completely inverted for the growing cohort of prisoners assessed as dangerous by the courts. While short sentence prisoners could still look forward to automatic release by the mid-way point of their sentence, often proceeded by a period of release on electronic tag, discretionary release was reserved for the prisoners serving the longest sentences whose release was contingent upon their ability to satisfy the Parole Board that they no longer represented a risk to the public (JUSTICE 2009). This shift towards risk as the central organizing principle of early release had begun with the Carlisle Committee (Home Office 1989) but it was transformed within a climate where penal populism, dangerousness, and a fear of the 'criminal other' were pervasive. Take, for example, the revised policy directions issued to the Parole Board on 1 May 2004 by the then Home Secretary David Blunkett following the passage of the Criminal Justice Act 2003:

> In deciding whether or not to recommend the release on licence, the Parole Board shall consider the risk to the public of a further offence being committed at a time when the prisoner would otherwise be in prison and whether any such risk is acceptable. This must be balanced against the benefit, both to the public and the offender, of early release back into the community under a degree of supervision, which might help rehabilitation and so lessen the risk of re-offending in the future. The Board shall take into account that safeguarding the public may often outweigh the benefits to the offender of early release. (as quoted in Padfield 2006 p.10)

As Hood and Shute had noted in an earlier study of parole decision-making the growing focus on risk-management has instilled a risk aversion that often saw decision makers overestimate the threat presented by certain individuals (2002 p.xvii). Moreover, with the main political parties locked into a narrowly defined political consensus on crime, and the Blair government unwilling to consider radical departures, the prison population continued to rise despite overall reductions in crime since the mid-1990s (see Maguire 2007 p.273). Root and branch reform of early release was politically unpalatable and policymakers were forced instead to pursue increasingly marginal gains within a bifurcated system of punishment where the only feasible option was to loosen the release arrangements of short determinate sentences. In a statement to Parliament on 19 June 2007, just five weeks after the creation of the Ministry of Justice, the Secretary of State for Justice and Lord Chancellor, Lord Falconer announced a package of reforms intended to reduce pressure on the prison estate that was struggling to accommodate a prison population which had reached 81,016, a record high for England and Wales at this time (Hansard: HC 19 Jun 2007 vol 693 c97). Alongside an acceleration of the existing prison-building programme, Lord Falconer signalled the introduction of a new 'End of Custodial Licence' (ECL) scheme. In an amendment to Rule 9 of the Prison Rules (Temporary Release) Lord Falconer informed Parliament that he was issuing new guidance to Prison Governors authorizing, 'release on licence, in accordance with existing prison rules, up to

18 days before their release date to those who have been sentenced to a determinate prison sentence of four years or less' (Hansard: HC 19 Jun 2007 vol 693 c98). Falconer was at pains to emphasize that the ECL licence was a 'temporary measure', but in practice, the scheme would remain in operation until April 2010, by which time over 80,000 prisoners had benefited from an ECL licence (Prison Service Instruction 15: 2010).

Over time, the aggregate effect of these changes has been to extend the scope of automatic release for prisoners serving determinate sentences and refocus discretionary parole not only on the most serious offences, but the growing number of prisoners deemed to be an ongoing threat to the public. Since the Criminal Justice and Immigration Act 2008, the core business of the Parole Board has largely consisted of mandatory and discretionary life sentences, extended sentences for public protection and the recall of some determinate sentence prisoners. This specialization has fundamentally altered the operation of parole in discretionary cases and many have questioned whether the Parole Board is fit for purpose given this radically redefined function (Samuel 2009). In their 2008 review of the parole system, the National Audit Office drew attention to both the quality and timeliness of the information provided to the Parole Board, the representativeness of the Parole Board membership and the frequency with which decisions were deferred pending further information. Such was the scale of the administrative backlog the NAO estimated that the compensation paid to prisoners because of deferred hearings and other administrative delays had cost the taxpayer £3 million between September 2006 and June 2007 (National Audit Office 2008 p.7). At a more fundamental level, the operation of the parole system has been increasingly difficult to reconcile with the emerging jurisprudence of the courts since the enactment of the Human Rights Act 1998 and the incorporation of the European Convention on Human Rights (ECHR) into English law. In 1991 the Home Office rejected the Carlisle Committee's call for a stronger Parole Board Chair and secretariat, favouring instead to preserve the Home Secretary's responsibility for the parole system. This proved unsustainable and in 1996 the Parole Board was reconstituted as a Non-Departmental Public Body (NDPB). Sponsorship initially sat with the Prison Service before moving to the National Offender Management Service (NOMS) in 2014 following the merger of the Prison and Probation Directorates that same year. Despite these changes in the machinery of government, the Home Secretary (and latterly the Secretary of State for Justice) retained responsibility for public appointments and, until 2016, continued to issue policy directions to the Parole Board setting the overarching framework for parole decision-making (Padfield 2006; 2016). Just as in 1967, the legal status of the Parole Board has remained a source of considerable controversy. In the case of *R v. Brooke*[1] the Court of Appeal held that the Parole Board was not sufficiently independent from the Secretary of State for Justice to discharge its responsibilities in accordance with the rule of law. At the initial hearing, heard in the Divisional Court, a number of claimants sought judicial review of their parole decisions on the grounds that the Parole Board did not meet the requirements of the common law and Article 5(4) of the ECHR for a court to have demonstrated objective independence from both the executive and the parties to the case. This argument was accepted by the Divisional Court, but legal redress was denied by Hughes LJ and Treacy J (as they then were) on the grounds that the claimants had not satisfied the court that a lack of independence had materially influenced the outcome of their parole hearings. This point of law was appealed by the government and the Court of Appeal was asked to consider the legal standing of the Parole Board. Affirming the judgment of the Divisional Court, the Lord Chief Justice Lord Phillips expressed his view that:

> Neither the Secretary of State nor his department had adequately addressed the need for the board to be and to be seen to be free of influence in relation to the performance of its judicial functions. Both by directions and by the use of his control over the appointment of members of the board the Secretary of State had sought to influence the manner in which the board carried out its risk assessment. The close working relationship between the board and the unit acting as its sponsor had tended to blur the distinction between the executive role of the former and the judicial role of the latter.[2]

Following this judgment sponsorship of the Parole Board was moved from NOMS to the Access to Justice Directorate of the Ministry of Justice. In June 2009, the government announced a public consultation on the parole system and in the accompanying

[1] [2008] EWCA Civ 29.
[2] [2008] EWCA Civ 29 at para. 78.

discussion paper *The Future of Parole* the Ministry of Justice (2009) invited views from the public on whether the Parole Board should be reconstituted as a court, tribunal, or another form of arm's length body. The consultation stimulated a wide-ranging literature on the operation of parole in England and Wales (JUSTICE 2009), but eagerly awaited proposals for reform were not forthcoming. The consultation ended shortly before pre-election Purdah for the 2010 General Election and no further action was taken when these restrictions were lifted (Padfield 2016). At the time of writing (January 2018) the Parole Board remains an executive non-departmental public body sponsored by the Ministry of Justice, although a review of the 'law, policy and procedure relating to Parole Board decisions' was announced by the Secretary of State for Justice in January 2018 following the controversial release of John Worboys.

2010–2017

The 2010 General Election marked a profound economic and political readjustment in England and Wales. The Labour Party, now led by Gordon Brown, was voted out of office after thirteen years of power and replaced by the first coalition government in the United Kingdom since the Second World War. In the aftermath of the 2008 global financial crisis the political agenda was dominated by macro-economic policy and the Coalition Agreement, signed by the Conservative Party and Liberal Democrats in May 2010, committed the government to achieve significant reductions in the structural deficit during the 2010–2015 Parliament. This emphasis on deficit reduction was quickly supplemented by an ambitious programme of public service reform Downes and Morgan have characterized as a 'New Conservatism', blending elements of traditional one nation conservatism with the nascent communitarianism of the 'Big Society' (2012 p.189). The key elements of this programme were articulated in the 2010 Public Spending Review:

- localizing power and funding, the removal of resourcing ring-fencing and 'extending the use of personal budgets for service users';
- 'cutting the burdens on frontline staff, including policing';
- increased diversity of provision in public services through further use of payment by results, removing barriers to greater

independent provision, and supporting communities, citizens and volunteers to play a greater role in shaping and providing services; and
- improving the transparent efficiency and accountability of public services. (HM Treasury 2010, as summarized by Downes and Morgan 2012 p.189)

The twin pressures of austerity and public service reform would come to define the management and delivery of public policy after 2010. In this context, the Coalition Government did initially express an appetite to break free from a rigid, cross-party consensus on crime, but in practice this was defined by a succession of false starts as efforts to import public service reform principles from health, education, and welfare were disrupted by changes in personnel and the demands of short-term political expediency. In May 2010, Kenneth Clarke was appointed Secretary of State for Justice and expressed alarm at the growth in the prison population since his tenure as Home Secretary in the early 1990s:

> I am amazed that the prison population has doubled since I was Home Secretary in the early 1990s. It stands at more than 85,000 today. This is quite an astonishing number which I would have dismissed as an impossible and ridiculous prediction if it had been put to me as a forecast in 1992. (Clarke 2010)

At a time of stringent austerity, Clarke argued, it was necessary to go 'back to basics' and in the Green Paper *Breaking the Cycle: Effective Punishment, Rehabilitation and Sentencing of Offenders* the Ministry of Justice (2010) set out its vision for a 'rehabilitation revolution' based upon prison reform, tougher community sentences and a payment by results approach to offender management. Clarke had promised a 'fundamental break with the failed and expensive policies of the past' (Clarke 2010) but, to the disappointment of many penal reformers, he was not in post long enough to realize this vision. In September 2012, David Cameron announced a major reshuffle of his Cabinet in a bid to re-energize his premiership and strengthen delivery of the government's ambitious public service reform programme. In a move intended to appease the right wing of the party, Clarke was side-lined as Minister without Portfolio and Chris Grayling was promoted to Justice Secretary. As the Minister of State for Employment, Grayling had overseen the implementation of the highly controversial Work Programme and his ascent to Secretary of State was intended to signify a 'tougher' position on law and order to his predecessor. The first task in the Minister's in-tray was implementation of the Legal Aid Sentencing and Punishment of Offenders (LASPO) Act 2012, which came into effect on 3 December 2012. The Act made significant changes to the release arrangements of short sentence prisoners. Under the Act, time spent on remand would be taken into account when determining a prisoner's release date and prisoners serving under twelve months would be released unconditionally at the half-way point of their sentence with no continuing liability for recall. Home Detention Curfew (HDC) was placed on a statutory footing and restrictions were placed on the availability of HDC for prisoners serving sentences of four years or more and those who have previously breached the terms of their HDC or prison licence. Faced with mounting judicial disquiet and a series of adverse legal challenges,[3] both the highly controversial sentence of imprisonment for public protection (IPP) and the little used extended sentence for public protection (EPP) were abolished for new cases (see Annison 2015 p.103). Significantly, this change did not apply retrospectively, and since the *Legal Aid Sentencing and Punishment of Offenders Act* came into effect thousands of IPP prisoners have remained in prison, post tariff, or on licence in the community with the possibility of recall for the rest of their lives. In their place, a new extended determinate sentence (EDS) was introduced to manage dangerous offenders where a life sentence would not be appropriate. Under the new arrangements the courts could impose an extended determinate sentence in cases where the offender was assessed as dangerous and the court had concluded that an extended licence period was necessary to protect the public from risk of harm. In such cases the individual would be denied release at the half way point of their sentence and would only become eligible for parole when they have served at least two-thirds of their prison sentence. By 2013, 656 offenders were serving an extended determinate sentence (Ministry of Justice 2014 p.7) and on 3 October

[3] Lang [2006] 1 WLR 2509, *R. (Wells) v. Parole Board; R. (Walker) v. Secretary of State for the Home Department* [2007] EWHC 1835, *R. (James) v. Secretary of State for Justice (Parole Board intervening); R. (Lee) v. Same (Same intervening); R. (Wells) v. Same (Same intervening)* [2009] UKHL 22; [2009].

2013, the Justice Secretary announced a further hardening of the sentencing framework. Under the changes announced, all individuals serving an extended determinate sentence would be denied release at the two thirds point of their sentence and could only expect to be released before the end of their sentence under strict conditions. The Parole Board was instructed to deny a positive release decision unless it was satisfied that the individual no longer 'posed a threat to society' and could demonstrate a positive record of sustained engagement with their own rehabilitation (Ministry of Justice 2013c). Justifying this approach in an inflammatory press release entitled *'Automatic "early release" axed for child rapists and terrorists'*, Grayling indicated that:

> It's outrageous that offenders who commit some truly horrific crimes in this country are automatically released from prison halfway through their custodial sentence, regardless of their behaviour, attitude and engagement in their own rehabilitation. This Government is on the side of people who play by the rules and want to get on. We need to teach criminals a lesson; you will be punished for your crime and you must earn your release, it is not an automatic right. (Ministry of Justice 2013c)

The announcement added a further layer of complexity to the already challenging workload of the Parole Board. Shortly after Grayling's announcement, the Supreme Court issued their long-awaited judgment in *Osborn Booth and Reilly v. The Parole Board*[4] which held that the Parole Board had breached both its common law duty of fairness and Article 5(4) of the European Convention on Human Rights (ECHR) by failing to offer the appellants an oral hearing as part of their parole review. The judgment required fundamental changes to how the Parole Board approached the exercise of oral hearings and the circumstances in which a prisoner was entitled to present their case in person. Since *Osborne,* far more oral hearings have been granted across the whole caseload referred to the Board and an internal review of parole case management, known as *Fair for the Future,* was launched to help clear the considerable backlog of cases that quickly developed following the Supreme Court ruling.

In parallel, Grayling signalled an acceleration of the 2010 Conservative Party Manifesto commitment to radically overhaul the management and resettlement of offenders in England and

[4] [2013] UKSC 61.

Wales. In January 2013, the government published a consultation document *Transforming Rehabilitation—A Revolution in the Way We Manage Offenders* setting out wide-ranging proposals for reform of offender management services in the community (Ministry of Justice 2013a). This was followed by a White Paper *Transforming Rehabilitation: A Strategy for Reform* (Ministry of Justice 2013b). Published in May 2013 the White Paper outlined the government's commitment to the partial privatization of the Probation Service, a reorganization of the prison estate intended to establish a 'through the prison gate' resettlement service and the extension of supervision on release to short sentence prisoners serving less than twelve months in custody.

> As we extend rehabilitation to short sentenced offenders, we will also put in place robust powers so that providers can ensure that this group engages with rehabilitation and can tackle their needs effectively. We will introduce legislation to make sure that for the first time in recent history engagement with rehabilitation is mandatory over a 12 month period for all prisoners released from short custodial sentences of up to 2 years (longer sentences already include licence periods in the community of at least 12 months). The new legislation will provide that all those released from short custodial sentences will now: first be subject to a standard licence period for the remainder of their custodial sentence served in the community; and then be subject to an additional supervision period for the purpose of rehabilitation. The licence period and supervision period together will last for 12 months. (Ministry of Justice 2013b p.12)

The new arrangements were given legal effect by the Offender Rehabilitation Act 2014. Under the Act, which came into force on 1 February 2015, the thirty-five existing Probation Trusts were abolished and replaced by a National Probation Service (NPS) and twenty-one privately run Community Rehabilitation Companies (CRCs). In many respects, the *Transforming Rehabilitation* change programme can be understood as the operational extension of penal bifurcation (Burke and Collett 2016 p.122). Under the new framework, the management of offenders assessed as low or medium risk transferred to the new CRCs, while the NPS retained responsibility for court liaison and 'dangerous offenders' considered to be of highest risk to public safety. For the first time, short sentence prisoners are now subject to a standard licence period of twelve months with a risk of recall if they fail to comply with the terms of their licence. The incremental reform of sentencing and release arrangements has fundamentally altered the composition of the prison population in England and Wales. Analysis by the Prison Reform Trust (2015) indicates that at the top end of the sentencing framework almost three times as many people were sentenced to prison sentences of ten years or more in the twelve months to March 2015 than during the same period in 2005. Perhaps of greater concern, 12,053 people were serving indeterminate sentences at the end of June 2015, compared with fewer than 4,000 in 1998 and 3,000 in 1992 (Prison Reform Trust 2015 p.21–22). The result is an ageing prison population comprising a growing core of prisoners serving long custodial sentences whose eventual release into the community will be conditional upon their ability to satisfy the Parole Board they are no longer a significant risk to the public.

Since the Offender Rehabilitation Act 2014 the countervailing pressures upon the criminal justice system have arguably become even more pronounced. The acceleration of the government's deficit reduction plan required the Ministry of Justice to find a further £1 billion of savings between 2015 and 2020, the equivalent to 15 per cent of the overall Departmental budget,. Like all areas of public policy, criminal justice has been shaped by the political fallout from the EU referendum. Following David Cameron's resignation in June 2016, Teresa May was appointed Prime Minister and in the subsequent cabinet reshuffle, Elizabeth Truss replaced Michael Gove as Justice Secretary. During her short tenure as Justice Secretary, Truss was beset by concerns over staffing levels, a high-profile riot at HMP Birmingham and the growing use of psycho-active substances within the prison estate. In parallel, Truss struggled to manage rising animosity within the legal profession for her failure, as Lord Chancellor, to publicly support the high court judges branded 'enemies of the people' for their judgment that the government could not invoke article 50 of the Lisbon Treaty without the prior consent of Parliament. A White Paper was published in November 2016 setting out proposals for reform of the criminal justice system, but a formative Prisons and Courts Bill was abandoned in April 2017 following the announcement of a snap General Election held on 8 June 2017. The Conservative Party were returned to power with a significantly diminished parliamentary majority and David Liddington was briefly appointed Secretary of State for Justice and Lord Chancellor before making way for David

Gauke in January 2018. It remains too early to judge what this extraordinary turnover of Ministers at the Ministry of Justice will mean for penal policy, but the basic challenge of reconciling the competing political, financial, and administrative pressures upon the prison system is likely to continue. In January 2018, the prison population in England and Wales stood at 84,574, an 85 per cent increase from the yearly average of 45,800 in 1992 when the Criminal Justice Act 1991 came into effect. With financial pressures likely to become even more pronounced, and no indication that the government is willing to countenance significant reform of sentencing policy or legislation at a time when Britain's exit from the European Union continues to dominate parliamentary business, the events described in this book suggest that calls for further reform of early release arrangements, particularly for those serving short sentence of imprisonment, are likely to grow.[5] The more things change, it seems, the more they stay the same.

[5] Indeed, as this book was being finalized, Andrea Albutt, the Chair of the Prison Governors Association (PGA), called publicly for the introduction of a system of executive release for sentences of under twelve months in order to reduce pressure on a prison system that was in 'crisis' <http://prison-governors-association.org.uk/pga-press-release-presidents-opening-address-10-october-2017/> accessed 9 March 2018.

Appendix 1
Early Release Key Event Timeline, 1960–1995

July 1964	Pubcrt, *Crime: A Challenge to Us All.*
October 1964	General Election. The Labour Party form new government.
August 1965	During the passage of the Murder (Abolition of Death Penalty) Act 1965, the government make a commitment to review the legal position of prisoners serving long determinate sentences.
December 1965	The Home Office publish *The Adult Offender* setting out proposals for the introduction of a system of parole in England and Wales.
March 1966	General Election. The Labour Party are returned to power.
October 1966	George Blake escapes from HMP Wormwood Scrubs. Roy Jenkins announces review of prison security by Lord Mountbatten.
July 1967	The Criminal Justice Act 1967 receives Royal Assent.
April 1968	The first tranche of 350 prisoners are released on parole.
June 1970	General Election. The Conservative Party form new government.
October 1972	The Criminal Justice Act 1972 receives Royal Assent. The Act empowers Local Review Committee's (LRC) to release certain categories of offender pre-agreed by the Parole Board.
February 1974	General Election. The Labour Party forms a minority government.
October 1974	General Election. The Labour Party form new government.
August 1975	Roy Jenkins makes Parliamentary statement announcing plans to extend the scope of the parole system to more categories of prisoner.
October 1976	The Lord Chancellor Lord Elwyn-Jones addresses the Annual General Meeting of the Magistrates Association and calls upon the courts to make greater use of shorter sentences.
July 1977	The Criminal Law Act 1977 receives Royal Assent. The Act introduces a new power to partly suspend determinate sentences.

May 1979	General Election. The Conservative Party form new government.
1980	Lord Chief Justice issues a series of practice judgements in *Bibi* and *Upton* calling upon the courts to make less use of custody.
May 1981	The Home Office publish *A Review of Parole in England and Wales 1981* calling for the introduction of a scheme of release on licence for short sentence prisoners.
October 1981	The Lord Chief Justice Lord Lane writes to the Home Secretary setting out judicial opposition to the proposed system of release on licence for short sentence prisoners.
October 1981	The Law and Order motion is defeated at the Conservative Party conference.
March 1982	The Home Office activate the partly suspended sentence provisions of The Criminal Law Act 1977.
October 1982	The Criminal Justice Act 1982 receives Royal Assent. The Act contains provisions relating to partly suspended sentences, emergency release and minimum eligibility for parole.
June 1983	General Election. The Conservative Party are returned to power.
October 1983	Leon Brittan addresses the Conservative Party conference and announces plans to limit parole eligibility for serious offenders.
July 1984	The threshold for parole eligibility is reduced from 12 months to 6 months.
November 1985	In the case of *Re Findlay* the House of Lords find that the Home Secretary had acted lawfully in issuing revised policy directions to the Parole Board restricting parole eligibility for serious offenders.
December 1985	Home Office establish a working group to review the operation of 's33 cases' of parole for short sentence prisoners.
June 1987	General Election. The Conservative Party are returned to power.
July 1987	Douglas Hurd addressed the House of Commons and introduces a system of 50 per cent remission and a review of parole in England and Wales.
September 1987	The Carlisle Committee is established and meets for the first time.
November 1988	The Carlisle Committee publish, *The Parole System in England and Wales*. The Report recommends sweeping changes to the operation of early release in England and Wales.

September 1989	The Home Office convene a conference of senior decision-makers at Ditchley Park to agree a long-term strategy for administration of the criminal justice system.
February 1990	The Home Office publish *Crime, Justice and Protecting the Public*. This includes a commitment to implement the recommendations of the Carlisle Committee.
April 1990	Riots at HMP Strangeways. Lord Woolf is asked to Chair an enquiry into disturbances at prisons across England and Wales.
November 1990	Thatcher resigns as party leader. In the ensuing Conservative Party leadership contest John Major becomes Prime Minister.
July 1991	The Criminal Justice Act 1991 receives Royal Assent.
April 1992	General Election. Conservative Party returned to power.
October 1992	The new Criminal Justice Act parole arrangements come into effect.
October 1995	Michael Howard addresses the Conservative Party conference and announces plans to abolish automatic early release.

Appendix 2
Biography of Key Actors

Sir Phillip Allen (Lord Allen of Abbeydale)	Joined the Home Office in 1934 and served in the War Cabinet 1943–1944, Deputy Secretary to the Ministry of Housing and Local Government 1955–1960. Deputy Secretary, Home Office 1960–1962, Second Secretary, HM Treasury 1963–1966 and Permanent Under-Secretary of State, Home Office 1966–1972.
Graham Angel	Assistant Under-Secretary of State, Criminal Department, Home Office, and Receiver of the Met Police, 1992–1996.
William Bohan	Home Office: Assistant Principal, 1952; Principal, 1958; Secretary, Committee on Immigration Appeals, 1966–1967; Assistant Secretary, 1967. Assistant Under Secretary of State, Home Office, 1979–1989.
Anthony Brennan	Principal Private Secretary to Home Secretary, 1963, Assistant Under Secretary of State, Criminal Department, 1971–1975, Immigration Department, 1975–1977; Deputy Under-Secretary. of State, Home Office, 1977–1982, Deputy Secretary, Northern Ireland Office, 1982–1987.
Leon Brittan (Lord Brittan of Spennithorne)	Minister of State, Home Office, 1979–1981; Chief Secretary to the Treasury, 1981–1983; Secretary of State for Home Department, 1983–1985; Secretary of State for Trade and Industry, 1985–1986.
Henry Brooke (Lord Brooke of Cumnor)	Conservative MP Hampstead, 1950–1966, Chief Secretary to the Treasury and Paymaster-General, 1961–1962; Home Secretary, 1962–1964.
Neil Cairncross	Home Office, 1948; a Private Secretary to the Prime Minister, 1955–1958, Deputy Secretary, Cabinet Office, 1970–1972, Deputy Under-Secretary of State, Home Office, 1972–1980.
Mark Carlisle (Lord Carlisle of Bucklow)	Parliamentary Under-Secretary of State, Home Office, 1970–1972; Minister of State, Home Office, 1972–1974; Secretary of State for Education and Science, 1979–1981. Chairman: Home Affairs Committee, 1983–1987; Parole Review Committee, 1987–1988.
Victor Collins (Lord Stonham)	Joint Parliamentary Under-Secretary of State, Home Office, 1964–1967, Minister of State, 1967–1969.
Sir Brian Cubbon	Home Office, 1951; Cabinet Office, 1961–1963, 1971–1975; Private Secretary to Home Secretary, 1968–1969; Permanent Under-Secretary of State, Northern Ireland Office, 1976–1979. Permanent Under-Secretary of State, Home Office, 1979–1988.

Sir Charles Cunningham	Entered Scottish Office, 1929. Private Secretary to Secretary of State for Scotland, 1935–1939; Assistant Secretary, Scottish Home Department, 1939–1941; Principal Assistant Secretary, 1941–1942; Deputy Secretary, 1942–1947; Secretary, 1948–1957; Permanent Under-Secretary of State, Home Office, 1957–1966.
Sir Maurice Drake	A Judge of the High Court of Justice, Queen's Bench Division, 1978–1995 Vice-Chairman., Parole Board, England and Wales, 1985–1986.
Sir Frederick Elwyn-Jones (Lord Elwyn-Jones)	Attorney General, 1964–1970, Lord High Chancellor of Great Britain, 1974–1979, Labour West Ham South, 1950–1974.
David Faulkner	Private Secretary to Home Secretary, 1969–1970, Assistant Under-Secretary of State, 1976; Under Secretary, Cabinet Office, 1978–1980; Home Office; Assistant Under-Secretary of State, Deputy Under-Secretary of State, 1982; Head of Criminal and Res. and Statistical Departments, 1982–1990; Principal Establishment Officer, 1990–1992.
Sir Lionel Fox	Chairman of Prison Commission for England and Wales, 1942–1960, Visiting Fellow Institute of Criminology, Cambridge 1960–1961.
Robert Fulton	Home Office, 1973–2003: Private Secretary to Permanent Secretary, 1977–1978; Radio Regulatory Department, 1978–1983; Police Department 1984–1988; Prison and Criminal Policy Deprtments, 1988–1991; Director of Prison Service Industries, 1991–1996.
Gerald Gardiner (Lord Gardiner)	Called to the Bar, 1925; KC 1948, Lord High Chancellor of Great Britain, 1964–1970.
John Harris (Lord Harris of Greenwich)	Special Assistant to Rt Hon. Roy Jenkins as Home Secretary, 1965–Nov. 1967, and as Chancellor, Nov. 1967–1970, Minister of State, Home Office, 1974–1979, Chairman Parole Board for England and Wales, 1979–1982.
Quintin Hogg (Lord Hailsham of St Marylebone)	Leader of the House of Lords, 1960–1963. Secretary of State for Education and Science, April-Oct. 1964; Lord High Chancellor of GB, 1970–1974 and 1979–1987.
John Hunt (Lord Hunt of Fawley)	Leader British Expedition to Mount Everest, 1952–1953. Chairman: Parole Board for England and Wales, 1967–1974.
Douglas Hurd (Lord Hurd of Westwell)	Minister of State, Home Office, 1983–1984; Secretary of State for Northern Ireland, 1984–1985, for Home Department, 1985–1989; Secretary of State for Foreign and Commonwealth Affairs, 1989–1995.
Roy Jenkins (Lord Jenkins of Hillhead)	Minister of Aviation, 1964–1965; Home Secretary, 1965–1967, 1974–1976; Chancellor of the Exchequer, 1967–1970; President of the European Commission, 1977–1981.

Robert Kilroy-Silk	Labour MP Ormskirk, Feb. 1974–1983; Knowsley N, 1983–1986. Member Home Affairs Select Committee, 1979–1984; Chairman: Party All-Party Penal Affairs Group, 1979–1986.
Geoffrey Lane (Lord Lane)	A Judge of the High Court of Justice, Queen's Bench Div., 1966–1974; a Lord Justice of Appeal, 1974–1979; a Lord of Appeal in Ordinary, 1979–1980, Lord Chief Justice of England, 1980–1992.
Francis Longford/ Pakenham (Lord Longford)	Personal assistant to Sir William Beveridge, 1941–1944, Lord Privy Seal, 1964–1965; Secretary of State for the Colonies, 1965–1966; Leader of the House of Lords, 1964–1968.
Sir Patrick Mayhew (Lord Mayhew of Twysden)	Minister of State, Home Office, 1981–1983; Solicitor General, 1983–1987; Attorney General, 1987–1992; Secretary of State for Northern Ireland, 1992–1997.
Michael Moriarty	Home Office Private Secretary to Parliamentary Under-Secretaries of State, 1957–1959, Private Secretary to Home Secretary, 1968; Head of Crime Policy Planning Unit, 1974–1975; Assistant Under-Secretary of State, 1975–1984. Deputy Under-Secretary of State and Principal Establishment Officer, 1984–1990.
Sydney George Norris	Principal Private Secretary to Home Secretary, 1973–1974; Assistant Secretary, 1974; seconded to HM Treasury, 1979–1981; Assistant Under Secretary of State, 1982; NI Office, Principal Establishment and Finance Officer, 1982–1985; Director of Operational Policy, Prison Department, 1985–1988; Police Department, 1988–1990; Principal Finance Officer, 1990–1996.
Hubert Parker (Lord Parker of Waddington)	Called to Bar, 1924, Judge of High Court of Justice, King's Bench Division, 1950–1954; a Lord Justice of Appeal, 1954–1958, Lord Chief Justice of England, 1958–1971.
John Patten (Lord Patten of Barnes)	Minister of State, Home Office, 1987–1992; Secretary of State for Education, 1992–1994.
Sir Louis Petch	Private Secretary to successive Chancellors of the Exchequer, 1953–1956, Second Permanent Secretary, Civil Service Department, 1968–1969, Chairman of the Parole Board Parole Board, 1974–1979.
Sir Arthur Peterson	Principal Private Secretary to Home Secretary, 1946–1949, Assistant Under-Secretary of State, Prison Department, Home Office, 1963–1964, Permanent Under-Secretary of State, Home Office, 1972–1977.
Sir Oliver Popplewell	Judge of the High Court of Justice, Queen's Bench Division, 1983–1999, Vice-Chm., Parole Board, 1986–1987 (Member, 1985–1987); Member, Parole Review Committee, 1987–1988.

Sir Frank Soskice (Lord Stow Hill)	Solicitor-General, 1945–1951; Attorney-General, 1951; Home Secretary 1964–1965; Lord Privy Seal, 1965–1966.
Vivien Stern (Baroness Stern)	Director NACRO, 1977–1996, Secretary-General, Penal Reform International, 1989–2006.
Norman Storr	Entered Indian Civil Service, 1930, Principal, Home Office, 1947; Principal, 1952, Principal, 1952, Establishment Officer, 1958, Comr and Secretary, 1962, Prison Commission; Assistant Secretary, Establishment Division Home Office, 1966–1967.
Christopher Train	Deputy Under Secretary of State, Home Office, and Director-General, Prison Service, 1983–1991, Visiting Professor, Department of Management Science, Strathclyde University, 1992–1995.
Dennis Trevelyan	Entered Home Office, 1950; Treasury, 1953–1954, Home Office: Assistant Under-Secretary of State, Broadcasting Department, 1976–1977; Deputy Under-Secretary of State and Director-General, Prison Service, 1978–1983, Deputy Secretary, Cabinet Office, 1983–1989, Principal, Mansfield College, Oxford, 1989–1996.
Sir Tasker Watkins	Lord Justice of Appeal, 1980–1993; Deputy Chief Justice of England, 1988–1993.
William Whitelaw (Lord Whitelaw)	Secretary of State for: N Ireland, 1972–1973; Employment, 1973–1974, Home Secretary, 1979–1983; Lord President of the Council and Leader, H of L, 1983–1988.
Lord Widgery	High Court Judge, 1961–1968; a Lord Justice of Appeal, 1968–1971, Lord Chief Justice of England, 1971–1980.
Barbara Wootton (Baroness Wootton of Abinger)	Professor of Social Studies, University of London, 1948–1952; Nuffield Research Fellow, Bedford College, 1952–1957, Royal Commission on Penal System, 1964–1966; Penal Advisory Council, 1966–1979.

Appendix 3
Carlisle Review Committee Membership and Terms of Reference

Membership

The Rt Hon the Lord Carlisle of Bucklow QC	Chair
Mr David Atkinson	Retired Prison Governor
Mr Navnit Dholakia JP	Member of Lewes Board of Visitors and an officer of the Commission for Racial Equality
Mr Nicholas Hinton CBE	Director General, Save the Children Fund
Dr Roger Hood	Director of the Oxford Centre for Criminological Research
Mr Martin Laing	Chairman, John Laing PLC
The Hon Mr Justice Popplewell	High Court Judge
Mrs Jenny Roberts	Chief Probation Officer of Hereford & Worcester
His Honour Judge Sir David West-Russell	President of Industrial Tribunals and a circuit judge
Mr Peter Wright CBE	Chief Constable of South Yorkshire
Mr W R Fittall	Secretary
Ms J M Langdale	Assistant Secretary

Terms of Reference

To examine the operation of the parole scheme in England and Wales, its relationship with the current arrangements for remission, time spent in custody on remand, and partly and fully suspended sentences and their effect on the time which offenders sentenced to imprisonment spend in custody after sentence; and to make recommendations on

(a) whether a parole scheme should be retained as a feature of the penal system; and, if so,

(b) its objectives
(c) any changes which should be made in law or practice affecting either eligibility or criteria; or, alternatively,
(d) any different scheme which night be introduced to provide for release before expiry of sentence, either generally or for particular categories of prisoners; and, in any case,
(e) the possibility of prisoners released before expiry of sentence being required to perform work of value to the community, having regard to the relative cost and effectiveness of custodial and non-custodial disposals;

having regard to the need for

i. fairness and consistency in the treatment of prisoners;
ii. a clear understanding of the relationship between determination of the original sentence by judicial decision and the proper limits of executive discretion in giving effect to it;
iii. public and judicial confidence in any new arrangements that might be proposed;
iv. the resource implications of any changes proposed.

Source: Home Office 1989c.

Bibliography

Adonis, A and Thomas, K (eds) (2004) *Roy Jenkins: A Retrospective*. Oxford: Oxford University Press.

Advisory Council on the Penal System (1978) *Sentences of Imprisonment: A Review of Maximum Penalties* (Chairperson: Baroness Serota). London, HMSO.

Allen, F (1981) *The Decline of the Rehabilitative Ideal: Penal Policy and Social Purpose*. New Haven: Yale University Press.

Allen, L (2004) 'A Young Home Secretary' in Adonis, A and Thomas, K (eds) *Roy Jenkins: A Retrospective*. Oxford: Oxford University Press.

Allott, AN (1976) 'It's My View' *The Magistrate*, January: 29.

Amenta, E (2009) 'Making the Most of an Historical Case Study: Configuration, Sequence, Casing, and the US Old-Age Pension Movement' in Ragin, CC and Byrne, D (eds) *The Handbook of Case-Oriented Methods*. Thousand Oaks, CA: Sage.

Anderson, P and Mann, N (1997) *Safety First: The Making of New Labour*. London: Granta.

Annison, H (2015) *Dangerous Politics: Risk, Political Vulnerability and Penal Policy*. Oxford: Oxford University Press.

Ashworth, A (1989) 'Criminal Justice and Deserved Sentences' *Criminal Law Review*, May: 242–251.

Ashworth, A (2010) *Sentencing and Criminal Justice* 5th edn. Cambridge: Cambridge University Press.

Audit Commission (1984) *Improving Economy, Efficiency and Effectiveness in Local Government in England and Wales*. London: HMSO.

Bachrach, P and Baratz, M (1962) 'Two Faces of Power' *American Political Science Review*, 56: 947–952.

Bachrach, P and Baratz, M (1970) *Power and Poverty: Theory and Practice*. London: Oxford University Press.

Bailey, V (eds) (1981) *Policing and Punishment in Nineteenth Century Britain*. London: Croom Helm.

Barker, V (2009) *The Politics of Imprisonment: How the Democratic Process Shapes the Way America Punishes Offenders*. New York: Oxford University Press.

BBC *Inside Story* (1979) '*Parole*' first aired BBC 2. 11 June 21:40.

BBC *Panorama* (1982) '*The Sentence of the Court*', first aired BBC1 22 February 20: 10.

Biderman, AD and Reiss, JR (1967) 'On Exploring the "Dark Figure" of Crime' *The Annals of the American Academy of Political and Social Science*, 374(1): 1–15.

Bottomley, AK (unpublished) *The Operation of Parole at Hull Prison 1969–1970.*

Bottomley, AK (1973a) *Decisions in the Penal Process.* London: Robertson.

Bottomley, AK (1973b) 'Parole Decisions in a Long Term Closed Prison' *British Journal of Criminology*, 13(1): 26–40.

Bottomley, AK (1981) The Pitfalls of Automatic Parole, *The Times*, 21 August 1981.

Bottomley, AK (1990) 'Parole in Transition: A Comparative Study of Origins, Developments and Prospects for the 1990s' *Crime and Justice*, 12: 319–374.

Bottoms, AE (1977) 'Reflections on the Renaissance of Dangerousness' *Howard Journal of Criminal Justice*, 16: 70–96.

Bottoms AE (1979) 'The Advisory Council and the Suspended Sentence' *Criminal Law Review*, 437–446.

Bottoms, AE (1981) 'The Suspended Sentence in England, 1967–1978' *British Journal of Criminology*, 21: 1–26.

Bottoms, AE (1995) 'The Philosophy and Politics of Punishment and Sentencing' in Clarkson, C and Morgan, R (eds) *The Politics of Sentencing Reform.* Oxford: Clarendon Press.

Bottoms, AE and Stevenson, S (1992) 'What Went Wrong? Criminal Justice Policy in England and Wales 1945–1970' in Downes, D (ed) *Unravelling Criminal Justice.* Basingstoke: Macmillan.

Bryman, A (2008) *Social Research Methods* 3rd edn. Oxford: Oxford University Press.

Bulpitt, J (1986) 'The Discipline of the New Democracy: Mrs Thatcher's Domestic Statecraft' *Political Studies*, XXXIV: 19–39.

Burke, L and Collett, S (2016) 'Transforming Rehabilitation: Organizational Bifurcation and the End of Probation as We Knew It?' *Probation Journal*, 63(2): 120–135.

Butler, D and Butler, G (2000) *Twentieth-Century British Political Facts, 1900–2000* 8th edn. Basingstoke: Palgrave Macmillan.

Cabinet Office (2016) *Independent Commission on Freedom of Information Report.* London: HMSO.

Callaghan, J (1982) 'Cumber and Variables' in RIBA (eds) *The Home Office: Perspectives on Policy and Administration Bicentenary Lectures.* London: RIPA.

Caro, R (2012) *The Passage of Power: The Years of Lyndon Johnson, Volume 4.* New York: Random House.

Cavadino, M and Dignan, J (2006a) 'Penal Policy and Political Economy' *Criminology & Criminal Justice*, 6(4): 435–456.

Cavadino, M and Dignan, J (2006b) *Penal Systems: A Comparative Approach.* London: Sage Publications.

Cavadino, M, Dignan, J, and Mair, G (2013) *The Penal System: An Introduction* 5th edn. London: Sage.

Cavadino, P et al. (1977) *Parole: The Case for Change*. Chichester: Rose [for the National Association for the Care and Resettlement of Offenders].

CCBH (2010) *Centre for Contemporary British History Witness Seminar: The Criminal Justice Act 1991*. Unpublished.

Clark, C (2014) *The Sleepwalkers: How Europe Went to War in 1914*. New York: Harper.

Clarke, K (2010) *The Government's Vision for Criminal Justice Reform, 30 June 2010*. London: Centre for Crime and Justice Studies <https://www.crimeandjustice.org.uk/resources/governments-vision-criminal-justice-reform>, accessed 5 March 2017.

Conservative Party (1966) *Crime Knows No Boundaries*. London: Conservative Party Office.

Conservative Party (1981) *Verbatim Report of the Platform Speeches: Conservative Party Conference, Blackpool, October 1981*. London: Conservative Party.

Conservative Party (1983) *Verbatim Report of the Platform Speeches: Conservative Party Conference, Blackpool, October 1983*. London: Conservative Party.

Conservative Party (1987) *The Next Moves Forward*. London: Conservative Party.

Conservative Party (2010) *Invitation to Join the Government of Britain*. London: Conservative Party.

Cross, R (1962) Indeterminate Prison Sentences *The Listener*, 15 February 1962.

Cross, R (1966) 'Penal Reform in 1965: A Mass of Unexplained and Unfounded Assumptions' *Criminal Law Review*, April: 184–194.

Crossman, R (1975) *The Diaries of a Cabinet Minister, Volume 1: Minister of Housing 1964–66*. London: Hamish Hamilton and Jonathan Cape.

Crossman, R (1976) *The Diaries of a Cabinet Minister, Volume 2: Lord President of the Council and Leader of the House of Commons 1966–68*. London: Hamish Hamilton and Jonathan Cape.

Dahl, R (1961) *Who Governs?* New Haven: Yale University Press.

Daily Express (1966) This is London 1966. *Daily Express*, 13 August 1966.

Daily Express (1975) Roy Opens the Cell Door. *Daily Express*, 5 August 1975.

Daily Express (1981) Willie is Howled Down. *Daily Express*, 14 October 1981.

Daily Express (1987) The Fatal Flaw in Hurd's Plan for Freedom. *Daily Express* 14 October 1987.

Daily Mail (1975) No Room in Jail. *Daily Mail*, 5 August 1975.

Daily Mail (1976) 'More Parole' to Ease Jail Crush. *Daily Mail*, 16 November 1976.

Daily Mail (1987a) Jails: 3,500 to Go Free. *Daily Mail*, 17 July 1987.
Daily Mail (1987b) Out for a Good Time. *Daily Mail*, 14 August 1987.
Daily Mirror (1966a) Storm over Mountbatten Jail Enquiry. *Daily Mirror*, 25 October 1966.
Daily Mirror (1966b) Five Escape on Day of Jail Report. *Daily Mirror*, 23 December 1966.
Daily Mirror (1966c) The Great Escape Rush: Jenkins Acts. *Daily Mirror*, 28 December 1966.
Daily Mirror (1968) Three Shot Dead after Killer is Given Parole. *Daily Mirror*, 12 August 1968.
De Certeau, M (1988). *The Writing of History*, trans. T. Conley. New York: Columbia University Press.
De Giorgi, A (2006) *Re-thinking the Political Economy of Punishment: Perspectives on post-Fordism and Penal Politics.* Aldershot: Ashgate.
Derrida, J (1996) *Archive Fever: A Freudian Impression*, trans. Eric Prenowitz. Chicago: University of Chicago Press.
Dignan, J (1984) 'The Sword of Damocles and the Clang of the Prison Gates: Prospects on the Inception of the Partly Suspended Sentence' *Howard Journal of Criminal Justice*, 23: 183–200.
Douglas, M (1986) *How Institutions Think*. London: Routledge & Kegan Paul.
Downes, D (ed) (1992) *Unravelling Criminal Justice*. Basingstoke: Macmillan.
Downes, D and Morgan, R (2002) 'The Skeletons in the Cupboard: The Politics of Law and Order at the Turn of the Millennium' in Maguire, M, Morgan, R, and Reiner, R (eds) *The Oxford Handbook of Criminology* 3rd edn. Oxford: Oxford University Press.
Downes, D and Morgan, R (2007) 'No Turning Back: The Politics of Law and Order into the Millennium' in Maguire, M, Morgan, R, and Reiner, R (eds) *The Oxford Handbook of Criminology* 4th edn. Oxford: Oxford University Press.
Downes, D and Morgan, R (2012) 'Overtaking on the Left? The Politics of Law and Order in the "Big Society"' in Maguire, M, Morgan, R, and Reiner, R (eds) *The Oxford Handbook of Criminology* 5th edn. Oxford: Oxford University Press.
Dutton, D (1997) *British Politics since 1945: The Rise and Fall and Re-Birth of Consensus* 2nd edn. Oxford: Blackwell.
Dworkin, R (1986) *Law's Empire*. London: Fontana Press.
Editorial (1989) 'Remission, Parole and Prison Sentences—Half a Loaf' *Criminal Law Review*, February: 81–86.
Eldredge, N and Gould, SJ (1972) 'Punctuated Equilibria: An Alternative to Phyletic Gradualism' in Schopf, TJM (ed) *Models in Paleobiology*. Freeman, San Francisco.

Elliott, M (2007) 'The Parole Board and the Changing Face of Public Law' in Padfield, N (ed) *Who to Release? Parole, Fairness and Criminal Justice*. Devon: Willan Publishing.

Farrall, S and Hay, C (2010) 'Not so Tough on Crime' *British Journal of Criminology*, 50: 550–569.

Farrall, S et al. (2014) *Using Ideas Derived from Historical Institutionalism to Illuminate the Long-Term Impacts on Crime of 'Thatcherite' Social and Economic Policies: A Working Paper*. Long-term Trajectories of Crime in the UK Working Paper No.1 <http://papers.ssrn.com/sol3/papers.cfm?abstract_id=2376136>.

Faulkner, D (1990) *Policy, Legislation and Practice, a Paper Presented to a Conference of European and Canadian Judges held in Breda, the Netherlands, October 1990*. Unpublished.

Faulkner, D (1991) *Continuity and Change in the Home Office*. An Occasional Paper written in 1991 for internal use within the Home Office <http://www.watersidepress.co.uk/acatalog/CCHO_paper.pdf>.

Faulkner, D (2006) *Crime the State and Citizen: A Field Full of Folk* 2nd edn. Winchester: Waterside Press.

Faulkner, D (2010) *Introductory Paper: The Criminal Justice Act 1991* in CCBH Centre for Contemporary British History Witness Seminar: The Criminal Justice Act 1991. Unpublished.

Faulkner, D (2014) *Servant of the Crown: A Civil Servant's Story of Criminal Justice and Public Service Reform*. London: Waterside Press.

Feeley, M and Simon, J (1992) 'The New Penology: Notes on the Emerging Strategy of Corrections and its Implications' *Criminology*, 30(4): 449–474.

Feeley, M and Simon, J (1994) 'Actuarial Justice: The Emerging New Criminal Law' in Nelken, D (ed) *The Futures of Criminology*. London: Sage.

Foucault, M (1977) *Discipline and Punish: The Birth of the Prison*, trans. A. Sheridan. London: Allen Lane-Penguin.

Foucault, M (1980) 'Prison Talk' in Gordon, C (ed) *Power / Knowledge: Selected Interviews and Other Writings*. New York: Pantheon Books.

Foucault, M (1991) 'Governmentality' in Burchell et al. (eds) *The Foucault Effect*. Harvester: Wheatsheaf.

Fox, L (1952) *The English Prison and Borstal Systems: An Account of the English Prison and Borstal Systems after the Criminal Justice Act 1948, with a Historical Introduction and an Examination of the Principles of Imprisonment as a Legal Punishment*. London: Routledge & Keegan Paul.

Freedom of Information/FOI: *BV3/26, Working Party on Parole*. Unpublished.

Freedom of Information/FOI: *BV3/30/2. Parole Board Policy Study Group to Review the Present Parole System*. Unpublished.
Freedom of Information/FOI: *BV3/35. Parole Board Policy Study Group to Review the Present Parole System*. Unpublished.
Freedom of Information/FOI: *BV3/38. Review of Parole in England and Wales by the Home Office*. Unpublished.
Freedom of Information/FOI: *BV3/47. Request from the Home Secretary for the Extension of the Parole System*. Unpublished.
Freedom of Information/FOI: *BV3/52. FULL Board Meeting 8th Annual Overnight Planning Conference at Cumberland Lodge 22–23 September 1977*. Unpublished.
Freedom of Information/FOI: *BV3/66. 43rd Meeting of the General Purpose Committee on 1/11/82*. Unpublished.
Freedom of Information/FOI: *BV3/8/2. Informing a Prisoner of the Parole Board's Reasons for not Recommending Parole; Pilot Experiment*. Unpublished.
Freedom of Information/FOI: *HO 291/2081. Prisons + Prisoners on Licence Miscellaneous + General. Working Group on Parole*. Unpublished.
Freedom of Information/FOI: *HO 291/2138. Prisons + Prisoners – Release on Licence. Parole*. Unpublished.
Freedom of Information/FOI: *HO 495/21. Penal Policy: Early Release for Short Sentence Offenders*. Unpublished.
Freedom of Information/FOI (January 2013) *Diversion of Offenders from Custody: Parole for Short Sentence Prisoners*. Unpublished.
Freedom of Information/FOI (May 2013) Includes:

- *9 October 1981: Letter from the Lord Chief Justice to the Home Secretary.*
- *23 December 1985: Letter from HO Official to Mr Justice Drake.*
- *23 December 1985: Letter from HO Official to Dr Douglas Acres.*
- *7 February 1986: Letter from Mr Douglas Acres to HO Official.*
- *5 April 1989: Submission on Working Group on the Carlisle Review of Parole.*
- *20 July 1989: Submission on Report of the Working Group on the Carlisle Review of Parole.*
- *1 March 1990: Submission on New Parole Scheme: Shape and Mechanics.*
- *19 March 1990: Submission on New Parole Scheme: The Legislative Framework—Shape and Mechanics.*
- *16 July 1990: Briefing: NACRO's Response to the White Paper and Meeting with the Home Secretary on 23 July 1990.*
- *20 July 1990: Submission on Home Secretary's Meeting with NACRO on 23 July 1990.*

• *18 Jan 1991: Submission on Parole.* Unpublished.

Freedom of Information/FOI (April 2014) *The Integrated Resource and Policy Planning Document, 1988–1989.* Unpublished.

Garland, D (1985) *Punishment and Welfare: A History of Penal Strategies.* Aldershot: Gower.

Garland, D (1996) 'The Limits of the Sovereign State: Strategies of Crime Control in Contemporary Society' *British Journal of Criminology,* 36(4): 445–471.

Garland, D (2000) 'The Culture of High Crime Societies' *British Journal of Criminology,* 40(3): 347–375.

Garland, D (2001) *The Culture of Control: Crime and Social Order in Contemporary Society.* Oxford: Oxford University Press.

Garland, D and Sparks, R (eds) (2000) *Criminology and Social Theory.* Oxford: Oxford University Press.

Gibson, B (2008) *The New Home Office* 2nd edn. Hook: Waterside Press.

Gibson, B et al. (1994) *The Youth Court: One Year Onwards.* Winchester: Waterside Press.

Green, D (2008) *When Children Kill Children: Penal Populism and Political Culture.* Oxford: Oxford University Press.

Gunn, S and Faire, L (eds) (2012) *Research Methods for History.* Edinburgh: Edinburgh University Press.

Hall, PA (1986) *Governing the Economy: The Politics of State Intervention in Britain and France.* New York: Oxford University Press.

Hall, PA (1993) 'Policy Paradigms, Social Learning, and the State: The Case of Economic Policy Making in Britain' *Comparative Politics,* 25(3): 275–296.

Hall, PA (2009) 'Historical Institutionalism in Rationalist and Sociological Perspective' in Mahoney, J and Thelen, K (eds) *Explaining Institutional Change: Ambiguity, Agency, and Power.* Cambridge University Press.

Hall, PA and Soskice, D (2001) *Varieties of Capitalism: The Institutional Foundations of Comparative Advantage.* Oxford: Oxford University Press.

Hall, PA and Taylor, R (1996) 'Political Science and the Three New Institutionalisms' *Political Studies,* 44(4): 936–957.

Hall, PA and Taylor, R (1998) 'The Potential of Historical Institutionalism: A Response to Hay and Wincott' *Political Studies,* 46(5): 958–962.

Hall-Williams, JE (1964) 'Alternatives to Definite Sentences' *Law Quarterly Review,* 80: 41–62.

Hall-Williams, JE (1975) 'Natural Justice and Parole' *The Criminal Law Review,* February: 82–97.

Hartley, LP (1953) *The Go-Between*. London: Hamish Hamilton.
Hawkins, K (1973) 'Parole Procedure: An Alternative Approach' *British Journal of Criminology*, 13(1): 6–25.
Hay, C (2002) *Political Analysis: A Critical Introduction*. Oxford: Oxford University Press.
Hay, C (2006) 'Constructivist Institutionalism' in Rhodes, RAW, Binder, S, and Rockman, B (eds) *The Oxford Handbook of Political Institutions*. Oxford: Oxford University Press.
Hay, C and Wincott, D (1998) 'Structure, Agency and Historical Institutionalism' *Political Studies*, 116: 951–957.
Hennessy, P (2012) *Distilling the Frenzy: Writing the History of One's Own Times*. London: Biteback Publishing.
Hermiston, R (2013) *The Greatest Traitor: The Secret Lives of Agent George Blake*. London: Aurum Press.
HM Inspector of Prisons (1982) *Annual Report of HM Chief Inspector of Prisons for England and Wales, 1981*: London: HMSO.
HM Inspector of Prisons (1987) *Annual Report of HM Chief Inspector of Prisons for England and Wales, 1986*: London: HMSO.
HMPS (2001) *The Comprehensive Review of Parole and Lifer Processes*. London: Home Office.
HMSO (1895) *Report from the Departmental Committee on Prisons, Report, Minutes of Evidence, Appendices and Index. (Gladstone Committee)*. C.7702. London: HMSO.
HMSO (1969) *Report of the Parole Board for 1968*. HC 290. London: HMSO.
HMSO (1970) *Report of the Parole Board for 1969*. HC 48. London: HMSO.
HMSO (1971) *Report of the Parole Board for 1970*. HC 437. London: HMSO.
HMSO (1972) *Report of the Parole Board for 1971*. HC 274. London: HMSO.
HMSO (1973) *Report of the Parole Board for 1972*. HC 272. London: HMSO.
HMSO (1974) *Report of the Parole Board for 1973*. HC 143. London: HMSO.
HMSO (1975) *Report of the Parole Board for 1974*. HC 380. London: HMSO.
HMSO (1976a) *Report of the Parole Board for 1975*. HC 432. London: HMSO.
HMSO (1976b) *Third Report from the Committee of Public Accounts together with the Proceedings of the Committee, part of the Minutes of Evidence and Appendices. Session 1975–76*. London: HMSO.
HMSO (1977) *Report of the Parole Board for 1976*. HC 388. London: HMSO.

HMSO (1978) *Report of the Parole Board for 1977.* HC 497. London: HMSO.
HMSO (1979) *Report of the Parole Board for 1978.* HC 105. London: HMSO.
HMSO (1980) *Report of the Parole Board for 1979.* HC 651. London: HMSO.
HMSO (1981) *Report of the Parole Board for 1980.* HC 340. London: HMSO.
HMSO (1982) *Report of the Parole Board for 1981.* HC 388. London: HMSO.
HMSO (1983) *Report of the Parole Board for 1982.* HC 16. London: HMSO.
HMSO (1984) *Report of the Parole Board for 1983.* HC 463. London: HMSO.
HMSO (1985) *Report of the Parole Board for 1984.* HC 411. London: HMSO.
HMSO (1986) *Report of the Parole Board for 1985.* HC 428. London: HMSO.
HMSO (1987) *Report of the Parole Board for 1986.* HC 5. London: HMSO.
HMSO (1988) *Report of the Parole Board for 1987.* HC 509. London: HMSO.
HMSO (1989) *Report of the Parole Board for 1988.* HC 412. London: HMSO.
HMSO (1990) *Report of the Parole Board for 1989.* HC 385. London: HMSO.
HMSO (1991) *Report of the Parole Board for 1990.* HC 481. London: HMSO.
HMSO (1992) *Report of the Parole Board for 1991.* HC 43. London: HMSO.
HMSO (1993) *Report of the Parole Board for 1992.* HC 712. London: HMSO.
HMSO (1994) *Report of the Parole Board for 1993.* HC 450. London: HMSO.
HMSO (1995) *Report of the Parole Board for 1994.* HC 531. London: HMSO.
HMSO (1996) *Report of the Parole Board for 1995 and 1995/96.* HC 506. London: HMSO.
HM Treasury (2010) *Spending Review 2010*, Cm 7942. London: HMSO.
HM Treasury (2011) *The Green Book: Appraisal and Evaluation in Central Government.* London: HMSO.
Hobsbawm, E (1997) *On History.* London: Abacus.
Home Office (1895) *Report from the Departmental Committee on Prisons (Gladstone Committee).* Cmnd 7702. London: HMSO.

Home Office (1958) *The After-care and Supervision of Discharged Prisoners. Report of the Advisory Council on the Treatment of Offenders*. London: HMSO.
Home Office (1959) *Penal Practice in a Changing Society: Aspects of Future Development (England and Wales)*. Cmnd 645. London: HMSO.
Home Office (1962) *Report of the Commissioners of Prisons for the Year 1961*. Cmnd 1798. London: HMSO.
Home Office (1963a) *Preventive Detention. Report of the Advisory Council on the Treatment of Offenders*. London: HMSO.
Home Office (1963b) *The Organisation of After-Care. Report of the Advisory Council on the Treatment of Offenders*. London: HMSO.
Home Office (1965) *The Adult Offender*. London: HMSO.
Home Office (1966) *Report of the Inquiry into Prison Escapers and Security (Mountbatten Report)*. Cmnd. 3175. London: HMSO.
Home Office (1973) *Report on the Work of the Prison Department 1972*. Cmnd 5375. London: HMSO.
Home Office (1975) *Criminal Statistics England and Wales 1974. Statistics Relating to Crime and Criminal Proceedings for the Year 1974*. Cmnd 6168. London: HMSO.
Home Office (1976) *Review of Criminal Justice Policy*. London: HMSO.
Home Office (1978) *Criminal Statistics England and Wales 1977. Statistics Relating to Crime and Criminal Proceedings for the Year 1978*. Cmnd 7289. London: HMSO.
Home Office (1979) *Report of the Committee of Inquiry into the United Kingdom Prison Services (May Committee)*. Cmnd 7673. London: HMSO.
Home Office (1980) *Criminal Statistics England and Wales 1979. Statistics Relating to Crime and Criminal Proceedings for the Year 1979*. Cmnd 8098. London: HMSO.
Home Office (1981a) *Parole—Your Questions Answered*. London: HMSO.
Home Office (1981b) *Review of Parole in England and Wales*. London: HMSO.
Home Office (1984) *Criminal Justice: A Working Paper*. London: HMSO.
Home Office (1985) *Criminal Statistics England and Wales 1984. Statistics Relating to Crime and Criminal Proceedings for the Year 1984*. Cmnd 9621. London: HMSO.
Home Office (1986a) *Criminal Justice: A Working Paper* rev edn. London: HMSO.
Home Office (1986b) *Criminal Justice: Plans for Legislation*. Cmnd 9658. London: HMSO.
Home Office (1987) *Report on the Work of the Prison Service 1986/87*. Cm 246. London: HMSO.

Home Office (1988a) *Punishment, Custody and the Community*. Cm 424. London: HMSO.
Home Office (1988b) *Prison Statistics England and Wales 1987*. Cm 547. London: HMSO.
Home Office (1988c) *Report on the Work of the Prison Service April 1987—March 1988*. Cm 516. London: HMSO.
Home Office (1989) *The Parole System in England and Wales. Report of the Review Committee*. Cm 532. London: HMSO.
Home Office (1990a) *Crime, Justice and Protecting the Public*. Cm 965. London: HMSO.
Home Office (1990b) *Statistics of Offences against Prison Discipline and Punishments, England and Wales*. Cm 1236. London: HMSO.
Home Office (1991) *Prison Disturbances April 1990; Report of an Inquiry by the Rt. Hon. Lord Justice Woolf and his Honour Judge Stephen Tumim*. Cm 1456. London: HMSO.
Home Office (1996) *Protecting the Public: The Government's Strategy on Crime in England and Wales'*. Cm 3190. London: HMSO.
Home Office (2000) 'Police Service Personnel, England and Wales, as at 31 March 2000. Home Office Statistical Bulletin' <http://webarchive.nationalarchives.gov.uk/20110218135832/http://rds.homeoffice.gov.uk/rds/pdfs/hosb1500.pdf>.
Home Office (2001) *Making Punishments Work: Report of a Review of the Sentencing Framework for England and Wales (The Halliday Report)*. London: HMSO.
Home Office (2002a) *Criminal Statistics England and Wales 2001. Statistics Relating to Criminal Proceedings for the Year 2001*. Cm 5696. London: HMSO.
Home Office (2002b) *Justice for All*. London: HMSO.
Home Office (2012) 'A Summary of Recorded Crime Data from 1898 to 2001/02' <https://www.gov.uk/government/uploads/.../rec-crime-1898-2002.xls>.
Hood, R (1965) *Borstal Reassessed*. London: Heinemann.
Hood, R (1974a) *Tolerance and the Tariff: Some Reflections on Fixing the Time Prisoners Serve in Custody*. NACRO Reprint No 11. London: NACRO.
Hood, R (1974b) 'Some Fundamental Dilemmas of the English Parole System and a Suggestion for Reform' in Thomas, DA (ed) *Parole: Its Implications for the Criminal Justice and Penal Systems*. Cambridge: University of Cambridge Institute of Criminology.
Hood, R (ed) (1974c) *Crime, Criminology and Public Policy: Essays in Honour of Sir Leon Radzinowicz*. London: Heinemann.
Hood, R and Shute, S (1994) *Parole in Transition: Evaluating the Impact and Effects of Changes in the Parole System—Phase One, Establishing the Baseline*. Oxford Centre for Criminological

Research, Occasional Paper 13. Oxford: Centre for Criminological Research.

Hood, R and Shute, S (2000) *The Parole System At Work: A Study of Risk Based Decision-Making.* Home Office Research Study No. 202. London: Home Office.

Hood, R and Shute, S (2002) 'The Changing Face of Parole in England and Wales: A Story of Some Well-Intentioned Reforms and Unintended Consequences' in Prittwitz et al. (eds) *Festschrift für Klaus Lüderssen (Nomos verlagsgessellschaft)*. Unpublished.

House of Commons (1978) *Fifteenth Report from the Expenditure Committee: The Reduction of Pressure on the Prison System, Volume I—Report, Volume II—Minutes of Evidence, Volume III Minutes of Evidence and Appendices, H.C. 662, Session 1977–1978.* London: HMSO.

House of Commons (1981) *Fourth Reports from the Home Affairs Committee: The Prison Service.* HC 412. London: HMSO.

House of Commons (2010) Social background of MPs. SN/SG/1528 <http://researchbriefings.files.parliament.uk/documents/SN01528/SN01528.pdf>, accessed 10 May 2016.

House of Lords (1989) *Report of the Select Committee on Murder and Life Imprisonment.* HL Paper 78. London: HMSO.

Howarth, D (2013) 'Lawyers in the House of Commons' in Feldman, D (ed) *Law in Politics, Politics in Law.* Oxford: Hart.

Howard League (1981) *Freedom on Licence: The Development of Parole and Proposals for Reform.* London: Quartermaine House.

Howard League (2009) *Do Better Do Less: The Report of the Commission on English Prisons Today.* London: The Howard League for Penal Reform.

Hunt, A and Wickham, G (1994) *Foucault and Law: Towards Sociology of Law as Governance.* Sterling VA: Pluto Press.

Hurd, D (1987) 'The Home Office Today' *The House Magazine*, 367(12): 14–15.

Hurd, D (2003) *Memoirs.* London: Little Brown.

Jenkins, R (1975) 'On Being a Cabinet Minister' in Herman, V and Alt, JE (eds) *Cabinet Studies: A Reader.* London: Macmillan.

Jenkins, R (1991) *A Life at the Centre.* London: Macmillan.

Jessop, B (1990) *State Theory: Putting Capitalist States in their Place.* Cambridge: Polity Press.

Jessop, B (2000) *Institutional (Re)turns and the Strategic-Relational Approach, Paper Presented at the Institutional Theory in Political Science Conference, Ross Priory, Loch Lomand, 18–19 October.* Unpublished.

Jewkes, Y and Bennett, J (eds) (2008) *Dictionary of Prisons and Punishment.* Cullompton Devon: Willan Publishing.

Jones, C (1993) 'Auditing Criminal Justice' *British Journal of Criminology*, 33(3): 187–202.
JUSTICE (2009) *A New Parole System for England and Wales*. London: JUSTICE.
Karstedt, S (2010) 'New Institutionalism in Criminology: Approaches, Theories and Themes' in McLaughlin, E and Newburn, T (eds) *The Sage Handbook of Criminological Theory*. London: Sage.
Kavanagh, D and Morris, P (1994) *Consensus Politics from Attlee to Thatcher*. Oxford: Blackwell.
King, MT (2012) 'Working With / In the Archives' in Gunn, S and Faire, L (eds) *Research Methods for History*. Edinburgh: Edinburgh University Press.
Kingdon, J (2003) *Agendas, Alternatives and Public Policies* 2nd edn. New York: Addison-Wesley Publishers.
Koffman L (2006) 'The Rise and Fall of Proportionality: The Failure of the Criminal Justice Act 1991' *Criminal Law Review*, 4: 281–299.
Kuhn, T (1962) *The Structure of Scientific Revolutions*. Chicago: University of Chicago Press.
Labour Party (1964a) *Crime: A Challenge to Us All (The Longford Report)*. London: Labour Party.
Labour Party (1964b) *Let's Go with Labour for the New Britain: The Labour Party's Manifesto for the 1964 General Election*. London: Labour Party.
Lacey, N (2008) *The Prisoners' Dilemma: Political Economy and Punishment in Contemporary Democracies*. Cambridge: Cambridge University Press.
Lacey, N (2013) 'The Rule of Law and the Political Economy of Criminalisation: An Agenda for Research' *Punishment & Society*, 15(4): 349–366.
Lacey, N, Soskice, D, and Hope, D (2017) 'Understanding the Determinants of Penal Policy: Crime, Culture and Comparative Political Economy', *Working Paper 13: LSE International Inequalities Institute* http://www.lse.ac.uk/International-Inequalities/Assets/Documents/Working-Papers/Working-Paper-13-Understanding-the-Determinants-of-Penal-Policy-crime-culture-and-comparative-political-economy.pdf, accessed 16 October 2017.
Laws, J (1995) 'Law and Democracy' *Public Law*, (72): 89.
Lester, A (ed) (1967) *Essays and Speeches by Roy Jenkins*. London: Collins.
Levi, M (1997) 'A Model, a Method, and a Map: Rational Choice in Comparative and Historical Analysis' in Lichbach, MI and Zuckerman, AS (eds) *Comparative Politics: Rationality, Culture, and Structure*. New York: Cambridge University Press.
Liebling, A (2007) 'Why Fairness Matters in Criminal Justice' in Padfield, N (ed) *Who to Release? Parole, Fairness and Criminal Justice*. Cullompton: Willan Publishing.

Loader, I (2006) '"Fall of the 'Platonic Guardians": Liberalism, Criminology and Political Responses to Crime in England and Wales' *British Journal of Criminology*, 46(4): 561–586.

Loader, I and Sparks, R (2004) 'For an Historical Sociology of Crime Policy in England and Wales since 1968' *Critical Review of International Social and Political Philosophy*, 7(2): 5–32.

Lodge, TS (1974) 'The Founding of the Home Office Research Unit' in Hood, R (ed) *Crime, Criminology and Public Policy: Essays in Honour of Sir Leon Radzinowicz*. London: Heinemann.

Loughlin, M (2003) *The Idea of Public Law*. Oxford: Oxford University Press.

Lowndes, V (2010) 'The Institutional Approach' in Marsh, D and Stoker, G (eds) *Theory and Method in Political Science* 3rd edn. Basingstoke: Palgrave MacMillan.

LSE Archive and Special Collections: *Morris T/6, Labour Party Study Group on Penal Reform (Longford Committee), 1963–1964. Outline of Group's Work and Memoranda of Evidence*. Unpublished.

LSE Archive and Special Collections: *Morris T/7, Labour Party Study Group on Penal Reform (Longford Committee), 1963–1964. Draft Reports, Correspondence and Background Papers, also Copy of Published Report ('Crime: A Challenge to Us All')*. Unpublished.

Lukes, S (1974) *Power: A Radical View*. London: Macmillan.

Lukes, S (1978) 'Power and Authority' in Bottomore, TB and Nisbet, R (eds) *A History of Sociological Thought*. London: Heinemann.

Macintyre, S (1999) *A Concise History of Australia*. Cambridge: Cambridge University Press.

Mackay, S (1980) *Prospects for Parole: A Review of the Present System and Attitudes towards it*. London: NACRO.

Maguire, M (1992) 'Parole' in Stockdale, E and Casale, S (eds) *Criminal Justice Under Stress*. London: Blackstone Press.

Maguire, M (2007) 'Crime Data and Statistics' in Maguire, M, Morgan, R, and Reiner, R (eds) *The Oxford Handbook of Criminology* 4th edn. Oxford: Oxford University Press.

Mahoney, J and Rueschemeyer, D (2003) *Comparative Historical Analysis in the Social Sciences*. Cambridge: Cambridge University Press.

March, JG and Olsen, JP (1984) 'The New Institutionalism: Organizati onal Factors in Political Life' *The American Political Science Review*, 78(3): 734–749.

March, JG and Olsen, JP (1989) *Rediscovering Institutions: The Organisational Basis of Politics*. New York: Free Press.

March, JG and Olsen, JP (2006) 'Elaborating the "New Institutionalism"' in Rhodes, RAW, Binder, S, and Rockman, B (eds) *The Oxford Handbook of Political Institutions*. Oxford: Oxford University Press.

Marsh, D and Stoker, G (eds) (2010) *Theory and Methods in Political Science* 3rd edn. Basingstoke: Palgrave Macmillan.

Marsh, D et al. (eds) (1999) *Post-war British Politics in Perspective.* Cambridge: Polity.

Martinson, R (1974) 'What Works? Questions and Answers about Prison Reform' *The Public Interest*, 35: 22–45.

Mathiesen, T (2006) *Prison on Trial.* Winchester: Waterside Press.

Matthews, R (2005) 'The Myth of Punitiveness' *Theoretical Criminology*, 9(2): 175–201.

McCabe, S (1985) 'The Powers and Purposes of the Parole Board' *Criminal Law Review*: 489.

McConville, S (1981) *A History of English Prison Administration, Volume 1, 1760–1877.* London: Routledge.

McKie, D and Cook, C (1972) *The Decade of Disillusion: British Politics in the Sixties*. London: Basingstoke.

McLaughlin, E (1994) *Community, Policing and Accountability.* Aldershot: Avebury.

Merton, RK (1967) *On Theoretical Sociology*. New York: Free Press.

Messner, S and Rosenfeld, R (2007) *Crime and the American Dream* 4th edn. Belmont: Wadsworth.

Ministry of Justice (2009) *The Future of Parole (Consultation Paper 14/09)*. London: HMSO.

Ministry of Justice (2010) *Breaking the Cycle: Effective Punishment, Rehabilitation and Sentencing of Offenders, Cm 7972.* London: HMSO.

Ministry of Justice (2013a) *Transforming Rehabilitation: A Revolution in the Way We Manage Offenders, Consultation Paper CP1/2013.* London: HMSO.

Ministry of Justice (2013b) *Transforming Rehabilitation: A Strategy for Reform.* London: HMSO.

Ministry of Justice (2013c) *Press Release: Automatic 'Early Release' Axed for Child Rapists and Terrorists, 4 October 2013.* Direct Gov Website. Accessed 9 July 2017.

Ministry of Justice (2014) *Offender Management Statistics Quarterly: July–September 2013* <https://www.gov.uk/government/uploads/system/uploads/attachment_data/file/276074/omsq-q3-2013.pdf>.

Molesworth, W (1838) *Report of the Select Committee of the House of Commons on Transportation; Together with a Letter from the Archbishop of Dublin on the Same Subject: And Notes by Sir William Molesworth, Bart. Chairman of the Committee.* London: Henry Hooper.

Moran, M, Rein, M, and Goodin, RE (eds) (2006) *The Oxford Handbook of Public Policy*. Oxford: Oxford University Press.

Morgan, N (1983) 'The Shaping of Parole in England and Wales' *Criminal Law Review*, 131–151.

Moriarty, MJ (1977) 'The Policy-Making Process: How It Is Seen from the Home Office' in Walker, N and Giller, H (eds) *Penal Policy-Making in England: Papers Presented to the Cropwood Round-Table Conference*. Cambridge: University of Cambridge Institute of Criminology.

Morris, P and Beverley, F (1975) *On Licence: A Study of Parole*. London: Wiley.

Morris RM (1980) 'Home Office Crime Policy Planning: Six Years On' *Howard Journal*, 19(3): 135–141.

Morris, T (1980) 'The Case for Abolishing Parole' *New Society*, 19 June 1980: 282–284.

Morris, T (1989) *Crime and Criminal Justice in Britain since 1945*. Oxford: Basil Blackwell.

Mullin, C (2010) *Decline and Fall*. London: Profile Books.

National Audit Office (1985) *Report by the Comptroller and Auditor General on Home Office and Property Services Agency: Programme of the Provision of Prison Places*. London: HMSO.

National Audit Office (2008) *Protecting the Public: The Work of the Parole Board (HC 239)*. London: HMSO.

Nelken, D (2009) 'Comparative Criminal Justice: Beyond Ethnocentrism and Relativism' *European Journal of Criminology*, 6: 291–311.

Nevitte, N (1996) *The Decline of Deference: Canadian Value Change in Cross-National Perspective*. Peterborough: Broadview Press.

Newburn, T (2003a) *Crime and Criminal Justice Policy* 2nd edn. London: Longman.

Newburn, T (ed) (2003b) *Handbook of Policing*. Cullompton, Devon: Willan.

Newburn, T (2007a) *Criminology*. Cullompton: Willan.

Newburn, T (2007b) '"Tough on Crime": Penal Policy in England and Wales' in Michael, T (ed) *Crime, Punishment and Politics in Comparative Perspective. Volume 36 of Crime and Justice: A Review of Research*. Chicago, IL: University of Chicago Press.

Newburn, T (2015) 'The 2011 English Riots in Recent Historical Perspective' *British Journal of British Criminology*, 55(1): 39–64.

Nichol, D (2007) 'Who Should We Keep Locked Up?' in Padfield, N (ed) *Who to Release? Parole, Fairness and Criminal Justice*. Cullompton: Willan Publishing.

North, D (1990) *Institutions, Institutional Change and Economic Performance*. Cambridge: Cambridge University Press.

Nuttall, C (1973) 'Parole Selection' *British Journal of Criminology*, 13(1): 41–45.

Nuttall, C et al. (1977) *Parole in England and Wales, Home Office Research Study No. 38*. London: HMSO.

Office for Budget Responsibility (2015) 'Historical official forecasts database' <http://budgetresponsibility.org.uk/pubs/Historical-official-forecasts-database1.xls>, accessed 1 September 2015.

O'Malley, P (1998) *Crime and the Risk Society*. Dartmouth: Ashgate.

O'Malley, P (2000) 'Criminologies of Catastrophe?: Understanding Criminal Justice on the Edge of the New Millennium' *Australian and New Zealand Journal of Criminology*, 33(3): 153–167.

ONS (2013) 'Crime in England & Wales, Year Ending March 2014—Bulletin Tables' <http://www.ons.gov.uk/ons/rel/crime-stats/crime-statistics/period-ending-september-2013/chd-figure-3.xls>, accessed 31 August 2015.

Oxford, Bodleian Library, Conservative Party Archive: Shelfmark: *CRD 4/30/7/26. 1987 General Election: Manifesto Planning Notes and Briefs (I), 1987*. Unpublished.

Oxford, Bodleian Library, Conservative Party Archive: Shelfmark: *LCC 1/2/7. Agendas, Minutes, LCC (66) 134–146, and Papers, LCC (66) 106–118, 7 November–19 December 1966: LCC (66) 115 Criminal Justice Bill by Mr. Hogg, 2 December 1966*. Unpublished.

Padfield, N (2006) 'The Parole Board in Transition' *Criminal Law Review*, 3: 3–23.

Padfield, N (ed) (2007) *Who to Release? Parole, Fairness and Criminal Justice*. Devon: Willan Publishing.

Padfield, N (2009) 'Parole and Early Release: The Criminal Justice and Immigration Act 2008 Changes in Context' *Criminal Law Review*, 3: 166–187.

Padfield, N (2016) 'Editorial: A New Chapter for the Parole Board' *Criminal Law Review* 6: 379–380.

Padfield N, Morgan R, and Maguire M (2012a) 'Out of Court, Out of Sight? Criminal Sanctions and Non-Judicial Decision Making' in Maguire, M, Morgan R, and Reiner R (eds) *The Oxford Handbook of Criminology* 5th edn. Oxford: Oxford University Press.

Padfield, N, Smit, DZ, and Dunkel, F (2012b) *Release from Prison: European Policy and Practice* 2nd edn. Abingdon: Routledge.

Parliamentary All-Party Penal Affairs Group (1980) *Too Many Prisoners*. Chichester: Barry Rose.

Parliamentary All-Party Penal Affairs Group (1981) 'Still Too Many Prisoners: An Assessment of the Government's Response to the Report "Too Many Prisoners" since June 1980'. London: P.A.P.P.A.G.

Penal Affairs Consortium (1996) *Protecting the Public: Comments on the White Paper*. News Release 19 July 1996.

Peters, BG (2005) *Institutional Theory in Political Science: The 'New Institutionalism'* 2nd edn. London: Continuum.

Pierson, P (1994) *Dismantling the Welfare State? Reagan, Thatcher, and the Politics of Retrenchment*. Cambridge: Cambridge University Press.

Pierson, P (2000) 'Increasing Returns, Path Dependence, and the Study of Politics' *The American Political Science Review*, 94(2): 251–267.

Pierson, P (2004) *Politics in Time*. Princeton: Princeton University Press.

Pimlott, B (1992) *Harold Wilson*. London: Harper Collins.

Plowden Report (1961) *Public Expenditure Planning and Control*. London: HMSO.

Poggi, G (1965) 'A Main Theme of Contemporary Sociological Analysis: Its Achievements and Limitations' *British Journal of Sociology*, 16(4): 283–294.

Popplewell, O (2003) *Benchmark: Life, Laughter and the Law*. London: I.B. Tauris.

Pratt, J (2007) *Penal Populism*. London: Routledge.

Prison and Borstal Governors' Branch of the Society of Civil and Public Servants (1977) *Reducing the Prison Population, Recommendations submitted to the Secretary of State by the Society of Civil and Public Servants on behalf of the Prison Governors*. Unpublished.

Prison and Borstal Governors' Branch of the Society of Civil and Public Servants (1978) *Memorandum from the Prison and Borstal Governors' Branch of the Society of Civil and Public Servants to the House of Commons Expenditure Committee's Inquiry into The Administration of the Prison Service, HMSO 1978*. Unpublished.

Prison Reform Trust (1987) *Parole System Review: Memorandum by the Prison Reform Trust*. London: Prison Reform Trust.

Prison Reform Trust (2015) Bromley Briefings Prison Factfile Autumn 2015 <http://www.thebromleytrust.org.uk/files/bromleybriefingsautumn2013.pdf>, accessed 15 October 2017.

Radzinowicz, L (1999) *Adventures in Criminology*. London: Routledge.

Radzinowicz, L and Hood, R (1986) *A History of the English Criminal Law and its Administration from 1750, Volume 5: The Emergence of Penal Policy*. Oxford: Oxford University Press.

Rawls, JA (1999) *A Theory of Justice* rev edn. Oxford: Oxford University Press.

Reiner, R (2000) *The Politics of the Police* 3rd edn. Oxford: Oxford University Press.

Reiner, R (2007) 'Political Economy, Crime and Criminal Justice' in Maguire M, Morgan R, and Reiner R (eds) *The Oxford Handbook of Criminology* 4th edn. Oxford: Oxford University Press.

Reiner, R (2010) 'Citizenship, Crime, Criminalization: Marshalling a Social Democratic Perspective' *New Criminal Law Review*, 13(2): 241–261.

Reiner, R (2016) *Crime, the Mystery of the Common-Sense Concept*. Cambridge: Polity Press.

Roberts, J and Hough, M (eds) (2002) *Changing Attitudes to Punishment: Public Opinion, Crime and Justice*. Cullompton: Willan Publishing.

Roberts, J et al. (eds) (2003) *Penal Populism and Public Opinion: Lessons from Five Countries*. Oxford: Oxford University Press.
Robson, C (2013) *Real World Research* 4th edn. Oxford: Blackwell.
Rock, P (1990) *Helping Victims of Crime: The Home Office and the Rise of Victim Support in England and Wales*. Oxford: Oxford University Press.
Rock, P (2005) 'Chronocentrism and British Criminology' *British Journal of Sociology*, 56(3): 473–479.
Royal Commission (1863) *Royal Commission to Inquire into the Operation of the Acts Relating to Transportation and Penal Servitude*. PP, [3190], XXI Session, 1863.
RIPA (1982) *The Home Office: Perspectives on Policy and Administration Bicentenary Lectures*. London: Royal Institute of Public Administration.
Rusche, G and Kircheimer, O (1939) *Punishment and Social Structure*. New York: Columbia University Press.
Ryan, M (1983) *The Politics of Penal Reform*. London: Longman.
Ryan, M (2003) *Penal Policy and Political Culture: Four Essays on Policy and Process*. Winchester: Waterside Press.
Samuels, A (2009) 'Early Release of Prisoners' *Criminal Law & Justice Weekly*, 21 (May): 173.
Sandbrook, D (2010) *State of Emergency—The Way We Were: Britain 1970–1974*. London: Allen Lane.
Sandel, M (1998) *Liberalism and the Limits of Justice* 2nd edn. Cambridge: Cambridge University Press.
Sanders, E (2006) 'Historical Institutionalism' in Rhodes, RAW, Binder, SA, and Rockman, BA (eds) *The Oxford Handbook of Political Institutions*. Oxford: Oxford University Press.
Sartori, G (1970) 'Concept Misformation in Comparative Politics' *American Political Science Review*, 64(4): 1033–1053.
Scull, A (2015) *Madness in Civilization: A Cultural History of Insanity, from the Bible to Freud, from the Madhouse to Modern Medicine*. London: Thames and Hudson Ltd.
Seale, G (1995) *Country Before Party*. London: Longman.
Sewell, WH (1996) 'Three Temporalities: Toward an Eventful Sociology' in McDonald, T (ed) *The Historic Turn in the Human Sciences*. Ann Arbor: University of Michigan Press.
Sewell, WH (2006) *Logics of History: Social Theory and Social Transformation*. Chicago: University of Chicago Press.
Shute, S (2003) 'The Development of Parole and the Role of Research in its Reform' in Zedner, L and Ashworth, A (eds) *The Criminological Foundations of Penal Policy: Essays in Honour of Roger Hood*. Oxford: Oxford University Press.
Shute, S (2013) 'On the Outside Looking In: Reflections on the Role of Inspection in Driving Up Quality in the Criminal Justice System' *Modern Law Review*, 76(3): 494–528.

Simon, J (2007) *Governing Through Crime: How the War on Crime Transformed American Democracy and Created a Culture of Fear.* New York: Oxford University Press.

Skocpol, T (1992) *Protecting Soldiers and Mothers.* Cambridge: Harvard University Press.

Smith, MJ, Marsh, D, and Richards, D (1993) 'Central Government Departments and the Policy Process' *Public Administration,* 71(4): 567–594.

Steinmo, S (2008) 'Historical Institutionalism' in Porta, DD and Keating, M (eds) *Approaches and Methodologies in the Social Sciences: A Pluralist Perspective.* Cambridge: Cambridge University Press.

Steinmo, S, Thelen, K, and Longstreth, F (eds) (1992) *Structuring Politics: Historical Institutionalism in Comparative Analysis.* New York: Cambridge University Press.

Streeck, W and Thelen, K (eds) (2005) *Beyond Continuity: Institutional Change in Advanced Political Economies.* Oxford: Oxford University Press.

Tata, C (1990) Coherence and Consensus: Parole Policy in England and Wales. Department of Politics, University of Hull. Unpublished.

The Churchill Archives Centre: *Churchill/HLSM 2/17/22, September 1966–January 1967. The Papers of Lord Hailsham: Political Miscellaneous Correspondence, O-P. Correspondence with Enoch Powell about the Criminal Justice Bill, December 1966 (2).With two posters about …* Unpublished.

The Churchill Archives Centre: *Churchill/HLSM 2/42/2/16, November 1966–December 1966. The Papers of Lord Hailsham: Minutes, agendas and papers of the Leader's Consultative Committee … (66) 114, 25 November 1966; 'Criminal Justice Bill' by Quintin Hogg, LCC (66) 115 … 8 December 1966; 'The Housing Subsidies Bill' by Geoffrey Rippon, LCC (66) 117.* Unpublished.

The Churchill Archives Centre: *Churchill/ILLD 2/14/10, July 1985–January 1989. The Papers of Sir Ian Lloyd: Home Office … Research Notes, Leaflets, Copy of the Criminal Law Bill, Parliamentary Questions. Correspondents include: Douglas Hurd …* Unpublished.

The Churchill Archives Centre: *Churchill/KNNK 2/3/1/42, September 1991. The Papers of Neil Kinnock: NEC Meeting … Draft Statement by Roy Hattersley on Crime; Draft Timetables and a List of …* Unpublished.

The Guardian (1974) Jenkins Promises Reforms to Cut Gaol Population. *The Guardian*, 22 May 1974.

The Guardian (1975) The Gaol Population Explosion. *The Guardian*, 24 July 1975.

The Guardian (1981a) Coming Clean on Parole. *The Guardian*, 11 June 1981.

The Guardian (1981b) Automatic Prison Parole Plans Dropped. *The Guardian*, 27 November 1981.
The Guardian (1984) Brittan's Parole Policy 'Risks Confrontation in Prisons'. *The Guardian*, 6 February 1984.
The Guardian (1985) Society Tomorrow: Honesty is the Best Policy/ Home Secretary Hurd and the Conservative Party's Conference Debate on Law and Order. *The Guardian*, 9 October 1985.
The Guardian (1987a) Crowding May Free 6,000 Prisoners. *The Guardian*, 12 March 1987.
The Guardian (1987b) Backdoor' Solution for Gaols: How Successive Home Secretaries have Failed to Resolve Prison Crisis. *The Guardian*, 13 July 1987.
The Guardian (1987c) Leading Article: Penal policy under the microscope. *The Guardian*, 22 July 1987.
The Guardian (1988a) The Personal Touch in Punishment—Recent and Sometimes Bizarre Examples of 'Creative Sentencing'. *The Guardian*, 17 November 1988.
The Guardian (1988b) Parole Changes too Timid, Say Reformers. *The Guardian*, 26 November 1988.
The Guardian (1989) Attacks Went on after Early Release/Murder of Anna Humphries. *The Guardian*, 6 July 1989.
The Guardian (1990) Softly, Softly along the Road to a New Sentencing Policy: John Carvel on How Bulging Prisons Forced the Home Office to Take a Deep Breath. *The Guardian*, 10 November 1990.
The Independent (1989a) Ministers Reject Radical Overhaul of Parole System. *The Independent*, 24 January 1989.
The Independent (1989b) New Pressure to Lift Parole Ban. *The Independent*, 17 July 1989.
Thelen, K and Steinmo, S (1992) 'Historical Institutionalism in Comparative Politics' in Steinmo, S, Thelen, K, and Longstreth, F (eds) *Structuring Politics: Historical Institutionalism in Comparative Analysis*. New York: Cambridge University Press.
The National Archives (TNA): *CAB 128/39/83. Cabinet Conclusions, 2 December 1965*. Unpublished.
The National Archives (TNA): *CAB 128/41. Cabinet Conclusion 5. Penal Reform, 4 August 1966*. Unpublished.
The National Archives (TNA): *CAB 129/24. Cabinet Memorandum. Criminal Justice Bill. Memorandum by the Secretary of State for the Home Department, 2 August 1966*. Unpublished.
The National Archives (TNA): *CAB 134/1997a. Home Affairs Committee Meeting, 5 August 1965*. Unpublished.
The National Archives (TNA): *CAB 134/1997b. Home Affairs Committee Meeting, 19 November 1965*. Unpublished.
The National Archives (TNA): *CAB 134/1997c. Home Affairs Committee Memorandum, 14 September 1965*. Unpublished.

The National Archives (TNA): *CAB 134/2001a. Home Affairs Committee Memorandum, 2 August 1965*. Unpublished.

The National Archives (TNA): *CAB 134/2001b. Home Affairs Committee Memorandum, 15 November 1965*. Unpublished.

The National Archives (TNA): *CAB 134/2001c. Home Affairs Committee Memorandum, 22 September 1965*. Unpublished.

The National Archives (TNA): *CAB 134/2001d. Home Affairs Committee Memorandum, 18 November 1981*. Unpublished.

The National Archives (TNA): *CAB 134/2956. Legislation Committee, 22 November 1966*. Unpublished.

The National Archives (TNA): *HO 223/4. Home Office Divisional Organisation and Functions, 1953–1963*. Unpublished.

The National Archives (TNA): *HO 263/148. United Kingdom Prison Services Committee: Evidence and Papers. Uncirculated Evidence and Papers. Incentive Remission*. Unpublished.

The National Archives (TNA): *HO 291/727 Home Office: Criminal (CRI and CCS Symbol Series) Files. Magistrates' Court Act 1952: Proposals for Amendments. Amendments which Might Be Included in Criminal Justice Bill 1966*. Unpublished.

The National Archives (TNA): *HO 291/1246. Home Office: Criminal (CRI and CCS Symbol Series) Files. Examining Further Ways of Reducing Prison*. Unpublished.

The National Archives (TNA): *HO 291/1509. Records Created or Inherited by the Home Office, Ministry of Home Security, and Related Bodies*. Unpublished.

The National Archives (TNA): *HO 303/98. Home Office: Publicity and Public Relations (PTY Symbol Series) Files. Parole Board: Publicity Proposals, including a Documentary Film*. Unpublished.

The National Archives (TNA): *HO 330/335. Home Office: Probation (PBN Symbol Series) Files. Criminal Justice Bill 1976: Consultation with Probation and After-Care Service*. Unpublished.

The National Archives (TNA): *HO 383/219. Home Office: After-care (AFC Symbol Series) Files. Prisons: Welfare Arrangements, Annual Reports, Inspectors' Reports. Central Council of Probation Committees: Future After-care Responsibilities of Committees*. Unpublished.

The National Archives (TNA): *HO 384/99. Early Release of Prisoners*. Unpublished

The National Archives (TNA): *HO 391/433. Home Office: Prison Department: General (PDG Symbol Series) Files. Young Offenders. Detention Centres. Remission: Increase from One-Third to One-Half of Term of Detention for Offenders Aged 14 to under 17 Committed to Detention Centres; Detention Centre (Amendment) Rules 1975*. Unpublished.

The National Archives (TNA): *HO 495/4. Crime Policy Planning Committee*. Unpublished.

The National Archives (TNA): *HO 495/9. Crime Policy Planning Committee*. Unpublished.

The National Archives (TNA): *HO 495/13. Crime Policy Planning Committee*. Unpublished.

The National Archives (TNA): *HO 495/14. Crime Policy Planning Committee*. Unpublished.

The National Archives (TNA): *HO 495/18. Crime Policy Planning Committee*. Unpublished.

The National Archives (TNA): *HO 495/23. Crime Policy Planning Committee*. Unpublished.

The National Archives (TNA): *HO 495/25. Crime Policy Planning Committee*. Unpublished.

The National Archives (TNA): *PCOM 9/665. Prison Commission and Home Office, Prison Department: Registered Papers: Series 2. Emergency Measures: Release of Prisoners and Borstal Inmates. See also PCOM 9/2351*. Unpublished.

The National Archives (TNA): *PCOM 9/2248. Prison Commission and Home Office, Prison Department: Registered Papers: Series 2. Release on Licence: Method of Selection; Criminal Justice Bill 1966*. Unpublished.

The National Archives (TNA): *PCOM /9/2261. Prison Commission and Home Office, Prison Department: Registered Papers: Series 2. Parole Board and Local Review Committees: Setting Up; Formulation of Rules*. Unpublished.

The National Archives (TNA): *PCOM 14/18. Prison Commission and Home Office, Prison Department: Board of Prison Commissioners and Prisons Board: Minutes and Papers. Meeting with Sir Philip Allen, PUS, Home Office, 16 December 1971: Minutes and Papers*. Unpublished.

The National Archives (TNA): *PREM 13/999. Prime Minister's Office: Correspondence and Papers, 1964–1970. LEGAL PROCEDURE. Proposals for Reform of Penal System Relating to Adult Prisoners: Provisions of Criminal Justice Bill*. Unpublished.

The National Archives (TNA): *T 353/104. Treasury: Public Sector Group and Home and General Registered Files (2HE and 2HG series). Public Expenditure Survey: Law and Order Programmes; Briefs for Ministerial Discussions*. Unpublished.

The Telegraph (2007) Obituary: Lord Allen of Abbeydale. *The Telegraph*, 29 November 2007.

The Times (1966) Mr. Jenkins Booed by Police. *The Times*, 21 October 1966.

The Times (1981) Wider Parole Proposed to Ease Crisis in Jails. *The Times*, 14 June 1981.

The Times (1983) Editorial: The Place of Parole. *The Times*, 3 December 1983.

The Times (1984) Brittan Policy 'Damaging Parole Board Morale'. *The Times*, 21 February 1984.

The Times (1987) Parliament: Hurd Moves Will Lessen Jail Overcrowding. *The Times*, 17 July 1987.

The Times (1989a) Hurd Faces Call to Monitor Violent Criminals; Conviction of David Evans. *The Times*, 6 July 1989.

The Times (1989b) Evans Gets Life Sentence for Schoolgirl's Murder; David Evans. *The Times*, 6 July 1989.

The Times (1995) Howard's Jail Plan Rejected by Taylor. *The Times*, 13 October 1995.

Thomas, DA (ed) (1974) *Parole: Its Implications for the Criminal Justice and Penal Systems: Cropwood Round-Table Conference.* Cambridge: University of Cambridge, Institute of Criminology.

Thomas, DA (1982) 'The Partly Suspended Sentence' *Criminal Law Review*, May 1982: 288–295.

Tilly, C (2006) 'Why and How History Matters' in Goodin, RE and Tilly, C (eds) *The Oxford Handbook of Contextual Political Analysis.* New York: Oxford University Press.

Tonry, M (ed) (2003) *Confronting Crime: Crime Control Policy Under New Labour.* Cullompton: Willan Publishing.

Turner, M (1966a) *Prison without Tears: An Examination of Parole.* Unpublished.

Turner, M (1966b) 'Prepared for Freedom' *The Listener*, 1 August 1966.

UK Statistics Authority (2014) *Statistics on Crime in England and Wales (Produced by the Office for National Statistics).* Assessment of Compliance with the Code of Practice for Official Statistics. Assessment Report 268 January 2014 <https://www.statisticsauthority.gov.uk/archive/assessment/assessment/assessment-reports/assessment-report-268---statistics-on-crime-in-england-and-wales.pdf>, accessed 15 October 2017.

Uslaner, EM (2002) *The Moral Foundations of Trust.* Cambridge: Cambridge University Press.

von Hirsch, A (1976) *Doing Justice: The Choice of Punishments.* New York: Hill & Wang.

von Hirsch, A (1985) *Past and Future Crimes: Deservedness and Dangerousness in the Sentencing of Criminals.* New Brunswick, NJ: Rutgers University Press.

von Hirsch, A and Ashworth, A (1998) *Principled Sentencing* 2nd edn. Oxford: Hart Publishing.

Wacquant, L (2005) *Urban Outcasts: Toward a Sociology of Advanced Marginality.* Cambridge: Polity Press.

Wacquant, L (2009a) *Punishing the Poor: The Neoliberal Government of Social Insecurity.* Duke University Press: Durham, NC.

Wacquant, L (2009b) *Prisons of Poverty.* Minneapolis: University of Minnesota Press.
Walker, N (1962) 'The Sentence of the Court' *The Listener*, 28 June 1962.
Walker, N and Giller, H (eds) (1976) *Penal Policy-Making in England: Papers Presented to the Cropwood Round-Table Conference.* Cambridge: University of Cambridge Institute of Criminology.
Watkins, A (1992) *A Conservative Coup: The Fall of Margaret Thatcher.* London: Duckworth.
Weir, M (1992) 'Ideas and the Politics of Bounded Innovation' in Steinmo, S, Thelen, K, and Longstreth, F (eds) *The New Institutionalism: State, Society and Economy.* New York: Cambridge University Press.
West, DJ (ed) (1972) *The Future of Parole: Commentaries on Systems in Britain and U.S.A.* London: Duckworth.
Whitelaw, W (1989) *The Whitelaw Memoirs.* London: Headline.
Williams, M (1972) *Inside Number 10.* London: Coward, McCann and Geoghegan.
Windlesham, L (1987) *Responses to Crime, Volume 1: Ministering to a Gentler Age.* Oxford: Clarendon Press.
Windlesham, L (1989) 'Life Sentences: The Paradox of Indeterminacy' *Criminal Law Review*, 244–252.
Windlesham, L (1993) *Responses to Crime,Volume 2: Penal Policy in the Making.* Oxford: Clarendon Press.
Windlesham, L (1996) *Responses to Crime, Volume 3: Legislating with the Tide.* Oxford: Clarendon Press.
Windlesham, L (2001) *Responses to Crime, Volume 4: Dispensing Justice.* Oxford: Clarendon Press.
Wootton, B (1959) *Contemporary Trends in Crime and its Treatment, The Nineteenth Clarke Hall Lecture.* London: Clarke Hall Fellowship.
Yin, RK (2003) *Case Study Research: Design and Methods.* Thousand Oaks: Sage Publications.
Young, J (1988) 'Radical Criminology in Britain: The Emergence of a Competing Paradigm' *British Journal of Criminology*, 28(2): 159–183.
Young, J (1999) *The Exclusive Society: Social Exclusion, Crime and Difference in Late Modernity.* London: Sage Publications.
Young, J (2003) 'In Praise of Dangerous Thoughts' *Punishment & Society*, 5(1): 97–108.
Young, J (2007) *The Vertigo of Late Modernity.* London: Sage Publications.
Zander, M (1988) *A Matter of Justice.* Oxford: Oxford University Press.
Zedner, L and Ashworth, A (eds) (2003) *The Criminological Foundations of Penal Policy: Essays in Honours of Roger Hood.* Oxford: Oxford University Press.
Zimring, F and Johnson, D (2006) 'Public Opinion and the Governance of Punishment in Democratic Political Systems' *Annals of the American Academy of Political and Social Science*, 605: 266–280.

Copyright acknowledgements

Frontispiece and figures 1.6, 3.4, and 6.1 reproduced with the permission of the National Archives.

Figures 1.4, 6.2, and 7.3 are Crown Copyright and are reproduced under the terms of the Open Government Licence <http://www.nationalarchives.gov.uk/doc/open-government-licence/version/3/>

Figures 4.1 and 7.1 are reproduced with the permission of the Daily Express/N&S Syndication.

Figure 9.1 is reproduced with the permission of Michael Bennett.

There are instances where we have been unable to contact the copyright holder. If notified the publisher will be pleased to rectify any errors or omissions at the earliest opportunity.

Index

Adult Offender, The (Home Office White Paper, 1965) 55, 73–8, 79
  background 73–5
  criticism 76
Advisory Council on the Penal System (ACPS) 117–18
Advisory Council on the Treatment of Offenders 67, 83
Aftercare and Supervision of Discharged Prisoners, The (Home Office, 1958) 67
after-care of prisoners, compulsory 67
All Party Penal Affairs Group (PAPPAG) 140, 141
Allen, P 61, 81, 98, 103
Allott, A 117
Amenta, E 26
Amory, D (Viscount) 90–1
Angel, G 167
archival records 49, 82, 105
  reliability concerns 11–12
  'snowballing' approach to data collection 47
  triangulation, data collection 50
Ashworth, A 227
Association of Chief Police Officers (ACPO) 152
Audit Commission 24
austerity, 'stop-go' periods of 63–4
automatic release 77, 145, 168, 206, 234, 236, 238 *see also* early release
  Criminal Justice Act 1991 186, 188
  on licence 127, 130, 234
  short-term prisoners question 126–30

Bachrach, P 41
Bacon, A 73, 78
Bailey, V 51
Baker, K 182
Ballantyne, A 156
Bampton, S/'Bampton Proposal' 131, 135, 155, 200, 219
Baratz, M 41
Baring, S 129
Barker, V 34
Beverley, F 96
Bickham, E 172
bifurcation, strategy of 231
Biggs, R 87
'Black Wednesday' (1992) 16, 187
Blair, T 16, 17, 27, 237
Blake, G (escape of, October 1966) 84, 85, 87, 214
Blom-Cooper, L 206
Bloomstein, Rex 129–30
Blunkett, D 237
Bohan, W 132, 167
borstal system 61, 97
Bottomley, K 135
Bottoms, AE 231
Breaking the Cycle (Green Paper, 2010) 241
Brennan, A 126
Bretton-Woods system, breakdown 107
Bristol Prison, damage to (1986) 151
British Crime Survey (BCS) 13
Brittan, L 115, 145, 151, 155, 158–9, 162, 184, 188, 215, 231
  curtailing of parole eligibility by 10, 137, 190, 248
  Party Conference 1983, maiden speech at 142, 143, 154, 228
Brooke, H 67–8, 86
Brown, G 17, 240
Bulger, J 27
Bulpitt, J 210
Butler, RA 31
'Butskillism' 15

Cabinet
  Home Affairs Sub-Committee 73–4, 75, 83
  reshuffle (1966) 79–80, 214

Cairncross, N 111
Caithness, Lord (MI Sinclair) 149, 173
Callaghan, J 95, 197
The Home Office: Perspectives on Policy and Administration 80–1
Cameron, D 245
Carlisle, M 103–4, 160
Carlisle Committee 27, 159–65, 173, 176, 180, 215, 216, 225, 236, 238, 248, 249
Criminal Justice Act 1991 183, 184, 187–8
fallout from report 166–70
meetings 160–1
Parole System in England and Wales report (1988–89) x, 57, 149, 161, 167, 191, 222, 248
recommendations 164, 164–5, 169, 170, 175, 176, 177, 182, 208
Carr, R 106
Cavadino, M 33, 231
cell sharing 20, 65, 151
Certeau, M de 47
Certified Normal Accommodation (CNA) 19, 104, 109, 151
Chief Inspector of Prisons *see* Her Majesty's Chief Inspector of Prisons
chronocentrism 229
Churchill, W 142
Churchill Archive University of Cambridge 48
Citizens Charter 24
Clark, C 40
Clarke, K 241
Clayton, M 200
Coalition Government 240, 241
collective action dilemmas 37
Command Papers 50
community power debate 41
Community Rehabilitation Companies (CRCs) 244
comparative historical perspective *see* history
Conservative Party, UK 15–16, 63
Bodleian Library Archive, University of Oxford 49, 82
Conservative Party Conference (1981) 142, 202
Conservative Party Conference (1983) 142, 143, 154, 228
Crime Knows No Boundaries (1966) 88
Crisis in Crime and Punishment 111
Manifesto (1979) 23
Manifesto (2010) 243
New Conservatism 240
Constitutional Reform Act 2005 208
Constitutional Reform and Governance Act 2010 49
contingency 214
continuity and change 219–26
convicts 56–9
corporal punishment, abolition in prisons 84
Court of Appeal 136
Cox, R 103, 105
crime
child abuse 243
control of 11–14, 16
crime figures, loss of status as official statistics 11–12
'dark figure' of 12–13
increasing propensity to report 13
less serious crimes 11
paternalistic approach to 31
rise in recorded 12–13, 14
serious 12, 56
sexual offences 231, 236
'tough on crime, tough on causes of crime' 17
victimless 12
'war on crime' 16
Crime, Justice and Protecting the Public (White Paper, 1990) 179, 183
Crime and Disorder Act 1998 232
Crime Policy Planning Unit 146, 199, 201
Crime Survey for England and Wales (CSEW) 11, 12, 13
Criminal Justice Act 1948 59
Criminal Justice Act 1961 67
Criminal Justice Bill 1965/66 74–5
Criminal Justice Act 1967 26, 28, 76, 78, 82, 83, 87–91, 103, 115, 141, 192, 205, 214, 221
background 79–91

Clause 22 of Criminal Justice Bill 1966/67 88–9
defining features 90
eligibility for parole following 93, 188
justification of 187
Part III 112
Royal Assent (July 1967) 91
Second Reading of Criminal Justice Bill 1966/67 88
Criminal Justice Act 1972 96, 129
Criminal Justice Act 1981 150
Criminal Justice Act 1982 140–5, 155
Criminal Justice Act 1988 180
Criminal Justice Act 1991 7, 10, 17, 27, 171, 181–7, 191, 214, 216, 232, 234, 246
backlash 187–90
Royal Assent (July 1991) 186
Second Reading of Criminal Justice Bill 1990/91 181, 182
Criminal Justice Act 2003 234–5, 236
criminal justice policy
contemporary history 31
elites, preserve of 33–4
flux in system 190
intentionalism 31
investigation of system 24
in optimistic period (1960s) 27, 61–7
politicization 14–17
post-war administration 197
public policy concern 10–24, 27
statecraft 210–11
US influence 34
Criminal Law Act 1977 119, 128, 131, 139
Criminal Law Review 191
criminology
analytical choices 45, 46
criminologist as historian 44–50
neighbouring disciplines 33
rebalancing of the applied and the analytical 46–7
'rendezvous subject' 33
'snowballing' approach to data collection and analysis 47
theory and methodology 45
crisis management 83–7
Croft, J 200
Crofton, W 57
Cropwood Round-Table Conference (1976) 26
Cross, R 69–70, 91
Crossman, R 75, 86
diaries 84–5
Cubbon, B 122, 127–8, 202
Cunningham, C 78, 80, 81, 98
Currie, E 138
custody 5, 8, 18–19, 59, 67, 68, 70, 92, 106, 107, 120, 127, 133, 143, 150, 176, 180, 227, 232
see also prisons; remand
'custody plus' 234–5
immediate 18, 105–7, 110, 117, 119, 123, 135, 136, 162, 166, 168, 172, 174
and non-custodial sentences 137
'short, sharp shock' of 118, 143, 183, 184, 187

De Gaulle, C 63
death penalty, moratorium on use 84
deflation 63
Derrida, J 223
Dicey, AV 121
Dignan, J 33
Ditchley Park conference (1989) 171, 175–81, 183, 208, 211
Douglas, M 61
Downes, D 15, 27, 33, 240
Drake, M 155, 168–9
Dutton, D 62

earliest date of release (EDR) 76
early release *see also* automatic release; release, early
breakdown of rehabilitative ideal 17–20
case studies 25–8
comparative historical perspective 3–28
crime control 11–14
criminal justice as public policy concern 10–24, 27
history in England and Wales 55–61
Home Office *see* Home Office
key event timeline (1960–1995) 27, 247–9

early release (*cont.*)
- on licence 6
- overarching objectives 7
- politicization of criminal justice 14–17
- politics of 188
- release rates 111, 114
- situating 10–24
- steady state operation 6
- when to release 6–10

Eldrige, N 220
Elwyn Jones, F (Lord) 73, 116, 117
End of Custodial Licence (ECL) scheme 237
Erlestoke Youth Custody Centre, escape from (1986) 151
European Convention on Human Rights (ECHR) 1950 225, 238
European Court of Human Rights (ECtHR) 184, 185, 224
European Exchange Rate Mechanism (ERM), withdrawal from (1992) 187
Evans, D 168–70, 184
extended sentence for public protection (EPP) 235, 242

Faire, L 46
Falconer, CL (Lord) 237, 238
Family Courts 71
Farrall, S 182
Faulkner, D xiii, 50, 152, 160, 168, 172–4, 176–9, 187, 197, 208
- Breda Conference address (1990) 204

financialization 3–8
Findlay, Re (1985) 144, 154, 215
'Fordist-Keynesian' settlement 32
Foreign Office 21
Foucault, M 45
Fox, L 66
Freedom of Information Act 2000 49
'Fresh Start Agreement' (1986) 152
Fulton, R 182

Gaol Act 1835 65
Gardiner, GA (Lord Chancellor) 71, 72, 73, 98
Garland, D 3–4
- *The Culture of Control* 5, 32, 33, 45

Gauke, D 245–6
General Election 1964 61, 73
General Election 1987 27, 28, 149, 156, 171–5, 180, 204, 221, 222
General Election 1992 16
General Household Survey (GHS) 13
Gladstone Committee/Report (1895) 58–9, 61, 68, 97
Gould, S 220
Gove, M 245
Grayling, C 241, 243
Great Train Robbery 87
Gunn, S 46

Hall, PA 38, 40–1, 42, 226
- *Policy Paradigms, Social Learning, and the State* 41
- *Political Science and the Three New Institutionalisms* 37

Halliday, J 233–4
- *Making Punishments Work* (2001) 234

Halliday Review (2000) 233
Hall-Williams, E 70, 223
Harris, J (Lord of Greenwich) 112, 115, 116, 120, 251
Hartley, LP 4
Hattersley, R 158, 182
Hay, C 39–40, 182
Heath, E 86
Hennessy, P 4
Her Majesty's Chief Inspector of Prisons 65–6, 110
- Prison Inspectorate 65

Heseltine, M 181
high crime society 11
historical sociology 46
historiographical operation 47
history
- comparative historical perspective 3–28, 226–9
  - early release 3–28
  - merits of study 226–9
  - practicalities 26
- criminologist as historian 44–50
- of early release in England and Wales 55–61

historical institutionalism
see under institutions/ institutionalism
significance, policy change 43–4
Hobsbawm, E 16
Hobson, J 89
Hogg, Q 86, 88
Home Detention Curfew (HDC) 232, 242
Home Office 81, 83–7, 110–11, 196–201
computation of parole release eligibility 77
Crime Policy Planning Committee 207
Criminal Statistics England and Wales (1960–1995) 18
criticism of 60
establishment (1782) 21
expenditure/funding 21, 23–4, 64, 65
First and Second Prison Sentences with Special Reference to Parole 78
internal division 21
Leeds Castle meeting (1987) 1715, 180, 211
mediating role 20–4
Mountbatten Report (1966) 20
organizational chart 21, 22
prison population forecasts 105–7
Research Unit 78, 128
and rising prison population 151
short-term prisoners question 124–5
staff numbers 21
stewardship function 196
use of custody 18
Hood, R 10, 51, 112, 131, 162, 227, 237, 254
Hosking, J 178
Hougoumont (convict ship) 57
House of Commons Expenditure Committee 124
Howard, M 27, 187
Howard League of Penal Reform 50, 67, 161, 217
Howe, G 181
Human Rights Act 1998 238
Humphries, A 168, 170, 184
Hunt, HCJ (Chairman of Parole Board) 92, 93
Hurd, D 151–3, 177, 198, 202–3, 215, 221–2
'five-point plan' (July, 1987) 156, 157, 171
Leeds Castle meeting (1987) 171–5, 180, 211
Queen Anne's Gate meeting (March, 1987) 149–50, 221

ideas, role of 41–3
Imbert, P 178
immediate custody 18–19, 110, 117, 119, 123, 162, 166, 168, 172, 174 *see also* custody
disinvestment 105–7
parole, review of 135, 136
imperfect knowledge 215–16
imprisonment *see* prisons
indeterminate sentences 68, 69
Indeterminate Sentence for Public Protection (IPP) 235, 242
inspections of prisons 65–6
institutionalism/institutions
concept of institutionalism 37
historical institutionalism 29, 36–44, 51
and individuals 38–40
'institutional turn' 36
mediating role of political institutions 29–35
'new institutionalism' 36
'old institutionalism' 34, 36
rational choice 37
sociological 37
structures 34
structuring of individual action 39–40
interviews 50

James, R 62
Jenkin, P 107
Jenkins, R 84–5, 86, 97, 115, 142, 150, 155, 216
Home Secretary 14–15, 79, 80, 82, 83, 97, 214
'Jenkins initiative' 103, 110–15
A Life at the Centre 81
Minister for Aviation 80
reforms 78

Johnson, D 34
Johnson, LB 202
judiciary 205–10
'just deserts' sentencing philosophy 14, 31, 162, 174
JUSTICE 161, 236
Justice for All (White Paper, 2002) 234

Karstedt, S 34
Kennedy, JF 62
Keynesianism 42–3
Kilroy-Silk, R 140
King, M 223
King, PG 56
Koffman, L 123
Kray Twins 87
Kuhn, T 42

Labour Party, UK 15, 16–17, 71, 182, 190, 240
  Human Rights Sub-Committee 115–16
  return to power in 1964 61–2
Lacey, N 35
Lamont, N 187
Lane, GD (Lord) 128, 139, 160, 176, 177
law and order 15, 28
Lawson, N 16
Legal Aid Sentencing and Punishment of Offenders (LASPO) Act 2012 242
Legislation Committee 83, 89
Levi, M 44, 216
Lewis, D 24
liberal democracy 6
liberal elitism 33, 34
liberalism 46
licence, release on 6
  short-term prisoners 127–8
Liddington, D 245
life sentences, mandatory 68
Lisbon Treaty 245
Lloyd, S 63
Loader, I 4, 31, 33–4, 46, 197, 199, 226
Local Review Committees (LRCs) 8, 92, 144, 145, 154, 155, 219, 224
  parole system 93, 96, 111, 186
  prison-based 8, 113, 129, 206
London School of Economics 49
Longford, Lord (Francis Aungier Pakenham) 71, 73, 78, 139
Longford Committee 72–3, 74, 78
  Crime: A Challenge to Us All (1964) 55, 71, 95
  'recognisable peak' argument 117
  Study Group 71
Lukes, S 41

McGregor, OR (Lord) 130
McLaughlin, E 24
Macmillan, H 61, 87
Maconochie, A 57, 188
Magistrates' Association 208
Magistrates' Courts 18, 106, 123
mandatory life sentences *see* life sentences, mandatory
Mahoney, J 196
Major, J 16, 181–2, 187
March, JG 36–7, 39, 195, 212
Maudling, R 103
May, T 245
May Review/Report (1979) 109, 125
Mayhew, P 118, 139, 178
minimum qualifying for parole (MQP) 154
Ministry of Justice 239–40, 241
  Access to Justice Directorate 239
Mitchell, F 86–7
Molesworth, W 57
monetarism 42, 43
Morgan, R 15, 27, 96, 240
Moriarty, M 26, 63, 111
Morris, B 121
Morris, P 96
Morris, T 62, 71
Morrison, H 80
Mountbatten, LFAVN (Lord) 86
Mountbatten Report (1966) 20, 86
Mullin, C 202
murder 12, 27
  life sentences 68
  Shepherd's Bush murders (August, 1966) 84, 87, 214
Murder (Abolition of Death Penalty) Act 1965 68

National Archives, Kew 47, 49
National Association for the Care and Resettlement of Offenders (NACRO) 50, 161

National Association of Probation Officers (NAPO) 204
National Audit Office (NAO) 24, 152
National Offender Management Service (NOMS) 238, 239
National Probation Service (NPS) 244
New Conservatism 240
New Labour 17
new public management 24
Newburn, T 19, 32, 189
Newman, K 152–3
Next Steps Agencies 24
Non-Departmental Public Body (NDPB) 238
Norfolk Island penal colony 57
Norris, SG 154, 199, 215
Northern Ireland model, release on licence 127–8
Northeye Prison, partial destruction of (1986) 151

Offender Rehabilitation Act 2014 244, 245
'Oil Crisis' (1973 Oil Crisis) 107
Olsen, JP 36–7, 39, 195, 212
  Rediscovering Institutions 36
O'Neill, KA 200
open door policy 67–8, 150
optical character recognition (OCR) 49
organizational factors, early release policy and practice 195–211
  Home Office 196–201
  judiciary 205–10
  policy change 36–44
  political power 201–5
overcrowding, in prison system 19–20, 96, 151
  drafts 20, 150

Padfield, N 225, 235
parole 6, 9, 69 *see also Review of Parole in England and Wales* (Home Office, 1981)
  clerks 186
  determinate sentences 9
  discretionary nature 77, 235
  discretionary release 8, 10, 55, 93, 168, 170, 206, 234, 236
    comparative historical perspective 227, 232
    short-term prisoners 129, 130
  eligibility 76, 96
    curtailing for serious offenders (Brittan) 10, 137, 190, 248
    extending to new categories of prisoners 111, 113, 215
    following Criminal Justice Act 1967 93, 188
    parole eligibility dates (PED) 76, 92
  evaluating 96–100
  first steps 91–6
  and indeterminacy 67–73
  introduction/origins of modern system 8, 25, 26, 60, 68
  reforms 98
  and remission 98
  scope of system 10
  short-term prisoners 128–30
  therapeutic approach to decision-making 25
  'ticket of leave system' 25, 56, 57
  use of 114
Parole Board 8, 10, 83, 89, 91, 99, 115, 154, 170, 186, 189, 237
  8th Annual Overnight Conference (1977) 117
  Annual Reports 224–5
  Chair 92
  composition 92–3
  Criminal Justice Act 1982 143, 144
  'Jenkins initiative' 111, 113, 114
  membership 224, 238
  organizational factors, early release policy and practice 204, 205, 206
  policy-making, real-world settings 215, 216
  quasi-legal status 25
  Quinquennial Review (2000) 233
  short-term prisoners 125, 128–30
  sponsorship 239
Parole System in England and Wales Report (Carlisle Committee, 1988–89) x, 57, 149, 161, 167, 191, 222, 248
Parole Unit 92

partly suspended sentences 103
Criminal Justice Act 1982 141
short sentence prisoners 117–19
short-term prisoners 131–2
use of (1982–90) 142
path dependence 43, 216–19
Patten, J 157, 173, 175, 177, 178, 182, 183
Payne v. Lord Harris of Greenwich (1981) 224
penal colonies 56, 57
penal populism 7, 11, 31, 35
Penal Practice in a Changing Society (Home Office, 1959) 5, 17
Penal Servitude Act 1853 58
penal welfarism 3–4, 230
penal zeitgeist 19
Perry, E 114
Petch, L 112, 113
Peterson, A 106, 112, 113
Pierson, P 27, 43, 44, 220–1
Poggi, G 29–30
Police Federation 84, 152
Police Service 23–4, 152
policy and politics *see also* general elections
compromise 215
contingency 214
evolution of policy
in 1990s 230–2
from 1997 to 2003 232–6
from 2004 to 2009 236–40
from 2010 to 2017 240–6
imperfect knowledge 215–16
key actors 27, 250–3
new directions 119–23
organizational factors 36–44, 195–211
paradigms 41–2, 226
perspectives on early release 213
policy change *see* policy change
political power 40–1, 201–5
political re-organisation (mid 1960s) 79–83
politicization of criminal justice 14–17
real-world settings, policy-making 212–16
temporal elements of policy development 43
unintended consequences, law of 213–14
policy change 29–51 *see also* public policy
'big picture' view 25, 46, 51
distribution of political power 40–1
'first order' 42, 91
historical institutionalism 29, 36–44
ideas, role of 41–3
institutions and individuals 38–40
mediating role of political institutions 29–35
organizational factors in political life 36–44
research strategies 30
'second order' 42, 91
short sentence prisoners 115–19
significance of history 43–4
'third order' 42, 91
political prisoners 127
politicization of criminal justice 14–17
Popplewell, O 161–2, 166–7
post-industrial society 62
post-war Britain, economic paradox 62–3
power
community power debate 41
distribution of 40–1
nature of 41
organizational factors 201–5
political 40–1, 51, 201–5
Preventive Detention Advisory Board 82, 83
Prison Act 1878 58
Prison Act 1898 59
prison authorities 6
Prison Commissioners 61, 66–7
Board of Prison Commissioners 58
Prison Department 20, 60, 61, 99, 109
Prison Governors 7, 74, 237
Prison Governors Association (PGA) 152, 204
Prison Governors Conference 150
Prison Officers Association (POA) 109, 152, 204
Prison Reform Trust 50, 245

Prison Rules 7, 59, 66, 125, 156, 215, 232
prison security 20, 86
Prison Service 19, 20
as Executive Agency 24
Prison Service Order (PSO) 233
prisoners *see also* prisons
after-care and supervision 67
average population 19–20
determinate 76, 94
early release *see* early release
indeterminate 68, 69
long-term, care of 67, 68
political 127
recommendation for parole 93
short sentence *see* short sentence/short-term prisoners
prisons *see also* custody; prisoners; remand
corporal punishment, abolition 84
disinvestment from prison building programme 103–10
drafts, overcrowding 20, 150
escapes from 84, 85, 86–7, 151, 214
harms of imprisonment 183
inspections of 66
limitations place on use of imprisonment 6
overcrowding in system 19–20, 96
population forecasts 105–7
rising population 65, 110, 150, 151–2
tactical management 20
Victorian 66, 71
Privy Council 56
Probation and Aftercare Department/Division 24, 92, 94, 198, 201
probation service 61, 67, 76, 77, 110, 119, 128, 156, 170, 175, 234
Community Rehabilitation Companies (CRCs) 244
Criminal Justice Act 1982 144, 146
and Home Office 198, 200
National Probation Service (NPS) 244
parole, review of 134, 135
Probation Trusts 244
short-term prisoners 125, 128, 129, 130
Profumo affair (1963) 61
Protecting the Public: The Government's Strategy on Crime in England and Wales (Home Office, 1996) 188
Public Accounts Committee (PAC) 24, 109
Public Expenditure Survey (PES) 49, 64, 103, 104, 108, 146, 172, 198, 204, 214
public order 16
public policy *see also* policy change
criminal justice as concern of 10–24, 27
Public Records Act 1958 49
Public Spending Review (2010) 240
punishment
forward looking approach to 69
harsher, impulses towards 35
'just deserts' sentencing philosophy 14, 31, 162, 174
justifications for 6
personalization of 69, 90
political economy of 34, 35
retribution 31
sociology of 33
Punishment, Custody and the Community (Green Paper, 1988a) 171, 175–81

qualitative data analysis (QDA) software (NVivo) 49

R v. Bibi (1980) 122
R v. Ian Albert Upton (1980) 122
Radzinowicz, L 51
rational choice institutionalism 37
Rayner Efficiency Unit 24
Reagan, R 44
realpolitik
administrative 145–6
parliamentary 62
rehabilitation
beliefs 68–9
ideal 11, 226
breakdown of 17–20
paradigm of 1960s 91
scepticism 14
Reiner, R 13, 16, 35

release on temporary licence (ROTL) 232, 233 *see also* automatic release; discretionary release; early release
remand 84, 110, 152, 242, 254
remission 6, 7–8, 10, 60, 218
 50 per cent, introduction of 50, 155–9
 abolition (1991) 7
 and parole 98
 remission time 7
 short-term prisoners 125–6
reprieves 56
retribution 31
Review of Parole in England and Wales (Home Office, 1981) x, 124, 132–7, 139, 248 *see also* Home Office; parole; parole eligibility
 organizational factors, early release policy and practice 207–9, 211
Robbins Committee on Higher Education 62
Roberts, H 83
Rock, P 229
Royal Commission on the Penal System 74
Royal Commission on Transportation and Penal Servitude 58
Royal Institute for Public Administration 197
Royal Prerogative of Mercy 6, 57
Rueschemeyer, D 196
rule of law 70
Rumbold, A 182
Ryan, M 197

Scull, A 51
Select Committee on Transportation 57
Sentence Review Board 70
sentencing *see also* early release
 50 per cent remission, introduction of 155–9
 determinate sentences 76, 94
 extended sentence for public protection (EPP) 235
 indeterminate sentences 68, 69
  indeterminate sentence for public protection (IPP) 235
 'just deserts' sentencing philosophy 14, 31, 162, 174
 mandatory life sentences 68
 organized pressure, application of 152–3
 partly suspended sentences *see* partly suspended sentences
 rising prison population 65, 110, 150, 151–2
 short sentence prisoners *see* short sentence/short-term prisoners
 truth in 149–70
Sentencing Council 136, 180, 182
Sewell, WH 44–5
sexual offences 231, 236
Sheerman, B 166
Shepherd's Bush murders (August, 1966) 84, 87, 214
short sentence/short-term prisoners 103–23
 discretionary release 129, 130
 'Jenkins initiative' 110–15
 licence, release on 127–8
 Northern Ireland model 127–8
 parole 128–30
 partly suspended sentences 117–19
 policy innovation 115–19
 probation service 125, 128, 129, 130
 question of 124–32
 remission 125–6
 two-tier system, proposed 129
Shute, S 10, 25, 96, 155, 227, 237
Simon, J 32
situational crime control 14, 16
Skocpol, T 20
'slopping-out' 151
Smith, G 178
Society of Civil and Public Servants Prison and Borstal Governors' Branch 125, 204
sociology
 historical 46
 institutionalism 37
 of punishment 33
 of scientific knowledge 42

Soskice, F 73–4, 78, 80, 81, 97
Sparks, R 4, 33, 46
stays of execution 56
Steinmo, S 38, 39
Stern, V 166
Storr, N 61, 76
Straw, J 189, 190
summary offences 11
Summerskill, E 115
suspended sentences
 mandatory, abolition 96
 new political directions 119–23
 partly suspended sentences *see* partly suspended sentences

Taylor, R 38, 40
 Political Science and the Three New Institutionalisms 37
temporal factors, in early release policy and practice 212–29
 path dependence 216–19
 policy-making, real-world settings 212–16
 temporal elements of policy development 43
terrorism 243
Thatcher, M 16, 24, 44, 139, 161, 181, 182, 214
'thirty-year rule,' public access to records 49
Thynne, Wilson and Gunnell v. United Kingdom (1991) 185, 224
'ticket of leave system' 25, 56, 57
Tonry, M 19
Train, C 149, 152, 173
Transforming Rehabilitation — A Revolution in the Way We Manage Offenders (2013) 244
Treasury 43, 63, 107, 204, 214, 217, 219
 disinvestment from prison building programme 103–9
 Green Book (2011) 213
Treatment of Offenders (Northern Ireland) Order 1976 127
triangulation, data 50
Truss, E 245
Tumim, S 151

unintended consequences, law of 213–14
United States
 criminal justice policy 34
 penal code 57
 Social Security System 44

victimization, increase in risk of 14
victimless crimes 12
Von Hirsch, A 191

Wacquant, L 46
Waddington, D 179, 181, 182, 185
Walker, N 70
Watkins, T 160, 168, 175, 177, 208
Weeks v. United Kingdom (1988) 224
welfare state 44
West, D 8, 25, 111
Whitelaw, WSI (Willie) 103, 120, 121, 125, 137–42, 155, 202, 203, 222
 'Whitelaw Mark I and Mark 2' 139
Williams, S 95, 217
Wilson, H 62, 73, 75, 84, 85
 Cabinet reshuffle (1966) 79–80, 214
Windlesham, Lord (DJGH Hennessey) 30–1
Woolf Report 20
Wootton, Baroness B 69, 179
Work Programme 242
World War Two 14

Young, J 14, 46
Younger, K 67

Zander, M 114
Zimring, F 34

The manufacturer's authorised representative in the EU for product safety is Oxford University Press España S.A. of el Parque Empresarial San Fernando de Henares, Avenida de Castilla, 2 – 28830 Madrid (www.oup.es/en or product.safety@oup.com). OUP España S.A. also acts as importer into Spain of products made by the manufacturer.

www.ingramcontent.com/pod-product-compliance
Lightning Source LLC
Chambersburg PA
CBHW071250180926
51613CB00001B/1
* 9 7 8 0 1 9 8 8 0 3 6 8 3 *